Management for Social Enterprise

Management for Social Enterprise

Bob Doherty, George Foster, Chris Mason,
John Meehan, Karon Meehan, Neil Rotheroe,
and Maureen Royce

Los Angeles • London • New Delhi • Singapore • Washington DC

SAGE Publications Ltd
1 Oliver's Yard
55 City Road
London EC1Y 1SP

SAGE Publications Inc.
2455 Teller Road
Thousand Oaks, California 91320

SAGE Publications India Pvt Ltd
B 1/I 1 Mohan Cooperative Industrial Area
Mathura Road, Post Bag 7
New Delhi 110 044

SAGE Publications Asia-Pacific Pte Ltd
33 Pekin Street #02-01
Far East Square
Singapore 048763

Library of Congress Control Number: 2008934764

British Library Cataloguing in Publication data

A catalogue record for this book is available from the British Library

ISBN 978-1-4129-4748-0
ISBN 978-1-4129-4749-7 (pbk)

Typeset by C&M Digitals (P) Ltd, Chennai, India
Printed in Great Britain by CPI Antony Rowe, Chippenham, Wiltshire
Printed on paper from sustainable resources

Mixed Sources
Product group from well-managed forests and other controlled sources
www.fsc.org Cert no. SGS-COC-2953
© 1996 Forest Stewardship Council

CONTENTS

LIST OF FIGURES AND TABLES

FIGURES

TABLES

ABOUT THE AUTHORS

All the authors are based at Liverpool John Moores University

Bob Doherty is Senior Lecturer in Social Enterprise and Corporate Responsibility

George Foster is Senior Lecturer in Accounting Finance and Economics

Chris Mason is Lecturer in Marketing

John Meehan is Senior Lecturer in Strategic Management

Karon Meehan is Senior Lecturer in Marketing

Neil Rotheroe is Senior Lecturer in International Business Ethics and Corporate Responsibility

Maureen Royce is Senior Lecturer in HMR

INTRODUCTION TO THE LANDSCAPE FOR SOCIAL ENTERPRISES

KEY THEMES

- The historical roots of social enterprises (SEs).
- The positioning of SEs within the social economy.
- The size and growth of the social enterprise sector internationally.
- International differences in the role of SEs.
- The role of national, regional and local government in facilitating the development of SEs within the economy.

HISTORICAL ROOTS

The SE (Social Enterprise) is a powerful idea, having its historical roots in the cooperative, community and voluntary sectors. The social enterprise sector can trace its origins back to medieval guilds, but it is the Rochdale Pioneers, founded in 1844, who are normally seen as symbolizing the start of the growth in numbers of SEs (Pearce, 2003). The cooperative principles of working together for a common social purpose worked to address the spiralling poverty levels for those in traditional trades who were displaced during the industrial revolution (Birchall, 1994).

Nearly 200 years later, cooperatives and new mutuals are undergoing a renaissance, offering new solutions and applying them in a modern context. These can range from football supporters' trusts and new models for childcare and care homes for the elderly, to maintaining vital services in rural communities and more traditional activities, such as retail and financial services.

In 1948, the UK government took prime responsibility for services such as health, education and social welfare, which led to the eventual decline of friendly societies. The policies of the Labour Government of the early 1970s stimulated the development of the community and voluntary sector. During Margaret Thatcher's Conservative Government (1979–1990), the social sector evolved in the opposite direction – partly as a response to the ideal of individualism behind the free market economic policy at that time (Bull, 2006). Under the Thatcher Government, the welfare state model was replaced by a social policy framework based on neoliberalism, the effects of which were deregulation, privatization and reliance on the market and private philanthropy, resulting in economic and social inequality (Tickell and Peck, 2003). More recently, social demographic changes and the economic problems surrounding the operation of a national health and wider welfare services are stimulating a renewal of SEs as suppliers of such services (Bull and Crompton, 2005).

SEs are part of the wider social economy (as shown in Figure 1.2 later in this chapter). A number of authors suggest that the social economy in the UK and Europe has nineteenth-century origins (Amin et al., 2002; Moulaert and Ailenei, 2005). The European Commission's Social Economy Unit defines the social economy as including cooperatives, mutual societies, associations and foundations and SEs. However, until 12 years ago, the term 'social enterprise' was rarely discussed. Since then, the term has made significant breakthroughs on both sides of the Atlantic (Defourney and Nyssens, 2006).

In 1993, the Harvard Business School in the USA launched its 'SE Initiative' followed by other US universities including Colombia, Stanford and Yale set-up training programmes for social enterprises or social entrepreneurs. In 1991 the Italian Parliament introduced Law 8/11/1991, n.381 to regulate a new legal form of cooperatives named 'social cooperatives' (see Exhibit 1.1 later in this chapter). Borzaga and Santuari (2003) argue that the growth in numbers of Italian social cooperatives is due to the community's needs not being met by public services.

Similar initiatives have emerged in other EU states and, in 1996, the European Research Network (EMES) was formed to study SEs within the EU. Defourney and Nyssens (2006) propose that European SEs are positioned at the crossroads of the market, public policies and civil society.

MODELS OF SOCIAL ENTERPRISES

Despite the growing interest in SEs, they remain clearly under-researched compared to conventional businesses, charities and the wider social economy. According to Bull and Crompton (2005), this is due to the lack of an agreed definition. Smallbone et al. (2001) identify 16 different forms of SE, dependent on which definition is used. According to Bull and Crompton (2005), SEs are referred to as comprising 'the third sector'– the not-for-profit sector, the social enterprise, non-profitmaking businesses, civil society organizations, non-governmental organizations (NGOs). These terms are used interchangeably, which makes it challenging to bring together the literature for a book of this type. In this respect, Figure 1.2 (later in this chapter), showing Pearce's three systems model, is useful for framing these different literatures and their associated terms. In agreement with Pearce (2003), MacGillivray et al. (1998) argue that SEs can be placed diagrammatically between charitable/voluntary organizations and the private sector.

In the North American model, a SE may be incorporated as either a for-profit or non-profit organization. In the USA, the term SE remains a very broad concept, referring mainly to market-focused economic activities serving a social goal (Defourney and Nyssens, 2006). In some cases SEs are seen as an innovative response to the funding problems of non-profitmaking organizations (Dees, 1998). In contrast, the UK definitions (see the beginning of Chapter 2) recognize the importance of making a profit and what is done with the profit (surplus) created. According to Moulaert and Ailenei (2005), non-profitmaking organizations can be defined as ones that are required to reinvest any profits in these organization, and their activities (charities), whereas not-for-profit organizations may distribute profits between members or stakeholders (cooperatives). In addition, there is a legal distinction in the USA between 'non-profitmaking' and 'not for profit': the former being an organization and the latter an activity, meaning that non-profitmaking organizations can engage in for-profits activities, although those profits will be taxed (Jones and Keogh, 2006).

SEs are described as the enterprising wedge of the social economy (Pearce, 2003). The term 'social economy' is only a recent phenomenon in the UK literature, previously being defined as the third, voluntary and/or not-for-profit sectors (Amin et al., 2002; Dart, 2004; Hudson, 2005). Laville and Nyssens (2001) suggest that SEs represent a new dynamic within the third sector. ECOTEC (2003) also provides a useful explanation by defining the social economy as the trading arm of the third sector/ system (see Figure 1.2 later in this chapter) and SEs as that part of the social economy primarily engaged in trading.

THE GROWTH AND POSITIONING OF SOCIAL ENTERPRISES

The recent growth of the social enterprise sector in industrialized countries has been well documented (Defourney and Borzaga, 2001; Pearce, 2003; Salamon et al., 2003). Salamon et al. (2003) report a growth in the third sector/social economy across the developed countries of North America, Western Europe, Central and Eastern Europe and in much of the developed world. SEs are now competing in a diverse number of market sectors, including, health and social care, housing, children's services, transport, food and farming, plus environmental services and leisure (Westall and Chalkley, 2007). In fact, Salamon et al. (2003) argue that the rise of the third sector in the late twentieth and early twenty-first centuries may prove to be as important as the rise of the nation state in the late nineteenth and early twentieth centuries.

Salamon et al. (2003), in their work on mapping the third sector in 35 different countries, identified variations between nation states. In more developed countries, the share of the economically active population employed in the third sector is larger than in developing countries. This does not highlight an absence of these activities in developing countries, as many countries have strong familial, clan and community networks that perform the functions of third-sector organizations. Rather, the variations from country to country in the third sector reflect their different cultural, social, political and economic histories.

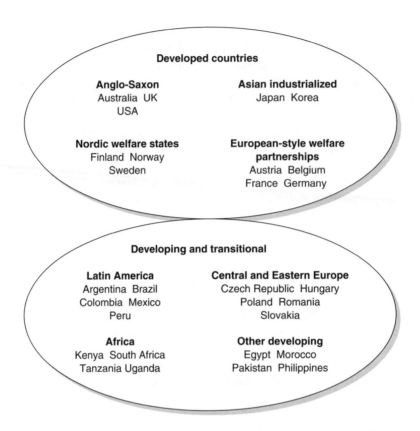

Figure 1.1   Sociopolitical clusters of countries (based on Salamon et al., 2003: 37)

Salamon et al. (2003) proposed a number of clusters (as shown in Figure 1.1). In the Anglo-Saxon group, the third sector plays a significant role and exhibits the largest average third-sector workforce of 8.2 per cent combined with a sizeable volunteer presence. Third-sector organizations in this cluster also derive a high proportion of their income from fees and charges.

The distinguishing characteristics of the Nordic cluster include a workforce of 2.5 per cent that is mainly comprised of volunteer labour and others receiving lower than average levels of pay. This is because of the broad welfare state policies adopted by these countries in the early twentieth century. The third sector in this cluster is characterized by strong advocacy and professional organizations staffed by volunteers, deriving income mainly from fees and government support.

The European-style welfare partnerships are characterized by a large civil society staffed in the main by paid employees who are predominantly engaged in social welfare service provision. The sector in this cluster derives significant income from tax revenues. It is important to note that this pattern is not universal across all European countries – Italy and Spain are exceptions (see the case study of Italy in Exhibit 1.1).

The Asian industrialized cluster is characterized by a small third sector – only 3.3 per cent of the economically active population is involved in the sector. The organizations in it are mainly involved in service provision of health and education, gaining most of their income from fees and receiving little state support.

The third sector in other developing and transitional economies has demonstrated stronger growth in recent years than before due to developments in communications technology and some international initiatives to empower the rural poor, particularly in Africa. The sector in this cluster is characterized in the main (except in Argentina) by lower than average levels of economically active people employed in the sector (both paid and unpaid), plus lower than average levels of government support. Third-sector organizations in these countries have depended heavily on both fees and international private philanthropy for their income.

A more recent development has been the growth in numbers of those organizations involved in ethical or fair trade (see Exhibit 1.4 later in this chapter) representing small-scale producer groups. Fair trade alone is claimed to provide benefits in improved livelihoods to over 7 million farmers and their families in developing countries (Fairtrade Labelling Organization, 2008).

The third sector in Latin America is larger than in other developing country clusters and is heavily orientated towards service functions such as education.

In Africa, third-sector organizations are limited by financial support. An exception to this is South Africa, where 40 per cent of revenue is derived from government compared to 5 per cent in Kenya.

The Central and Eastern Europe cluster demonstrates yet another pattern. It reflects the influence of the Soviet-style regimes that came to power in the aftermath of World War II. The third sector in this cluster is smaller in scale than in both Latin America and Africa due to the direct provision of social welfare services by the state in these countries. Exhibits 1.2 and 1.3 later in this chapter, which discuss the development of the social economy in Poland and Slovenia respectively, illustrate this dynamic.

In the last decade, Britain's third sector has grown significantly (Cabinet Office, 2007):

- the number of registered charities has grown from 120,000 in 1995 to 160,000 in 2005;

- the number of people volunteering once a month rose from 18.4 million in 2001 to 20.4 million in 2005;

- charities' turnover has increased from £16 billion in 1997 to over £27 billion in 2004/2005.

In addition, an important dynamic in the development of the third sector is the growth in numbers of SEs. It was reported in the UK 'Small business survey' of 2006 that there are now more than 55,000 SEs in the UK, generating more than £27 billion in turnover and contributing more than £8 billion to GDP, which is over 1 per cent of the UK's total. SEs account for 5 per cent of all UK businesses with employees (IFF, 2005).

The same survey proposed that 475,000 people are employed by SEs, 63 per cent of whom are full-time employees with the majority of SEs also employing some staff on a part-time basis. In addition, two thirds of SEs make use of volunteer labour, estimated to number 300,000 people. This blend of paid and volunteer labour is a unique feature of SEs.

SEs are part of the wider social economy, illustrated by Pearce's (2003) three system's framework (as shown in Figure 1.2). The diagram separates the private, public and

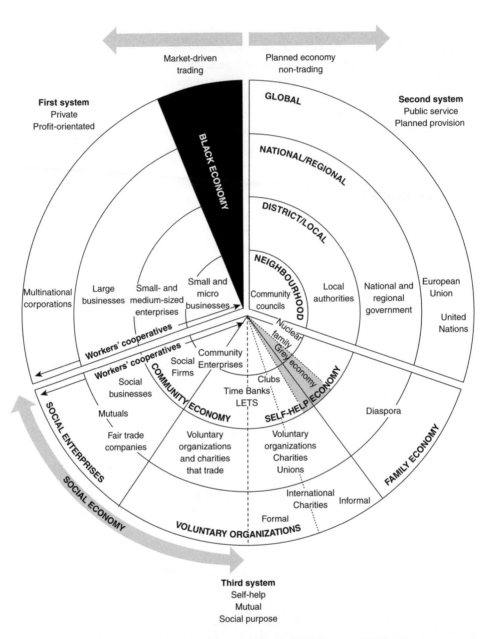

Figure 1.2   Pearce's three systems of the economy model (Pearce, 2003: 25)

mutual systems (the third system) within the economy and then splits the social economy from within the mutual economy where trading is a dimension of the sector, in contrast to the planned economy of the public sphere. SEs are positioned within the market-driven economy, which is one of the key discussion points covered in Chapter 2. Often the terms social economy, SEs and third sector are used interchangeably, so Pearce's three systems framework is a very useful diagram for explaining the differences between them and where each is positioned in the wider economy.

Pearce's model also shows the diversity and complexity of the social economy. The umbrella term 'SE' also covers a range of organizational types that vary in terms of size, legal structure, activity, geographic scope, income sources, motivations, level of profit orientation, relationship with communities, ownership and culture (see Chapter 2 for forms of SEs).

There are also different conceptions internationally. The USA views SEs more as non-profitmaking social organizations that are clearly delineated from commercial businesses, although sometimes working in partnership with them via activities such as cause-related marketing (Austin, 1999).

THE POTENTIAL OF SOCIAL ENTERPRISES

In Europe, the social economy is a fast-growing sector, significantly outstripping the private sector in terms of job creation (Hudson, 2005). The social economy within the EU has been estimated to cover nearly a tenth of all enterprises and employment, representing nine million full-time jobs. Of these about half (4.8 million) are employed in Europe's 300,000 cooperatives (Hudson, 2005).

According to Hudson (2005) the EU views SEs as an essential part of the European economic model and the European Commission has established a Social Economy Unit in the Directorate General for Industry. For example, almost one third of Europeans are insured by mutual insurers against the risks of illness or old age and about 140 million citizens are members of cooperatives (Hudson, 2005).

In some countries where SEs have been explicitly recognized for the work they do in tackling employment and social issues, they play a very significant role. For example, around 7 per cent of Spain's (GDP) is produced by cooperatives and labour-owned companies (SEL, 2000). Similarly, Branco (2007) explains that the Italian social economy accounts for more than 12 per cent of Italy's total GDP. The social economy in Italy is supported by a detailed and advanced legislative and normative framework that is both fully integrated and integral to the Italian economy and a specific credit system (Branco, 2007). Its key stakeholders are extremely integrated vertically, horizontally and trans-sectorally (the social regional innovation system) within the social economy. According to Branco (2007), SEs in Italy are enterprises run with entrepreneurial attitude to achieve social aims, as shown in Exhibit 1.1.

Exhibit 1.1   The social economy and SEs in Italy (www.teses.eu)

The weight of the 'social economy' in Italy

The social economy sector in Italy accounts for 12 per cent of the total GDP and, in some of the most industrialized regions in Northern Italy, such as Veneto and Emilia-Romagna, this value rises to more than 15 per cent. The size of the social economy in Italy is shown in Table 1.1.

(Continued)

(Continued)

Table 1.1   The social economy and third sector/total employed in Italy

Number	Employees	% of total workforce	Members/ volunteers (millions)	Income (€ billion)
Total social economy >250,000	1.3 million	5.4	<10	136
Third Sector (not-for-profit organizations) >235,000	490,000	2.0	<3.3	40
Cooperatives >50,000	814,000	3.4	>9	96

Source: Branco, 2007

According to Branco (2007), the Italian social economy sector is made up of four key organizational forms:

- the SEs;
- the cooperatives and social cooperatives;
- the Organizzazioni non lucrative di utilita sociale (ONLUS);
- the new social holdings.

SEs are regulated by art.1, comma 1, D.L. 24/0372006, n.155, defined as:

> A business with primarily social objectives whose surpluses are principally reinvested for that purpose in the business or in the community, rather than being driven by the need to maximize profit for shareholders and owners.

There are specific and clear conditions that need to be fulfilled in order to be considered a SE. The 'non-lucrative organizations of social utility' (the translation of the Italian, organizzazioni non lucrative di utilita' sociale, abbreviated as ONLUS) are not-for-profit organizations registered, if conditions prescribed by the law are satisfied, in the official book of ONLUSs. If an organization is registered as ONLUS, it benefits from fiscal deduction and value-added tax (VAT) exemption for part of its institutional activities.

A phenomenon particular to Italy is the system of cooperatives and social cooperatives, which conform to a specific legal framework and possess specific characteristics and benefits. The system is fully supported by a specific banking system based on credit cooperative banks (and ethical banks).

The social cooperatives' main purpose is to improve the lot of people and bring about the social integration of citizens through community development. The typical characteristics of social cooperatives include that they:

- are small in size;
- are connected with the local community;
- are very close to the world of volunteering;
- generate social services that are not in competition with existing public services;
- have a social and economic targets;
- create new employment opportunities;
- ensure the active participation of members in the organization.

There are three registration types for social cooperatives including:

- *Type A:* for the management of social health and educational services;
- *Type B:* for the introduction to the labour market of disadvantaged people (this is the fastest-growing of the three types);
- *Type C:* a consortium of cooperatives, with at least 70 per cent of the organizations being social cooperatives.

To be eligible for registration as a social cooperative, it is compulsory to fulfil the requirements of Law 381 and be registered in a special official book kept at local government offices.

The 'social holdings' organizational type – gruppo cooperativo paritetico – introduced in 2004 by the art. 2545-septies Italian civil code, represents the most recent legislative development in the Italian social economy sector. Social holdings are groups of at least two organizations that are SEs, ONLUS, private institutions, public institutions, cooperatives, agencies and so on where the majority of members (and votes – 1 member = 1 vote) are cooperatives.

Social holdings allow for the:

- participation of different organizations, both public (municipalities, regions) and private, for-profit companies (limited by shares);
- ability, by so doing, to cover different fields of action and work on local, national and international tenders;
- combining of strengths that can allow for increased contractual power, improved cost efficiency and greater lobbying power.

An example of a social holding is the Gruppo Paritetico Promolavoro, based in the Veneto region in north east Italy. It is the sum of seven cooperatives, supplying services for the benefit of both elderly people and young nursery children of one to five years of age.

As a result of joining the European Union, transition states such as Poland have experienced an increasing interest in SEs. There exists a political will for new solutions to emerge from the social economy sector (Reichel and Kozakiewicz, 2007). Initiatives are under way in Poland to formulate regulations concerning a new legal form of SEs and/or criteria that would allow other organizations to be classified as SEs. This will result in the enactment of concrete legislative proposals in the area of the Polish social economy (Reichel and Kozakiewicz, 2007). The modern history of the social economy in Poland is outlined in Exhibit 1.2.

Exhibit 1.2   The social economy and SEs in Poland

The social economy has a strong tradition in Poland. However, in the past, because of historical circumstances (120 years of occupation under the rule of Prussia, Russia and the Austro-Hungarian Empire), it was mainly a tool for sustaining Polish identity.

(Continued)

(Continued)

Between the two World Wars there existed more than 20,000 cooperatives and mutual insurance associations had 50 per cent of shares in the Polish insurance market. After World War II, social economy organizations, including cooperatives, were downgraded or eliminated by the communist regime.

Currently in Poland there is evidence of a growing interest in social economy organizations and an increase in their numbers. It is claimed that the main source of this increase is the non-governmental sector – still young, yet dynamic. EU integration has also caused an increased interest regarding the role of the social economy in Poland. However, there is still low awareness in Poland regarding the terms social economy, SE or social entrepreneurship (Reichel and Kozakiewicz, 2007).

Hotel Klos (www.klos.tpn.org.pl) is a good example of a new SE that has been set up in Poland, with support from the Equal fund (a European social fund). This SE, based near Lodz in Poland, rehabilitates people who are suffering from schizophrenia. As part of this rehabilitation, Hotel Klos provides training and employment in all aspects of running a hotel.

The inspiration for this SE came after a visit to the Forth Sector (www.forth sector.org.uk/index.htm), an SE based in Scotland, that has developed a number of successful SEs to develop employment opportunities for those excluded by mental health problems. One of its SEs is the St Mary's Place guesthouse in Edinburgh.

Hotel Klos was opened in 2005 with a mixture of financing from the European Equal project, National Fund for the Disabled, National Health Care Agency and the municipality of Lodz. Hotel Klos is a good example of NGO partnerships, with European, national and local authorities working together. This SE is also supported by the Polish Social Economy Centre, which provides advice and help.

The rehabilitation centre situated near to the hotel site provides support for patients in the form of group discussion and group activities (there is a riding stable and so on in the grounds of the hotel), emotion and stress support, creative training and life skills training. Sheltered employment training in the hotel is provided in all areas, including catering, front-of-house reception duties, secretarial, restaurant waiting skills, plus the duties of porters and cleaners. Physiological support is also provided to beneficiaries during the training programme.

The first 31 beneficiaries taken through the hotel training programme have already found jobs in the developing Polish tourist industry. This is an early sign of success and the next set of beneficiaries are currently being trained in the hotel.

To achieve financial sustainability, Hotel Klos aims to build up its occupancy rate. It aims to target the residential conference market by selling its services to other third-sector organizations and the socially responsible corporate sector. (A study visit was undertaken by the author in April 2008.)

In addition, the social economy in Slovenia is also in an early stage of development, as shown in Exhibit 1.3.

Exhibit 1.3   The social economy and SEs in Slovenia (www.teses.eu)

The social economy in Slovenia has its historical roots in the cooperative movement. The first law on cooperatives was adopted in 1873 (when Slovenia was part of the Austro-Hungarian monarchy, but under Austrian administration). In 1937, when it was part of the kingdom of Yugoslavia, Slovenia also passed the law on economic cooperatives (1937). This law made it possible for small groups of people to establish a cooperative with the aim of supporting the development of individual and family entrepreneurship through mutuality and solidarity. Cooperatives at this time were mainly set up by cattle and sheep farmers, wood processors, vine-growers and milk producers. The cooperatives shared their income or profits between their members and developed their own saving and lending financial institutions.

In the period 1944–1949, the Yugoslav communist government decreed that existing cooperatives were to be owned by the state and guided by political committees in order to serve national plan objectives (the Soviet model). Thus, they became alienated from their members and the memberships' ownership of their cooperatives was lost.

Currently, a new type of social economy in Slovenia is evolving after the dissolution of the socio-economic self-governance system and the associated labour law of the former federal country Yugoslavia, of which Slovenia was one of the federal republics.

Unfortunately, two transitions – first, from state capitalism to a socialist self-governance society in the period 1945–1990 and, then, to a market economy – resulted in confusion for the Slovenian public. Before 1990, under self-managed socialistic communities and societies, Slovene citizens experienced both high levels of employment and social welfare services. Therefore, the majority of Slovenian citizens are still quite confused about the terms 'social economy' and 'social entrepreneurship'. Also, this is partly due to the fact that 'entrepreneurship' during the transition time became associated with entrepreneurs who had no social conscience.

Today, Slovenia is trying to structure new socio-economic tools to balance conflicting development goals, increase economic efficiency and create social justice. To reach these socio-economic aims, the Slovenian government has recognized that the social economy and social entrepreneurship must play an extremely crucial role. The Slovenian government believes that community stakeholder participation is key to maximizing the potential benefits from the development of the social economy (Bunc et al., 2007).

Exhibits 1.1, 1.2 and 1.3 appear to agree with the analysis of Defourney and Borgaza (2001), who propose that international differences tend to reflect different levels of social and economic development – in legal frameworks, the nature of welfare systems and the historical development of the social economy in the different countries.

WHY THE GROWTH OF SOCIAL ENTERPRISES?

The recent growth in the social enterprise sector across industrialized countries has been well documented. According to Salamon et al. (2003) this growth is due to a number of factors, including a reawakening of active citizenship due to advances in information technology and rising literacy levels. The increasing number of educated people see third-sector organizations as vehicles for making a difference to societies affected by perceived state or market failures. Other factors include liberal developments in institutions such as the Catholic church, particularly in Latin America, stimulating the formation of many community groups. In addition, the work of Western charitable foundations committed to empowering the poor is also important. More recently, there has been recognition by multilateral organizations such as the World Bank (WB) of the importance of engaging citizens when implementing development agendas.

Globalization has resulted in significant expansion of world trade (more than ten fold), resulting in an increase in global per capita wealth. However there have been some negative consequences of this, including human rights abuses, environmental degradation, climate change, public health scares, a widening gap between rich and poor nations, declining commodity prices and growing poverty in less developed countries, and these are of concern to civil society (Doppelt, 2003; Elkington, 1997). According to Bornstein (2004) the gap between the poorest and richest countries continues to grow, resulting in the poorest 50 per cent of the world's population accounting for just 5 per cent of global income.

Civil society has responded in a number of ways. Social entrepreneurship has emerged as a global phenomenon, led by social activists and their networks, providing new market models for solving community problems (Nicholls, 2006). Consumers have responded, resulting in a growth in ethical consumption. The Co-operative Bank's 'Ethical purchasing index 2005' (Co-operative Bank, 2005) reports that ethical consumerism in UK markets is worth £29.3 billion per year. Spending on ethical food (organic, fair trade and free-range) was up by 18 per cent to £5.4 billion. A further £11.6 billion was accounted for by ethical finance, up from £10.6 billion in the previous year. The rapid development of fair trade SEs, such as Cafédirect and Divine Chocolate (formerly Day Chocolate), is an example of such a response, combining social entrepreneurship with a growth in ethical consumption (see Exhibit 1.4).

Exhibit 1.4   The growth of fair trade

Civil society has responded to the predicament of marginalized producers by the rapid emergence of the fair trade market, both within the UK and internationally (Barratt Brown, 1993; Crane and Matten, 2004; Lowe and Davenport, 2005). UK fair trade sales have grown to a level of £490 million (Fairtrade Foundation, 2007), demonstrating a growth of 80 per cent on 2006 sales.

Fair trade is a system aimed at offering the most disadvantaged producers in developing countries the opportunity to move out of poverty by creating market access under beneficial rather than exploitative terms. The objective is to empower producers to develop their own businesses and wider communities through international trade (Nicholls and Opal, 2004: 6). Fair trade is defined as 'a trading partnership based on dialogue, transparency and respect that seeks greater equity in international trade. It contributes to sustainable development by offering better trading conditions to, and securing the rights of marginalized producers and workers – especially in the South' (Lowe and Davenport, 2005: 499).

A number of authors report that ethical factors are increasingly important in influencing consumers' buying behaviour (Nicholls, 2002; Shaw et al., 2006). Harrison et al. (2005) propose that the exploitation of developing countries is high on the list of consumer issues. Consumers are now not only concerned with the intrinsic properties of the product but also supply chain and production issues such as human rights.

Ethical consumption is the conscious and deliberate choosing of certain products and services over others based on personal moral beliefs and values. It is about making decisions that are about more than self-interest. Worldwide, consumers spent over £1.6 billion on products being the Fairtrade Mark in 2007. This is a 47 per cent increase on 2006 and now means that over 7.5 million producers and workers across 58 developing countries are benefiting from fair trade (Fairtrade Labelling Organization, 2008).

The 'Ethical purchasing index' also reported that more people than ever said they recycled (94 per cent), supported local shops and suppliers (80 per cent), avoided a product or service on the basis of the company's reputation (55 per cent) or actively chose a product or service on the basis of a company's reputation (61 per cent)

Also vital to the growth of SEs in the UK has been the change in emphasis by the government, moving away from providing grants and towards giving contracts via the competitive tendering process. Further, the deregulation, devolution and privatization of welfare states across the world during the past 20 years is a key factor in this growth (Goerke, 2003).

Demographic changes, such as ageing populations, combined with changing attitudes to health issues in society has also meant that governments have responded by promoting the social enterprise sector. This response is a way of both modernizing public services and delivering new solutions to new challenges. There is evidence to show that SEs can be effective providers of public services. The success of Greenwich Leisure in London lies in the fact that it is linked to some 30 other UK local councils contracting their leisure/recreational services to other SEs (leisure trusts). In addition, 30 of England's top ten councils' recycling services are run by SEs (Allan, 2004). SEs also contribute to the production of social capital – those bonds of trust and reciprocity that have been found to be critical preconditions for democracy and economic growth (Salamon et al., 2003). One government interested in the social economy is the UK's New Labour Government, which came to power in 1997. The role of this government will now be explored.

THE ROLE OF THE GOVERNMENT IN THE UK

Pearce explained, 'The striking development of the last five years has been the growth in political and administrative support for SE in the UK, especially since the 1997 General Election' (Pearce, 2003: 91).

The Government in the UK has identified SEs as being an important part of its economic and social policy. In Prime Minister Gordon Brown's words, 'SE is the new British success story, forging a new frontier of enterprise' (Westall and Chalkley, 2007: 6).

SEs are proposed as catalysts for revitalizing disadvantaged UK communities through employment and countering welfare dependency (OECD, 2003). It is also important to note here that this drive towards a more enterprising orientation within the third sector is coupled with a reduction in grant funding for voluntary and charity-sector organizations. In 1999, the Treasury first identified a role for SEs in tackling social exclusion as part of its strategy to stimulate enterprise in disadvantaged communities (HM Treasury, 1999). This led to the development of the Phoenix Fund, which closed in March 2006, but has provided support for the creation of community development finance institutions (CDFIs), some of which provide access to funding for SEs, and funding for business development support projects in disadvantaged communities, a number of which have focused on SEs (see Exhibit 1.5). Following work by the Social Investment Taskforce, a new tax credit to promote enterprises in disadvantaged communities was also introduced that can support the capitalization of CDFIs.

Exhibit 1.5   Community Loan Fund North West (CLFNW)

The CLFNW, established in May 2000, is a CDFI working in the North West of England, providing loan finance to the voluntary and community/social economy sector. The funders include the Co-operative Bank, Northwest Regional Development Agency (NWDA), British Nuclear Fuels (BNFL), AMEC, Granada, Riverside, Cheshire Building Society and Liverpool Housing Trust. Priority is given for loans of up to £250,000 to those organizations that contribute to economic regeneration and social inclusion. The maximum repayment period is 10 years with interest rates 2.5 to 5 per cent above the base rate.

SEs in the North West that have received funding include social firm Dove Designs and Lister Steps Limited, a community nursery based in Liverpool. The CLFNW could play a growing role in the future, due to reduced grant funding available from European (SRB, ERDF and ESF) and Lottery Fund sources (interview with Roy White, 2007).

In 1999, the Government's strategy for neighbourhood renewal identified the need to better understand SEs in order to provide improved levels of support (DTI, 2002). In 2000, Patricia Hewitt, then Junior Minister of State, brought a focus on SEs to the Department of Trade and Industry (DTI). In 2001, the SE Unit was set up within the DTI to both coordinate policymaking and be a champion for SEs. Nigel Griffiths MP was also appointed the first junior minister for SEs. The Unit's 'social enterprise: a strategy for success' document, launched in 2002 (DTI), identified barriers to growth and made recommendations for overcoming them in order to make SEs better businesses.

This strategy document highlighted the need to create an enabling environment, make SEs better businesses and establish the value of SEs (DTI, 2002). To enable SEs, the document highlighted the need to coordinate SEs activities across national, regional and local government and educate both local authority procurement officers about the value of SEs and managers of SEs about the process of public procurement.

To make SEs better businesses the document identified the need to provide support and training via both UK business links and the Small Business Service and improve the finance and funding landscape for SEs by working with partners to increase the capitalization of community development finance institutions (CDFIs). By September 2003, 23 CDFIs were in existence.

In parallel to social enterprise: 'strategy for success', the Cabinet Office carried out research into reforming legal structures such as provident society legislation and the creation of community interest companies – a new legal form for SEs. Similarly, other new legal forms for SEs, mainly of the cooperative model, exist in France, Portugal, Spain and Greece. For example, the Portuguese 'social solidarity cooperative' was created in 1997. This type of cooperative provides services with the objective of integrating socially excluded groups.

A significant development in May 2006 has been the establishment of the Office of the Third Sector (OTS) within the Cabinet Office. According to the OTS, 'we have been set up to drive forward the Government's role in supporting a thriving sector, and bring together sector-related work from across government' (interview with Steven Wallace, 2006). Figure 1.3 shows how both the SE Unit at the DTI and the Active Communities Directorate (ACD) at the Home Office have been combined in the Office of the Third Sector (OTS). This move will counter some of the criticisms made of the government that have centred on the lack of joined-up thinking across different government departments. The OTS has allocated £515 million to support third-sector programmes to build capacity in the sector.

Westall and Chalkley (2007) argue that the forming of the OTS is due to the difficulties of clearly differentiating SEs from voluntary and community organizations. In November 2006, the OTS launched the new 'social enterprise action plan: scaling new heights'. This policy document declares the following intentions.

The action plan will drive change in four areas:

- embedding the cultural change that is already under way, especially by inspiring the next generation to start thinking about the social impact of business;

- improving the advice and support available to start-up and growing SEs;

- tackling the barriers to accessing finance that restrict the growth of SEs;

- enabling SEs to work effectively with government in pursuit of common goals.

The action plan builds on the first 2002 government strategy, 'social enterprise: a strategy for success' (DTI, 2002). In addition, other government departments have also launched initiatives for SEs, including the Department of Health (DoH), which, in 2006, set up its SE Unit to work with SEs to identify pathfinders that will lead the way in delivering innovative health and social care services. A SE fund of £73 million over four years has been established from April 2007 to help with set-up costs (Marks and Hunter, 2007).

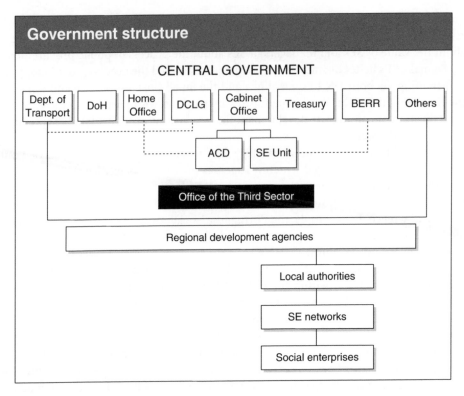

Figure 1.3 The UK government departments concerned with Social Enterprise (interview with Khan, 2007)

In addition, the Department for Environment, Food and Rural Affairs (DEFRA) recognizes the important role SEs can play in achieving its strategic objectives, particularly in sustainable development (DEFRA, 2007). SEs have also been identified as playing an important role by local government. The Department for Communities and Local Government (DCLG) published its Local Government White Paper, 'Strong and prosperous communities' (DCLG, 2006) and has announced a £2 billion fund for neighbourhood regeneration and strengthening communities (2008–2011) to be focused on disadvantaged areas in the UK. Also, the Department for Culture, Media and Sport has announced that it will engage with the third sector to ensure local communities are fully involved in the development of the 2012 Olympics (OTS, 2008).

Further, other recent UK government policy initiatives include Partnership for Public Services (PPS). The aim of PPS is to support innovative approaches and learn from the third sector, build its role in holding services to account, plus effective commissioning and improving procurement.

The PPS plan lists five key outcomes:

- coordinated specialist guidance and support with commissioning services from the third sector;

- increased understanding of the third sector among commissioning and procurement officers;

- provision of awareness training for councillors and public-sector officers on the benefits of third-sector involvement in the shaping and delivery of public services;

- provision of awareness and skills training for the most significant 2000 commissioners concerned with correctional, employment, children's, education and training, health and social care services as well as other local services.

- Improved third-sector bidding capacity, particularly among smaller organizations.

Clearly the aim is to develop a partnership culture between SEs and the UK public sector. This shows that public-sector procurement is a key aspect of the relationship between the social economy and the public sector. The support of SEs appears to fit with the political agenda to reform public services by contracting out services via the public sector's procurement and tendering process. This modernization, using SEs, is potentially more acceptable to many stakeholders, particularly trade unions, than awarding contracts to purely private-sector providers. However, progress in this area is not uniform across the different sectors in which SEs compete. SEs have broken into the procurement of a range of services, including leisure, homecare, waste and the employment, plus the training of the long-term unemployed (worker integration). Why SEs have not made the progress expected in public-sector procurement will be explored further in Chapter 2.

For New Labour, successful SEs can play an important role in helping deliver on many of the Government's key policy objectives. The OTS (2006) set out a range of attributes associated with SEs:

- helping to drive up productivity and competitiveness and increase levels of enterprise;

- contributing to socially inclusive wealth creation by tackling some of society's most entrenched social and environmental challenges;

- enabling individuals and communities to work towards regenerating their local neighbourhoods;

- set new standards for ethical markets, raising the bar for corporate responsibility and, in some cases, transforming markets;

- showing new ways to deliver public services;

- helping to develop an inclusive society and active citizenship;

- deliver sustainability;

- attract new people into enterprise.

There is also a strong focus in the Government's policy on increasing the business capacity of both the voluntary and charity sectors in the UK, particularly where public-sector contracting is concerned. It means that a number of voluntary and charity-sector organizations are in transition, moving towards becoming SEs. This is demonstrated by the dominant income source of UK charities now being *earned* income, recorded at 47 per cent. Voluntary income represents 45 per cent, with investment income at 8 per cent (Cabinet Office, 2007).

This SE political agenda is not popular, however, with all voluntary and charity-sector organizations. There are those that do not see the virtue in subscribing to this market-based agenda. Seanor and Meaton 2008 propose that the move from grant funding to contracting is complex. It can create tensions and lead to social mission drift, which can result in reduced trust between the organization and some of its key stakeholders, including staff and beneficiaries. There is a debate as to why SEs are any more able than the state or the voluntary sector at responding to the needs of disadvantaged groups.

We saw in Figure 1.3 where the OTS is positioned in relation to other government departments and regional and local government. Both regional development agencies and local authorities have also facilitated the setting up of networks of SEs. One such network is Social Enterprise London (SEL), described in Exhibit 1.6.

Exhibit 1.6   Social Enterprise London (SEL) (interview with Sabina Khan, Director of Policy and Research, 2007)

SEL was set up in 1998 and has developed a network of over 500 members that are SEs. Figure 1.4 shows the distribution of SE organizations that are members of SE within London. Of London residents between 18 and 64 years

Figure 1.4   Map of the social enterprise network in London, spring 2005

of age, 8.5 per cent are engaged in social entrepreneurship (Harding, 2004). All ethnic groupings are more likely than their white counterparts to be social entrepreneurs. Black Africans are three times more likely as whites people to be social entrepreneurs and black Caribbeans are twice as likely.

SEL's work includes offering business advice, delivering training programmes, network events, policy and research work and consultancy services.

London is made up of 33 different local authorities. In April 2004, SEL, with the support of the London councils, set up LA Connects, which is the first UK forum to bring together local authorities regarding the development of SEs to create a pan-London SE strategy (interview with Khan, 2007). According to Sabina Khan (interview, 2007), 'the aim is to build a consensus around SE. SEL also plays an active role in ensuring SE features in the 2012 Games. We are running a programme "Winning with 2012" in conjunction with the Cabinet Office and the SE Coalition to deliver on this'.

Within the United Kingdom, other such networks exist at a regional level that work very closely with the Social Enterprise Coalition (see Exhibit 1.7).

Exhibit 1.7   The Social Enterprise Coalition (SEC) (www.socialenterprise.org.uk)

The SEC is the UK's national body for SEs and has a combined membership of 10,500 organizations working in the social enterprise sector. It aims to share best practice and influence government policy at all levels to create an enabling environment for SEs.

The SEC has had a significant impact on central government, with all key government departments now containing SE units of their own (see Figure 1.3). It also works with banks and legal bodies to forward the interests of the sector and raise awareness.

Set up in 2003 on the recommendation of the All-Party Parliamentary Group on Social Enterprises, the SEC was funded by a small innovation grant from the DTI. The SEC's board is 25 people strong and they represent its key members, which include national representative bodies such as the National Council for Voluntary Organizations (NCVO), Co-operatives UK, Social Firms UK, Sporta and seven regional SE networks with their own subregion groupings. The SEC's key departments include business development and policy and research.

According to Cherry Read, former Head of Policy and Communications at the SEC (interview, 2007), 'we need to discuss where we will have maximum future impact? Do we build the sector via more SEs, further infrastructure support, building SEs' management capacity or raising the awareness of the sector?' Cherry also believes that the impact of SEs goes beyond the social enterprise sector: 'we are a catalyst for change within both the private and public sectors. We hope to see more convergence from all parts of the economy to the SE paradigm shift. Our aim should be to change society'.

The Government's vision is of a dynamic and sustainable social enterprise sector strengthening an inclusive and growing economy. Emerging from the devolution of the welfare state, privatization, deregulation and the drive for the 'Third Way', SEs have much to accomplish (Amin et al., 2002; Giddens, 1998).

Although social enterprise has been identified a growth sector, there have been difficulties encountered in fulfilling its potential. One of the major barriers to growth in the social enterprise sector identified by the SE Unit of the DTI is 'complexity and lack of coherence within the sector, combined with widely varying skills and knowledge bases'. Therefore, central to the Government's strategy for success in the sector is the policy of working more closely with training providers and encouraging SEs to move away from grant dependency and towards self-financing their activities. Pivotal to the Government's strategy for the sector is the Social Enterprise Coalition (SEC).

Managers of SEs are thus challenged to constantly adapt to a changing environment – a balancing act that requires strategic reflection and analysis to achieve ongoing sustainability. Pressures to improve performance have led to the adaptation of business practices in the third sector. It is important to note here that, in the UK, the social enterprise is being viewed by all political parties as a solution to many societal challenges (Westall and Chalkley, 2007).

Beyond the UK Peredo and Chrisman (2006) identify social enterprise in the Asian Pacific area as a route to both building small-to-medium-sized business' capacity and an approach to business that will foster sustainable development in the region. Both the UN (2001) and World Bank (2001) forecast that poverty will rise in poor countries and are particularly concerned about the negative aspects of globalization. Of the world's poor, 75 per cent live in rural communities in poor countries, leading to out migration to already overcrowded cities. This leads to an increasing economic burden on the women and children left behind (Peredo and Chrisman, 2006).

SEs are emerging from civil society organizations (CSO)/non-governmental organizations (NGOs) in the emerging markets of Latin America, Asia and Africa. Faced with the reduction of international charitable donations, such organizations are developing entrepreneurial strategies to generate income to further their social missions (Etchart and Davis, 2003). According to Peredo and Chrisman (2006), community-based enterprises (CBEs) that are managed and governed to pursue economic and social/environmental goals can result in local sustainable development. These organizations, led by social entrepreneurs, face high levels of uncertainty and risk, stemming from both political and economic instability and lack of access to capital markets.

One such organization is the Association of Craft Producers (ACP), based in Kathmandu, Nepal (see Exhibit 1.8). The ACP is led by Meera Bhatari (its Executive Director), who was awarded the Ashoka Fellowship in 1992 for her contribution to women and development in Nepal. The Ashoka Fellowship is awarded to extraordinary individuals with unprecedented ideas for effecting change in their communities. Ashoka is a global non-profitmaking organization that searches the world for inspirational social entrepreneurs (www.ashoka.org).

Exhibit 1.8   The Association of Craft Producers (ACP), Nepal

The ACP, established in 1984, works with over 1000 groups of small-scale women producers in 17 districts throughout Nepal. It provides design, marketing, management and technical services for the low-income, primarily female craft producers there. The aim is to empower the women to earn regular, adequate wages to improve their overall standard of living.

Nepal is an extremely poor country, despite four decades of development, and remains one of the poorest in South Asia, with two out of three Nepalese people living in poverty and 38 per cent of the population living on less than US$1 a day (DFID, 2003). The country has also been faced with civil war due to the Maoist insurgence.

Meera Bhatari (2007) explains that, 'ACP is involved in the whole development process. We have changed the notion that crafts are only for hobbies and part-time work, and women can be quickly and effectively trained to produce high-quality crafts'. Meera is keen to stress that 'ACP is not a charitable institution but operates very much on a business base with full accountability'. The ACP also believes in inclusivity, attaching equal importance to both urban and rural poor, while also trying to maintain a balance between the range of ethnic groups living in Nepal. The ACP maintains two shops – one in Kathmandu of 3600 square feet and one in Pokhara with 2000 square feet. Despite a growth in total sales of 34 per cent since 1997, Meera is still not satisfied with the ACP's sales performance: 'to meet the demands of our international customers we need to improve our access to relevant and timely market information. This is difficult for a country so far away from some of its key markets such as the US'. (*Source*: Interviews with Bhatari, 2003 and 2007)

CONCLUSIONS

There are clear international differences concerning the role of SEs. This demonstrates the impact of different levels of social and economic development, specific legal frameworks and the nature of different welfare systems.

Previous international research has tended to focus on comparisons between Europe and North America. However, there is literature emerging that relates to the role of SEs in international development and from regions such as Latin America and Asia.

It is also clear from this chapter that, in both Italy and the UK, SEs are embedded within the third sector. In these countries, too, SEs are involved in a wide range of activities. However, there are differences between the countries approaches. Italian laws stress a particular governance model through a requirement to involve the various stakeholders. The British model highlights the business character of SEs as usually 50 per cent of their income needs to be market-based for these enterprises to be seen as SEs.

The role of the UK's New Labour Government in setting policies specific to SEs is an illustration of how policy can influence the growth of SEs. It fits with the 'Third Way' political agenda, which promises to combine social justice with economic innovation. It is also clear that networks and other support structures are important if SE growth is to be facilitated.

This chapter has shown the scale of the social enterprise sector and the contribution SEs make to economies and societies worldwide. Although this is difficult to quantify accurately, there appears to be universal agreement that it has grown significantly. Despite this growth, we must also be aware of the challenges facing those voluntary and charity organizations that are making the transition to becoming towards SEs and develop support frameworks that recognize this dynamic.

REFERENCES

Interviews

Meera Bhatari, Executive Director, Association of Craft Producers, Kathmandu, Nepal, interviewed both 4 January 2003 and 10 January 2007.
Sabina Khan, Director of Policy and Research, Social Enterprise London, interview 14 June 2007, London.
Cherry Read, former director of Policy, Social Enterprise Coalition, 20 June 2007, London.
Stephen Wallace, Deputy Director, Office of the Third Sector, 13 March 2007, London.
Roy White, Fund Manager, Community Loan Fund North West, interviewed 23 July 2007.

Allan, B. (2004) Social Enterprise, through the eyes of the consumer. A think piece prepared for the National Consumer Council.
Amin, A., Cameron, A. and Hudson (2002) *Placing the Social Economy*. London and New York: Routledge.
Austin, J.E. (1999) 'The collaboration challenge: making the most of strategic alliances between non-profits and corporations'. Social Enterprise Series No. 6, Harvard Business School, Cambridge, MA.
Barratt Brown, M. (1993) *Fair Trade: Reform and realities in the international trading system*. London and New Jersey: Zed Books.
Birchall, J. (1994) *Co-op: The people's business*. Manchester and New York: Manchester University Press.
Bornstein, D. (2004) *How to Change the World: Social entrepreneurs and the power of new ideas*. Oxford: Oxford University Press.
Borzaga, C. and Santuari, A. (2003) 'New trends in the non-profit sector in Europe: the emergence of social entrepreneurship', in OECD (ed.), *The Nonprofit Sector in a Changing Economy*. Paris: OECD.
Branco, D. (2007) 'Country case study of social enterprise in Italy'. Available at: www.teses. eu/index.php?id=28 [accessed 29 September 2008] (www.teses.eu)
Bull, M. (2006) *Balance: Unlocking performance in social enterprises*. Manchester: Centre for Enterprise, Manchester Metropolitan University.
Bull, M. and Crompton, H. (2005) 'Business practices in social enterprises', *Social Enterprise Journal*, 2 (1): 42–60.
Bunc M., Kovac, Z. and Kociper, T. (2007) 'An exhaustive economic, training and educational needs analysis in Slovenia in the sector of social economy and social entrepreneurship'. Available at www.teses.eu/index.php?id=28 accessed 29 September 2008.
Cabinet Office (2007) 'The future role of the third sector in social and economic regeneration: final report', Cabinet Office, London.
Co-operative Bank (2005) 'Ethical purchasing index 2005', Co-operative Bank, Manchester.
Crane, A. and Matten, D. (2004) *Business Ethics*. Oxford: Oxford University Press.

Dart, R. (2004) 'The legitimacy of social enterprise', *Nonprofit Management and Leadership*, 14 (4): 411–24.

DCLG (2006) 'Strong and prosperous communities', Local Government White Paper, DCLG, 26 October. Available at: www.communities.gov.uk/publications/localgovernment/strongprosperous

Dees, J.G. (1998) 'Enterprising nonprofits', *Harvard Business Review*, 76 (1): 54–66.

Defourney, J. and Borgaza, C. (2001) *The Emergence of Social Enterprise*. University of Trento, Italy, University of Liege, Belgium.

Defourney, J. and Nyssens, M. (2006) *Defining Social Enterprise: Social enterprise at the crossroads of market, public policies and civil society*. London and New York: Routledge, Taylor and Francis.

DEFRA (2007) DEFRA, London. Available at: www.defra.gov.uk/rural/social-enterprise/default.htm#1

DoH (2006) 'No excuses. Embrace partnership now. Step towards change!'. Report of the third sector commissioning task force. Available at www.dh.gov.uk/en/Publicationsandsatistics/Publications/Publications/PolicyAndGuidance/DH_4137144

DFID (2003) 'DFID Nepal: country assistance plan 2003–2007', draft, DFID, London. Available at: www.dfid.gov.uk/Pubs/files/cap_nepal_draft.pdf

Doppelt, D. (2003) *Leading Change Toward Sustainability: A change management guide for business, government and civil society*. Sheffield: Greenleaf Publishing.

DTI (2002) 'Social enterprise: a strategy for success', DTI London.

ECOTEC (2003) ' Guidance on mapping social enterprise: final report to the DTI Social Enterprise Unit, DTI London.

Elkington, J. (1997) *Cannibals with Forks: The triple bottom line in the 21st century*. Oxford: Capstone.

Etchart, N. and Davis, L. (2003) 'Unique and universal lessons from emerging field of social enterprise in emerging market countries', Nonprofit Enterprise and Self-sustainability Team (NESsT), Turlock, CA.

Fairtrade Foundation (2007) 'Fairtrade Foundation annual report 2007', Fairtrade Foundation, London.

Fairtrade Labelling Organization (2008) 'FLO annual report', FLO, Bonn, Germany.

Giddens, A. (1998) *The Third Way: The renewal of social democracy*. Cambridge: Polity Press.

Goerke, J. (2003) 'Taking the quantum leap: nonprofits are now in business: an Australian perspective', *International Journal of Nonprofit and Voluntary Sector Marketing*, 8 (4): 317–27.

Harding, R. (2004) 'Social enterprise: the new economic engine', *Business Strategy Review*, 15: 39–43.

Harrison, R., Newholm, T. and Shaw, D. (2005) *The Ethical Consumer*. London: Sage.

HM Treasury (1999) '*Enterprise & social exclusion: national strategy for neighbourhood renewal*', Policy Action Team 3, HM Treasury, London.

Hudson, R. (2005) 'The social economy beyond the local? Developmental possibilities, problems and policy considerations', *Urbanistical*. Available at: http://eprints.dur.ac.uk/archive/00000049

IFF (2005) 'A survey of social enterprises across the UK', research report for the Small Business Service, IFF Research Ltd.

Jones, D. and Keogh, W. (2006) 'Social enterprise: a case of terminological ambiguity and complexity', *Social Enterprise Journal*, 2 (1): 11–26.

Laville, L.J. and Nyssens, M. (2001) 'The social enterprise: towards a theoretical socio-economic approach', Chapter 18 in J. Defourney and C. Borgaza, *The Emergence of Social Enterprise*. pp. 312–32.

Lowe, W. and Davenport, E. (2005) 'Postcards from the edge: maintaining the "alternative" character of fair trade', *Sustainable Development*, 13: 143–53.

MacGillivray, A., Conaty, P., Doling, J. and Mullineux, A. (1998) *Low Flying Heroes: Micro-social enterprises below the radar screen*. London: New Economics Foundation.

Marks, L. and Hunter, D. (2007) 'Social enterprises and the NHS: changing patterns of ownership and accountability', Centre for Public Policy and Health, Durham University/Unison.

Moulaert, F. and Ailenei, O. (2005) 'Social economy, third sector and solidarity relations: a conceptual synthesis from history to present', *Urban Studies*, 42 (11): 2037–53.

Nicholls, A.J. (2002) 'Strategic options for fair trade retailing', *International Journal of Retail and Distribution Management*, 30 (1) 6–17.

Nicholls, A. (2006) '*Social Entrepreneurship: New models of sustainable social change*. Oxford: Oxford University Press.

Nicholls, A. and Opal, C. (2004) *Fair Trade: Market-driven ethical consumption*. London: Sage.

OECD (2003) 'The non-profit sector in a changing economy', OECD, Paris.

OTS (2006) 'Social enterprise action plan: scaling new heights', OTS, London.

OTS (2008) 'The future role of the third sector in social and economic regeneration: final report', Office of the Third Sector, London.

Pearce, J. (2003) *Social Enterprise in Anytown*. London: Calouste Gulbenkian Foundation.

Peredo, M.A. and Chrisman, J.J. (2006) 'Towards a theory of community-based enterprise', *Academy of Management Review*, 31 (2): 309–28.

Reichel, J. and Kozakiewicz, M. (2007) An exhaustive economic, training and educational needs analysis in Poland in the sector of social economy and social enterpreneurship. Available at www.teses.eu/index.php?id=30 Accessed 29 September 2008.

Salamon, M.L., Sokolowski, W.S and List,. R. (2003) 'Global civil society: an overview', The Johns Hopkins Comparative Study for the Nonprofit Sector Project, Institute for policy studies, Centre for Civil Society, Baltimore, MD.

Seanor, P. and Meaton, J. (2008) 'Learning from failure, ambiguity and trust in social enterprise', *Social Enterprise Journal*, 4 (1): 24–40.

SEL (2000) 'Social enterprise in a regional context: main findings from a study visit to Valencia, Spain', SEL, London.

Shaw, D., Newholm, T. and Dickinson, R. (2006) 'Consumption as voting: an exploration of consumer empowerment', *European Journal of Marketing*, 40 (9/10): 1049–67.

Smallbone, D., Evans, M., Ekanem, I. and Butters, S. (2001) 'Researching social enterprise final report to the Small Business Service Centre for Enterprise and Economic Development Research', Middlesex University, London.

Tickell, A. and Peck, J. (2003) 'Making global rules: globalization or neoliberalisation', in J. Peck and H. Yeung (eds), *Remaking the Global Economy: Economic–geographical perspectives*. London: Sage. pp. 163–81.

United Nations (2001) 'UNDP poverty report: overcoming human poverty'. New York: United Nations.

Westall, A. and Chalkley, D. (2007) *Social Enterprise Futures*. London: The Smith Institute.

World Bank (2001) 'World development report', World Bank, Washington DC.

2

SOCIAL ENTERPRISES IN CONTEXT – THE STORY SO FAR

KEY THEMES

- To understand the discourse regarding the definition of social enterprise (SE).
- The different organizational and legal forms of SEs.
- The scale and scope of SEs.
- Management challenges for SEs.

DEFINITIONS OF SOCIAL ENTERPRISE

Despite the importance of the social economy and SEs to the UK and Europe, there is significant discourse over both the definition and identification of such organizations (Adams et al., 2003). Currently, SEs are defined by organizational type, legal structure and value characteristics. A number of authors have argued that different legal structures and organizational forms (see Forms of SEs later in this chapter) make any generalizations regarding SEs challenging (Dees, 1998; Westall, 2001). However, the lack of a universal definition is argued by some to lead to a slippage of key terms and also be a hindrance to research in the sector, particularly when mapping the SE sector (Haugh, 2005; Nicholls, 2006; Shaw and Carter, 2007). Jones et al. (2007) argue that definitions are important to both differentiate SEs from other organizations in the private and public sectors and also highlight the differences between specific models of SEs.

According to Peattie and Morley (2008) the problems with defining SEs is linked to a tendency by certain authors to focus on particular characteristics and these cannot be applied across the sector. For example, SEs are often described as not generating profits for distribution to shareholders when it is clear that a number of SEs, such as Traidcraft, and other SEs set up as community interest companies (CICs), are intended to share an element of profit with their shareholders. Also, SEs are often described as being small and democratic. Austin et al. (2005) argue there is nothing that prevents SEs from being large and there is an emerging concept of 'corporate social entrepreneurship'. Some authors also approach definitions from a normative position, arguing that SEs should be non-profitmaking or democratic.

Peattie and Morley (2008) argue that SEs are distinguished from other organizations by the simultaneous possession of two attributes.

- SEs trade in goods and/or services in a market (so they are an 'enterprise' and not simply a voluntary or community organization).

- The primacy of social aims. The primary purpose of SEs lies outside the commercial outcomes related to their trading of goods and/or services in a market (beyond the generation of profit or the growth of the enterprise itself). That is what makes them 'social'.

Both attributes reflect the delineations in Pearce's model (as shown in Figure 1.2 in Chapter 1) between SEs and the private sector.

The most widely used definition in the UK is (DTI, 2002):

> **A social enterprise is a business with primarily social objectives whose surpluses are principally reinvested for that purpose in the business or in the community rather than being driven by the need to maximize profit for shareholders and owners.**

This definition from the DTI highlights the importance of both the not for private profit and use of the surplus elements, which are what differentiate SEs from other organizations in the social economy. The DTI (2002) proposes that 50 per cent of the income from the trading of goods and services must be targeted at operationalizing the SEs' social and environmental missions through a business model of competitively trading for a social (or environmental) purpose. The DTI (2002) also describes the locus of SEs (see Figure 2.1), illustrating third sector organizations' funding orientation regarding trading. According to Westall and Chalkley (2007) this DTI definition prioritizes both profit use and financial self-reliance and supports calls by government to encourage the wider third sector to move towards greater financial self-sufficiency. This is set against a background of reduced grant funding for voluntary/community-based organizations.

The locus of SEs is particularly useful for third-sector organizations if you consider that, while some SEs start off as businesses, such as Divine Chocolate (formerly Day Chocolate), some are in transition, having begun as voluntary and community sector organizations. For example, Collins and Glossop (2006) reported that up to 35 per cent of general registered charity income is derived from trading activities. Jones et al. (2007) propose that a distinction is now made in the UK between established SEs (which receive 50 per cent plus income from trade) and emerging SEs (which receive less than 50 per cent, or 25 to 49 per cent, income from trade). This could suggest that the two attributes suggested by Peattie and Morley (2008) do not take into account charities or voluntary organizations that are in transition, moving towards an enterprise orientation.

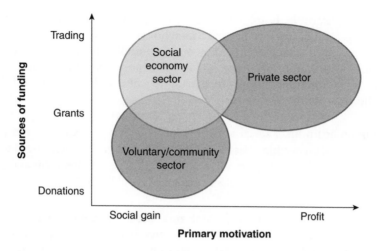

Figure 2.1   The locus of the social economy sector

Ed Miliband (2007) also proposes that SEs put ethics at the centre of their businesses, not just as a bolt-on. He argues for SEs competing on the basis of ethical values, particularly in consumer markets. He also argues that, by competing on these values, standards in the private sector will be raised and this will also transform public services.

This ethical dimension is also highlighted by Nicholls and Opal (2004), who propose that the core product of fair trade SEs is the ethical element. Fair trade, according to Nicholls and Opal (2004), is, in a Kantian analysis, deontological. This approach to supply chain relationships establishes the need to treat others fairly, as one would wish to be treated. Deontological ethics (ethics of duty) prioritize personal moral duty to others and are the foundation for the ethics of rights and justice (Crane and Matten, 2004). Authors in the neoclassical tradition, however, identify all economic agents as being egoistic, ignoring deontological considerations (Beauchamp and Bowie, 1988). Pearce (2003) also explores a values-based approach as underpinning the SE sector, including values, cooperation, empowerment by investing power in people and communities, inclusivity, good work (active citizenship), sustainability, democracy and being people-centered (embracing people, culture, environment).

There are similarities between the DTI's definition and that of the UK's Social Enterprise Coalition (2003), which proposes that an SE is 'an organization that trades in the market for a social purpose and who shares three common characteristics'.

- *Enterprise orientation*   They are directly engaged in providing goods or services to a market.

- *Social aims*   They have explicit social aims, such as job creation, training or the provision of local services. Their ethical values may include a commitment to building skills in local communities. Their profits are principally reinvested to achieve their social objectives. Increasingly, SEs measure their social impact.

- *Social ownership*   They are autonomous organizations, the governance and ownership structures of which are normally based on participation by stakeholder groups (for example, employees, users, clients, local community groups and social investors) or trustees or directors who control the enterprise on behalf of a wider group of stakeholders. They are accountable to their stakeholders and the wider community for their social, environmental and economic impact. Profits can be distributed as profit sharing to stakeholders or used for the benefit of the community.

This definition again links social aims with an enterprise orientation and places an emphasis on social ownership. Westall (2001) argues that governments need to be clear about what SEs are, but does propose that SE is still a developing term and its looseness could actually be an advantage. She explains (Westall, 2001: 1):

> SE is a loose umbrella term which raises the awareness of a variety of organizations that highlight alternative ways to do business that directly incorporate social and environmental concerns. This gives the possibility of creating revenue streams that enable an organization to create sustainable social change without being reliant on time-limited funding or charitable donation.

According to Westall (2001), such a definition can therefore raise the awareness of diversity, create new initiatives and new innovative models. Birch and Whittam (2006) appear to support this position by proposing that a market emphasis could encourage the development of new forms of organization.

Westall (2001) herself proposed the 'spaces for SE' model (see Figure 2.2) to illustrate where new innovations could be created. The axes show relative independence from government (top to bottom) and, from left to right, a spectrum from dependence on grants and donations to being fully self-financing and from no owners or multi-stakeholder governance to pure outside shareholding. The overlaps of the sectors illustrate the range of models possible incorporating different stakeholder involvement or ownership and also the lack of clear distinctions between sectors. The SEs featured in Exhibit 2.2 have been positioned in Figure 2.2 for the purposes of discussion.

Westall (2001) also argues that, while many SEs aim to be self-sufficient, they may also make use of a variety of income streams, including donations, public money and in kind support. Pearce (2003) also argues for mixed income streams. According to Pearce (2003), the primary purpose of a SE is social/environmental, the commercial activity being the means of achieving this primary purpose. Pearce (2003) and Drayton (2005) see SEs as being part of a social movement providing a radical model. Fair trade SEs, such as Divine Chocolate and Cafédirect, have their roots in the solidarity movements of the 1970s and 1980s (Lowe and Davenport, 2005).

In contrast to the definition used in the UK, the SE Alliance in the USA defines an SE as, 'An organization or venture that advances its social mission through entrepreneurial earned income strategies'. This definition appears to focus on the enterprise with a social mission. The US approach appears to see SEs as forming a subset of social entrepreneurship, focusing in the main on earned income as a method to achieve social aims. Many European definitions of SEs view participation as being of equal importance to trading and emphasize their role in developing a more diverse

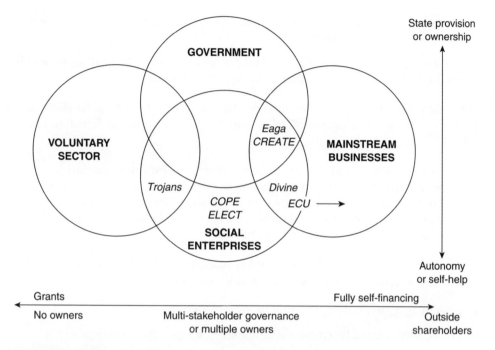

Figure 2.2 Spaces for social enterprise model (adapted from Westall, 2001: 9)

and pluralistic democracy. They also highlight their role in a social economy as pointing to another way of organizing the market (Westall and Chalkley, 2007).

Kerlin (2006) summarizes some of the key differences between the American and EU approach to SEs and argues that the key emphasis in the US is on generating revenue while the main emphasis in Europe is on bringing about social benefits.

The European Research Network's (EMES) definition of SEs proposes four criteria that distinguish between both economic and social indicators:

- directly involved in the production of goods or services to people on a continuous basis, the productive activity representing one of the key reasons for the existence of SEs;
- created by a group of people on the basis of an autonomous project and governed by these people – they are not managed by public authorities or other organizations (federations, for-profit private firms and so on);
- a significant level of economic risk;
- a minimum amount of paid work.

EMES also propose five criteria to capture the social dimensions of SEs:

- an explicit aim to benefit the community or a specific group of people;
- an initiative launched by a group of citizens who share a well-defined need or aim – this collective dimension must be maintained over time and the

importance of leadership, often embodied in an individual or small group of leaders, must not be neglected;

- decisionmaking power is not based on capital ownership, but, rather, generally on the principle of 'one member, one vote' is followed.

Other international perspectives include that of the Organisation for Economic Co-operation and Development(OECD), which provides a broader definition of SEs (OECD, 2006):

> Organizations with different legal forms in different countries, which are organized in an entrepreneurial spirit to pursue both social and economic goals. Social goals prioritize solutions to unemployment, social cohesion and social exclusion. These organizations can be urban or rural based.

The OECD (2006) has identified a list of key economic and social characteristics that define SEs in all the different countries in which they exist:

- directly engaged in the provision of goods or services;
- voluntarily created by citizens and managed by groups of citizens;
- stakeholders have the right to participate in them;
- involve a significant level of economic risk;
- have a minimum number of paid employees;
- the decisionmaking power is shared by stakeholders and is not based on capital ownership;
- participatory in nature;
- avoid profit maximization behaviour and involve the limited distribution of profits;
- have as an explicit aim to benefit a specific group of people.

In Central and Eastern Europe, there are fewer SEs (OECD, 2006) and political and historical challenges remain (see Exhibits 1.2 and 1.3). However, definitions of what SEs are have been stated in Slovenia (see Exhibit 2.1) and elsewhere in the region.

Exhibit 2.1   Definition of SEs in Slovenia (Bunc et al., 2007)

SEs in Slovenia are regarded as companies or organizations that have been set up with the aim of promoting social well-being and fulfil the following criteria:

- *economic:*
  - they are manufacturers or service-based;
  - they are autonomous (not state owned);

- market-orientated;
- have a defined share of voluntary work;

- *social:*

  - established as a result of civilians' initiatives;
  - decisionmaking is not related to share of capital (one stakeholder, one voice);
  - the active participation of all stakeholders is ensured;
  - work to benefit their members, targeted beneficiaries or the community;
  - the major share of the profits is reinvested back into their activities or the wider community (the primary goal is not maximizing profits for their owners).

Like elsewhere, therefore, any SE in Slovenia should combine its market-orientated business activities with its social aims, motives and needs. It should seek to succeed, as any other business entity (private profit and public profit-orientated) would, in creating and establishing its market share and making a profit. However, it should also emphasize the long-term benefits for its employees, its customers and the members of its living–working community.

The one common characteristic in all of these international definitions is the drive towards creating an enterprise culture to achieve social aims. This focus on generating an income from trading activities differentiates SEs from companies the broader social economy. Defourney and Nyssens (2006) agree and argue that SEs apply the methods of the private sector to achieving the types of primary social aims more normally associated with the public and voluntary sectors. This makes SEs a form of organizational hybrid (see also Dees (1998) on the SE hybrid spectrum).

A number of authors have identified sustainability as being key in their respective definitions of SEs (Birch and Whittam, 2006; Pearce, 2003). The UK Government's Sustainable Development Unit lists sustainable communities as being one of its four key aims.

> Sustainable communities are places where people want to live and work, now and in the future. From global to local we aim to improve the lives of people in deprived communities and socially excluded groups who experience poor quality of life, including poor local environmental quality and poor access to services such as health-care, education and transport (www.sustainable-development.gov.uk/key/local-global.htm).

Birch and Whittam (2006) discuss sustainable development in the social enterprise sector in relation to the production and promotion of social capital. They argue that SEs can play a crucial role in developing social capital by building new relationships and networks. Despite SEs focusing on economic sustainability, recent work has emphasized the double or triple bottom line, arguing for the debate regarding the sustainability of SEs to be widened to include social and environmental sustainability. Doherty and Thompson (2006) discuss the double and triple bottom line in relation to SEs.

It is interesting to note instances of leading SEs focusing on the triple bottom line as a key part of their business strategy. The ECT Group, for example, one of the UK's famous SEs, states, 'our commitment to the triple bottom line is the foundation of ECT's business model. It relates directly to sustainability and we are an example of a fully developed triple bottom line company committed to social and environmental outcomes as well as economic results' (ECT, 2007).

Reid and Griffith (2006) have also suggested the potential SEs have to tackle the quadruple bottom line–the blending of economic, social, ecological and community concerns. Related to this discussion is the question should we be looking at both financial and economic outcomes as two distinct areas?

Despite the discourse surrounding definitions, the need for organizations that have primarily a social mission, achieved by reinvesting profits derived from trading, is clear. It is this profit, termed surplus, and the reinvestment of this surplus in the social mission that clearly differentiates SEs from other companies (Bull 2006).

The kind of trading engaged in should not be limited to the sale of goods and services. The work of Pearce (2003) and Westall (2001) is useful in this respect. We also need to take account of the international variations in definitions and types of SEs. In this respect, the summary provided by the OECD is useful. However, it does not reflect all types of SEs, such as NGOs that trade–ACP in Nepal (see Exhibit 1.8), for example.

Pearce proposes that 'we need an international definition that is more encompassing of different SE forms' (interview: with Pearce, 2007). However, the key aspect on which there *is* agreement is that the primary focus of SEs is on a social aim, which means that, instead of customers and shareholders being prioritized, key stakeholders for SEs include a range of disadvantaged groups. These include;

- producers who have not been fairly paid for their products, in the case of fair trade organizations such as Divine Chocolate (see Exhibit 2.2 later in this chapter);

- the long-term unemployed, in the case of intermediate labour market companies such as CREATE (see Exhibit 2.2);

- those excluded by the established financial services providers in the case of credit unions such as the Enterprise Credit Union (see Exhibit 2.2);

- marginalized women, in the case of the ACP (see Exhibit 1.8);

- the environment, in the case of ECT (see Exhibit 2.3).

Building successful stakeholder relationships with the targeted disadvantaged groups is key to the success of SEs – the effective ones establishing high degrees of trust. Many SEs have been created to deliver products and services into sectors including healthcare, the arts and culture, employment, housing, social care, education and training, environmental and recycling services, financial services, food and beverage manufacturing (for example, fair trade models), regeneration, provision of leisure services, retail, transport and agriculture.

Although this is not a book on social entrepreneurship, it is important to discuss the distinction between SEs and social entrepreneurship, so we shall turn to this next.

SOCIAL ENTREPRENEURSHIP

In recent years, a number of excellent books have been written in this important area (see Dees, 2001; Nicholls, 2006). A number of authors have described social entrepreneurs as heroic, bold individuals or groups of people who provide innovative solutions that create and sustain social value (Dees, 2001; Vega and Kidwell, 2007). While there are many examples of this, Spear (2006) also argues that success in SEs often comes from teams and groups who use distributed entrepreneurship and circles of entrepreneurial activity. This debate does highlight the research tradition paradox mentioned by Peattie and Morley (2008), who contrast social entrepreneurship and its strong emphasis on the heroic individual with the literature on the cooperative movement, which emphasizes collectivism.

The literature on social entrepreneurship also highlights international differences. The term 'social entrepreneur' and the heroic individual perspective has, until recently, been particularly emphasized by American organizations, such as Ashoka. In contrast, the European literature has discussed the collective nature of the social enterprise more (Defourny and Nyssens, 2006).

According to Vega and Kidwell (2007), social entrepreneurs develop solutions to social problems that have not previously been applied by the private, public or voluntary sectors. In this way they can act as catalysts for change (see Exhibits 2.3 and 2.4 later in this chapter). Conceptualizations of social entrepreneurship stress the social innovation processes undertaken by social entrepreneurs. The concept is also now being used to describe a wide spectrum of initiatives, not only within the SE sector but also within the voluntary and corporate sectors (Nicholls, 2006). Two different types of social entrepreneur are described:

- those whose belief in a social cause inspires them to become entrepreneurial;

- entrepreneurs who decide to apply their business skills to solve a social problem.

These individuals may set up SEs, but they could also set up other types of organizations or networks or alter public policy frameworks.

Bull (2006) argues that, as in the SME (small medium enterprise) literature, it is naïve to suggest that the SEs are entirely made up of entrepreneurs. He also argues that the success of a social entrepreneur should be viewed not only in terms of economic success but also in terms of organizational entrepreneurialism and social success. Thompson (2008) agrees and proposes that, while SEs may create both social and economic wealth, they need not be run by entrepreneurial characters and their behaviour does not have to conform to what we understand as entrepreneurial.

Parkinson and Howorth (2007) found significant differences between the language used by social entrepreneurs and that of mainstream private-sector entrepreneurs. Concepts of community, collectivism, localness and the desire to focus business on community needs or not were the key differences.

A developing demographic trend that may create the potential for new social entrepreneurs is that of 'downshifting'. Research by Prudential Insurance showed that 1.4 million

Britons had already reduced their incomes in exchange for a better quality of life. There may be an opportunity to attract these 'downshifters', who may possess strong business acumen, to a career in social entrepreneurship. It is clear that SE as a term prioritizes organizational forms that trade to achieve their social mission over individuals who do so (Birch and Whittam, 2006).

For further reading on conceptualizing social enterprise and social entrepreneurship, see Professor John Thompson's paper in the *Social Enterprise Journal* (see the References section at the end of this chapter for further details).

FORMS OF SEs

Legal structure is viewed by some as helping to define SEs, but this is complicated by international variations in the legal format (Jones and Keogh, 2006). Some argue that it is purpose/mission that defines a SE rather than structure (Shaw and Carter, 2007). The legal structures commonly associated with SEs include the following:

- charity that trades;
- trusts;
- community interest company (CIC);
- company limited by guarantee;
- company limited by shares;
- community benefit society;
- industrial and provident society;
- unincorporated association.

Until the recent introduction of CIC, SEs in the UK have not been defined by a legal form. They have therefore used many organizational forms, including social firms, intermediate labour market (ILM) companies, development trusts, cooperatives, employee-owned companies, community enterprises, housing associations, football supporters' trusts, leisure trusts' charities with trading arms, and credit unions, among others. Exhibit 2.2 gives some examples of UK SEs that have adopted different organizational forms. The diversity of these forms demonstrates the innovative nature and richness of the social enterprise sector.

Exhibit 2.2   Some forms SEs can take

Social firms

These are businesses created to provide integrated employment and training for people with a disability or other disadvantage in the labour market (Social Enterprise Coalition, 2003). COPE, which stands for

---

Community Opportunities for Participation in Enterprise, established on the Shetland Islands in 1997, is an example of a social firm. COPE creates employment and training opportunities for people with learning disabilities by running businesses involved in soapmaking and catering to supply the tourist industry. COPE is a limited company with charitable status and employs more than 40 staff, trainees and volunteers.

Development trusts

Such trusts are community enterprises that are locally based and engaged in regeneration activities through a wide range of trade and service delivery operations and partnerships with other sectors. Common activities include community development, training, property development and management, environmental improvements, business development, building restoration and managed work space.

A development trust is not a legal structure in itself, but is usually registered as either a company or an industrial and provident society.

ELECT, based in Merseyside, is a development trust. It was set up in 1998 to regenerate disadvantaged communities by forming SEs in order to create job opportunities. ELECT has set up over 30 SEs, including daycare services, youth and health projects. Its turnover has grown from £69,000 to £1.5 million and it employs 25 staff (interview with Allen, 2007).

Cooperatives

Cooperatives are structured and run in accordance with the cooperative principals:

- voluntary and open membership;
- democratic member control;
- economic participation by members;
- autonomy and independence;
- education, training and information;
- cooperation between cooperatives;
- concern for community.

The members who own and control the cooperative can be employees (a worker coop, see Doherty and Thompson 2006 for the Suma Case study), customers (a consumer coop, such as Co-operative Food), tenants (a housing coop) or a combination of these groups.

The Midcounties Co-op is known for some interesting ventures, including retail, funeral care and car dealership (www.osg.coop). It is the fourth largest regional consumer coop in the UK, with a turnover of £300 million. In 2002 it launched a new social venture called Imagine Co-operative Childcare (www.imagine.coop) to provide affordable childcare across its trading area. The childcare SE now boasts five nurseries.

(Continued)

(Continued)

Community enterprise and intermediate labour market (ILM) company

CREATE (Community Recycling and Training) is a SE with four aims:

- to recycle used white goods;
- provide affordable white goods for low-income households;
- provide employment for long-term unemployed adults (this is the ILM part);
- be viable and sustainable.

This enterprise is based in Merseyside and has ILM contracts with Liverpool, St Helens and Knowsley councils (local government authorities). CREATE's income is made up in the following way: 56 per cent from the sale of raw or refurbished appliances, 42 per cent from training contracts and 2 per cent from grant income. It is worth noting here that, in 1998, 53 per cent of CREATE's income was derived from grants. CREATE's turnover has grown from £650,000 in 2001 to £2.1 million in 2006/2007. Greg Walker (its Chief Executive) explains that 'our transition from grant income to trading was achieved through a combination of having a board with a shared vision, a human resource plan that recognizes the skills of each employee, a passionate management team committed to raising the standard of our service.' Greg also explains that, 'We provide a professional service that provides a 12-month guarantee for reconditioned electrical goods and achieves a less than 10 per cent returns rate. This compares favourably with an average 12 per cent returns rate from new appliances from competitors in the private sector. The enterprise works across all economic sectors and searches for win-win situations' (interview with Walker, 2007).

Employee-owned businesses

These are companies that are wholly or substantially owned by the people who work in them (www.employeeownership.co.uk).

Eaga is an example of a large employee-owned SE. It has a turnover of £345 million and provides energy-efficient solutions for vulnerable people living in cold, damp and energy-inefficient homes. Since 1990 Eaga has improved the energy efficiency of 5 million disadvantaged households by providing sustainable services and products that address the government's environmental, social and energy efficiency objectives.

On 7 June 2007, Eaga was floated and admitted to the London Stock Exchange. The flotation was to raise £220 million for new investment in the business, but 51 per cent of Eaga's shares remain in employee ownership.

Fair trade SEs

Wholly fair trade companies challenge conventional international trade by aiming to improve the livelihoods of small-holder farmers in less developed countries.

One such company is Divine Chocolate (formerly Day Chocolate) which won SE of the Year at the Enterprise Solutions Awards 2007.

Divine shares with its partners a mission to improve the livelihoods and opportunities of small-scale cocoa farmers in West Africa by establishing a dynamic, branded company in the valuable UK chocolate market (Doherty and Tranchell, 2005; Tiffen, 2002). The cocoa farmers' cooperative Kuapa Kokoo (KK) in Ghana is the joint owner of Divine, with a shareholding of 45 per cent, and has two seats on the board. Divine Chocolate pays both a fair trade price and a 'social premium' for all the cocoa purchased from KK (Doherty and Tranchell, 2005). Consequently, its branded products, Divine and Dubble, all carry the Fairtrade Mark. Despite the competitive conditions of the UK confectionery sector, Divine has managed to grow, since it was set up in 1998, to a turnover of £10 million by developing fair trade brands that appeal to an increasing number of ethical consumers.

Charities with trading arms

The Trojans Scheme is an educational and training charity based in South West London (NCVO, 2008; Social Enterprise Coalition, 2003). Its trading arm, Kids City, runs out-of-school play activities for children aged 4–11 years plus activity schemes for teenagers aged 14–19. In addition, the SE provides volunteering, employment and training opportunities for adults living in areas of high unemployment. Kids City employs 85 staff – 14 full-time and the remainder part time – and over 110 volunteers. Kids City operates in areas ranked among the 10 per cent most deprived in England. It works with 14 schools in Lambeth and Wandsworth, with 2300 children using the service each week. Its income has grown from £97,000 in 1997 to over £1 million in 2006. The organization has adopted a SE model to boost its sustainability.

Credit unions

These are third-sector lenders within the economy. They are financial not-for-profit cooperatives offering savings and loans facilities to their members with the aim of financial inclusion.

All credit unions are regulated and supervised by the Financial Services Authority. There are 3.3 million households nationally outside the mainstream financial services market. The Association of British Credit Unions states that there are currently 561 credit unions in the UK. One such is the Enterprise Credit Union (ECU), based in Huyton in Knowsley, Merseyside.

The 2004 Index of Deprivation placed Knowsley as the third most deprived borough nationally. The ECU aims to address the stark problems of financial exclusion and now has 3426 members in a 17.5 square mile geographic area. The ECU offers a number of financial services, including instant accounts, low-interest loans, savings accounts and insurance.

Collectively, SEs are not registered by any central body. However, since July 2005, they have been able to register as a new legal form – the community interest company (Social Enterprise Coalition, 2008). The office of the Regulator (2005) defines this form as follows:

> **A limited liability company which carries on a social activity and it must be able to generate surpluses to support its activities, maintain its assets, makes its contributions to the community and in some cases make limited returns to its investors.'**

The Community interest company (CIC) is a new limited company structure for SEs that secures an 'asset lock' for the community and focuses on community benefit (Dunn and Riley, 2004). It has been designed to make incorporation simple for SEs wishing to use the familiar corporate form with a separate legal identity from its members.

Compared with other limited companies, CICs are subject to additional regulation to ensure that the community benefits (www.cicregulator.gov.uk).

The registration of a company as a CIC has to be approved by the regulator, who also thereafter has a monitoring and enforcement role. To apply for registration, the SE must provide the regulator with evidence that it satisfies the community interest test. In order to determine whether or not a company satisfies (or will satisfy) the test, the SE needs to consider:

- the purposes for which it has been set up;

- the range of activities it is engaged in;

- who will be seen as benefiting from its activities (Community Interest Companies, 2006).

There are now over 2000 organizations in the UK registered as CICs (www.cicregulator.gov.uk). Each CIC is required to report to the regulator on what if delivers for the community and its stakeholder involvement. In addition to the 'asset lock', CICs are subject to a dividend cap. This means that, unlike most companies, CICs may only declare a dividend by an ordinary or special resolution of its members (a dividend cannot be declared by the directors alone).

Julie Court (Deputy Regulator for Community Interest Companies) explains: 'I have been involved in community work over many years and see the creation of CICs as a major addition to the development and expansion of community-orientated activities. This additional legal form is complementary to what is already available' (interview with Court, 2006). However, recent reports highlight that a growing member of people are of the opinion that both the dividend and interest caps associated with CICS may be too restrictive. Attracting start-up and growth capital from private investors is proving challenging. Another school of thought is that the respective caps *enhance* the CIC brand (*Social Enterprise Magazine,* 2008a). Certainly the asset lock is an attractive mechanism for those involved in community asset transfer. Perhaps lifting the rate of the dividend cap is one solution.

ECT, described in Exhibit 2.3, is an example of well-known SE that converted to being a community interest company in 2005.

Exhibit 2.3   ECT

ECT, with a turnover of £60 million and over 1000 staff, is the largest SE to be awarded CIC status (ECT, 2007).

ECT began life 23 years ago as Ealing Community Transport, enabling residents with mobility difficulties to get out and about. Today, ECT has grown and diversified into a range of other community services, including recycling, street cleaning, waste management, public transport and healthcare, delivering services to over 20 UK local authorities. The ECT Group, alongside its wholly owned subsidiaries ECT Recycling and ECT Bus, are now registered as community interest companies (ECT, 2006).

ECT often competes with larger private providers for public service contracts. According to Stephen Sears (ECT's Chief Executive), the CIC status provides ECT with a clear and defined structure that gives ECT legitimacy in the eyes of key decisionmakers. Sears explains, 'decisionmakers have sometimes opted for profit-driven companies as they see them as less risk. The perceived risk of dealing with SEs comes from a lack of understanding. The fact that CICs will be registered at Companies House drives home the reality that we are a legitimate enterprise' (ECT, 2007).

Since this case study was written, ECT announced in July 2008 the sale of its recycling arm, ECT Recycling, to May Gurney – a large, private-sector maintenance and support services company – in a deal worth £15.3 million. Sears explains that ECT recycling will remain a CIC – after all, protecting the asset was the point of becoming a CIC in the first place. May Gurney is also keen to acquire the expertise of ECT, perhaps as part of its corporate social responsibility strategy. The move raises some key questions for discussion.

- Will future contracts won from the legitimacy provided via the CIC legal form be operated through the ECT CIC?
- How will the future of employees' terms and conditions be affected?
- What about those commissioners and local residents who thought that they were supporting a SE when the contracts were given to ECT. How do they feel?

There is no doubt that, in parts of local government, contracts are getting larger. Perhaps the move by ECT to team up with this private partner could be one way to enable SEs to scale up. The true test going forward will be whether or not the social objectives remain the same and the community need continues to be fulfilled (Hampson, 2008).

Other European countries also have specific legal forms for SEs, including the Italian social cooperative status (see Exhibit 1.1), Belgium's companies with a social purpose and Portugal's, social solidarity cooperatives (see the Defourny and Nyssens (2008) for a more in-depth look at specific legal forms by nation state).

THE SCALE AND SCOPE OF SEs

Due to the lack of any central body for SEs, it is challenging to get some measure of both the actual contribution and potential of SEs when placed within the context of the wider social economy (which we have seen referred to as the third sector), particularly if the current trends for social economy organizations to move towards more business, market-orientated modes of operation are taken into account. In the UK, the turnover of cooperatives is around £20 billion – consumer cooperatives alone have a turnover of £12.5 billion and 9.8 million members (www.co-operatives-uk.coop). There are 60 building societies with assets of £305 billion, more than 15 million savers and 2.5 million borrowers (www.bsa.org.uk). Housing corporation accounts for 2006 show that there are 1950 housing associations managing 2.2 million properties worth £74 billion (www.housingcorp.gov.uk). In the charitable and not-for-profit sector, there are between 500,000 and 700,000 organizations. Within this, there are 169,000 'general charities' with an income of £26.3 billion in 2003/04 and a paid workforce of at least 608,000 (www.ncvo-vol.org.uk). Since 2000, the sector has seen a net increase of 28,000 organizations (NCVO, 2006).

A number of types of SEs are growing fast. The past 10 years have seen the creation of 110 leisure trusts, where local authority in-house leisure services have been turned into SEs. They now have a combined turnover of more than £500 million, employ over 13,000 people and have in excess of 118 million customer visits per year (www.sporta.org). Development trusts (a form of community enterprise based on the use of community-owned assets that generate income to meet local needs, often in areas of greatest economic decline) have also seen rapid growth. There are now 385 such trusts with a combined turnover in the region of £210 million and £340 million-worth of assets in community ownership, employing 5000 staff (Development Trusts Association, 2006).

Another organizational form SEs can take that was outlined above is the social firm. Nearly one in five people of working age in Britain is disabled. Almost half of these 6.9 million people are unemployed. Since 1997, the number of social firms has grown from just 5 SEs to 137 social firms by 2007, creating a total of 1625 jobs for disabled people (Reynolds, 2007b). Social Firms UK (SFUK) now has its own quality mark. Insufficient employment opportunities for disabled and disadvantaged people is a worldwide problem. In 2007 SFUK launched the International Social Firms Association with the aim of providing solutions to common challenges and sharing best practice (Reynolds, 2007a).

In addition, another form for SEs that is displaying growth is the fair trade company. Total fair trade sales in the UK reached £490 million in 2007 (see Exhibit 1.4), but this figure includes sales of supermarkets' own brands and sales from private-sector companies that have recently launched fair trade products – for example, Nestlé plc with Nestlé Partners Blend. Those 100 per cent fair trade companies that have as their mission alleviating poverty in commodity supply chains are regarded by Lowe and Davenport (2005) as radical mainstreaming projects that maintain the transformative message of fairtrade These include fair trade companies such as Cafédirect, Divine Chocolate, the fresh produce business Agrofair and the fair trade nut company called Liberation (at the time of writing it has just been launched and is in its first year of

Table 2.1   Fair trade sales growth by 100 per cent fair trade companies

SEs	Annual sales in 2007 £ million	% growth
Agrofair	7.6	56
Cafédirect	22	3
Divine Chocolate Ltd	11	19
Traidcraft	16.5	5

Source: Annual reports of all companies, 2007

trading), all of which are examples of alternative approaches to the market with southern hemisphere producer organizations being shareholders in these northern hemisphere fair trade companies. You can also add to this list Traidcraft Plc. The growth in sales of these companies are highlighted in Table 2.1.

It is important to note that SEs come in all shapes and sizes. Many start small and will remain locally based businesses operating in niche markets, meeting local needs. Others operate nationally or even internationally. The largest in the UK is probably the Co-operative Group, which has a turnover in excess of £8 billion, more than 70,000 employees and 5.5 million members. Others such as Greenwich Leisure are also very significant businesses. Greenwich Leisure has a turnover of £28.5 million and over 3000 staff (www.socialenterprise.org.uk). Another example is Eaga – an employee-owned business based in Newcastle-upon-Tyne that has a turnover approaching £345 million and more than 500 staff (www.eaga.com). According to the Employee Ownership Association, this group of enterprises is worth £20 billion annually and is growing. The John Lewis Partnership is another good example of an employee-owned business.

The 2005 survey of SEs for the Small Business Review Service, however, considered only two forms of SEs: companies limited by guarantee (CLG) and industrial and provident societies (IPS). It is clear that they do not account for all forms of SEs, hence the need for a new comprehensive mapping study of the sector. Work being carried out by Professor Fergus Lyon at Middlesex University will be useful in this respect. He calls for a common set of methodologies for mapping the sector and outlines the gaps in previous studies, which failed to capture those charities involved in trading. Added to this, some organizations do no not see themselves as SEs, but they are involved in social enterprise activities.

Lyon (2008a) argues for the application of the DTI's definition in the mapping of SEs and proposes three tests for them, namely:

- social ownership – they are autonomous organizations with an element of participatory governance involving stakeholders and trustees, with profits used for the community or shared with stakeholders;

- enterprise orientation – income comes from trading;

- social aims – social (and environmental) benefits that are not limited to a restricted group.

Lyon (2008a) supports this approach to mapping the SE sector by going into these tests in further detail.

Social ownership

Social ownership is defined by ECOTEC (2003) as 'autonomous organizations with a governance and ownership structure based on participation by stakeholder groups and trustees'. The key categories include community interest companies, companies limited by guarantee, industrial and provident societies, housing associations and registered charities with trading income. In each of these, there are elements of democratic governance. They should be autonomous and institutionally separate from government.

Using ownership structures to distinguish between the for-profit and social enterprise sectors is also challenging where there are social firms or fair trade organizations registered as companies limited by shares. Companies limited by shares are therefore included where they are identified by local mapping exercises and where more than 50 per cent of any surplus or profit goes towards achieving social goals.

Trading income

Trading income refers to 'income from sale of goods and services' and 'payments received in direct exchange for a product, service' and indicates an enterprise orientation. While some studies propose a cut-off of 50 per cent of income from trading to define social enterprises, others, such as the IFF (2005), use a 25 per cent threshold so as to include organizations that are moving towards a SE model. However, this arbitrary cut-off point can exclude those organizations aiming to increase their SE activities.

Lyon (2008a) explains that, based on previous mapping studies, income should be included from contracts and service-level agreements with public bodies, but exclude grants, subsidies, fundraising, membership fees from supporters without specific benefits, voluntary contributions and donations.

Social aims

Lyon builds on the definition of a SE, saying that it is 'primarily social (including environmental) objectives and it principally reinvests its surplus in the business or in the community, in pursuit of these objectives'. However, Lyon also argues that this is open to some degree of interpretation.

Key issues here include the following:

- Social benefits should extend beyond a membership group, unless these are socially disadvantaged/excluded. In this we are guided by the community interest and charitable interest tests from the CIC guidance.

- CIC guidance states that a 'reasonable person' test should be applied regarding what constitutes community/wider public interest. Access to benefits provided by the organization should be 'widely available and not confined to an unduly restricted group'.

- The CIC test guidance also indicates that political parties and organizations, the purposes of which are support for a political party or political campaigning, should be excluded.

- The charitable status test is that 'charities must benefit the community at large or a substantial section within it. They must not entirely exclude those of limited means'.

There are several difficult cases, such as housing associations, that should be included if they are registered as charities and have social objectives, such as the provision of sheltered or affordable housing and targeting disadvantaged groups. Difficulties may arise where organizations are working purely in a commercial environment or housing stock is moved from a local authority with considerable local authority control still being exerted.

See further work on this subject by Fergus Lyon (2008b).

Building capacity

The DTI's 'Social enterprise: a strategy for success' document in 2002 identified a lack of understanding by the financial sector as a barrier to building capacity in the social enterprise sector. There are now several specialist banks working in this sector, including the Charity Bank, Triodos Bank (2007), plus community development finance institutions (see Exhibit 1.5). In addition, there are private equity groups such as Venturesome and Bridgeventures, plus specialist units within mainstream banks. One such example is the not for profit team at NatWest Bank (part of the Royal Bank of Scotland).

A 2003 Bank of England report into the financing of SEs found a small demand for conventional venture capital or business angel-type financing. This occurs for a number of reasons, including risk aversion, availability of cheaper funding sources, such as grants, limited profits for shareholders, lack of a conventional exit strategy and the unwillingness on the part of SEs to cede ownership to external investors. Both the SEs and venture capitalists must share a long-term vision. This issue is illustrated by the SE Poptel, which arose from the workers' cooperative movement. Poptel competed in the technology sector and set up the people's Internet service Easinet. To further expand the business, Poptel attracted venture capital investment. However, when the external drivers in the market changed, the venture capital provider did not have the long-term vision required to lower its expectations.

Harding (2006) argues that weak management teams and inadequate business planning cause problems regarding accessing appropriate finance. However, the report did find that 40 per cent of SEs (larger, established SEs) do use a range of external financing techniques involving banks and other lenders, such as CDFIs (see Exhibit 1.5). There is also evidence to suggest that banks can be risk-averse. Tiffen (2002) explains that Divine Chocolate, when it was set up in 1998, struggled to secure loan finance from a range of banks. A breakthrough came in the form of a loan guarantor agreement from the Department for International Development, which secured its initial start-up finance from the National Westminster Bank (part of the Royal Bank of Scotland).

Recent literature regarding SEs identifies a growth in innovative forms of investment, such as loans, near-equity and patient capital (Jones et al., 2007). In the USA, there has been the emergence of 'venture philanthropy' (Letts et al., 1999). There is also the development of longer-term patient finance from social banks such as Triodos, which means that they are prepared to accept lower returns in exchange for measurable social outputs (Brown and Murphy, 2003).

There is an ambition, both within the sector and externally, to scale up SEs to manage rapidly developing expectations, particularly in areas such as waste services (Darby and Jenkins, 2005). New approaches such as 'social franchising' are emerging to support them as they build capacity (Litalien, 2006). Other potential approaches include a social stock exchange and private partnerships, the move by ECT being a good example of this (see Exhibit 2.4).

The SEs' funding mixes and the combination of grant and trading income are a unique aspect of SEs. A number of banks have specialist teams working in the social economy sector in order to develop capacity. One such bank, NatWest Bank (now the Royal Bank of Scotland) is discussed in Exhibit 2.4.

Exhibit 2.4   Help for SEs from NatWest and others

The not for profit team at the NatWest Bank (now the Royal Bank of Scotland) consists of eight business managers and six support staff who together support between 550 and 600 third-sector organizations. David Brinsford (interview, 2007), the head of the unit, explains:

> Our assessment of a SE and its risk potential is no different from our assessment of other small-to-medium-sized enterprises. However, it is important to understand the differences in the structure of the balance sheet. You need to understand that from start-up to break-even point can be a longer time period. We often work on a consortia approach with a blend of finance including ourselves, a CDFI and other partners.

Brinsford also argues that SEs need to have a strong social mission combined with excellent products and services and be dedicated to quality.
There are some other investment initiatives worthy of mention here, including the following.

- Asset development. The 'making assets work: the Quirk review' (DCLG, 2007) highlighted the importance of a sustainable asset base for SEs. To this end, the UK government is committed to funding community anchors. This is particularly useful for development trusts (OTS, 2007).
- Raising share capital. Cafédirect is one example of a SE raising share capital. In 2004, it raised £5 million in a share issue sponsored by Triodos Bank. The company's shares are not listed on an exchange but on a matched bargaining system called ETHEX run by Triodos Bank. Currently, the OTS is supporting research into the feasibility of a 'social' capital market where investors interested in a blended social and financial return could make and trade investments (OTS, 2007).
- There is a government initiative, in partnership with the bank and building society sector, to develop a scheme to access unclaimed assets lying dormant in accounts and reinvest them to benefit community projects (HM Treasury, 2005).
- The UK government announced that £10 million is to be made available for co-investment with the private sector in SEs.

According to Peattie and Morley (2008) SEs' relationships with the private sector are relatively undeveloped when compared with their relationships with the public sector. Private companies can benefit from relationships with SEs by both accessing key expertise and enhancing their reputation (Young, 1999). Groundwork SE in the UK is offering help in this area by providing consultancy advice in environmental management for private-sector firms (interview with Smith, 2007). There are also examples of private-sector firms building links with SEs to provide volunteer opportunities for employees, leading to improved staff motivation and retention. The UK-based Brighton and Hove SE Partnership is a good example of this approach (see Exhibit 2.5).

Exhibit 2.5   The Brighton and Hove Business Community Partnership (www.bhbcp.org.uk)

The Brighton and Hove Business Community Partnership (BCP) is a membership-based SE that brings together commercial, community and voluntary-sector organizations to support community developments and encourage social entrepreneurship. Based in Brighton, it brings together third-sector organizations including SEs and private-sector companies to work in a partnership network to promote positive community change.

Since 1996, the partnership has brokered deals in kind between private businesses and third-sector organizations to the value of £3 million. It is funded by a range of revenue streams, including membership subscriptions, consultancy fees and charity grants. Its key services include its corporate social responsibility programmes, which enable private-sector companies to provide a range of services to third-sector organizations, including:

- mentoring support;
- in kind donations of services;
- volunteer time;
- trustee and management committee members;
- training and work placement opportunities.

In 2006/2007, the BCP's employee volunteering programme enabled 756 business volunteers to support 42 different third-sector organizations. This represents an investment of £79,380 to the community but also results in the development of leadership, strong teams and company values within participating businesses.

The BCP illustrates the two-way opportunities that accrue from SE and private-sector companies working together. This innovative support programme for SEs has led to the growth of SEs in Brighton. From a mapping study carried out in collaboration with the University of Brighton, it was found that 110 SEs operate in the Brighton and Hove district, contributing £21 million to the economy and employing 1262 people. Further analysis reveals that 20 per cent of these SEs obtain 91 per cent of their income from trading, 66 per cent of them work with volunteers, giving a total of 3042 volunteers work in the sector, and 52 per cent employ staff from disadvantaged groups (BCP, 2007).

The Community Action Network (CAN) Match winners initiative is another good example of how SEs can build mutually beneficial partnerships with the private sector (Community Action Network, 2006). As discussed earlier in this chapter (see Exhibit 2.4), there has also been the private-sector purchase of ECT Group. Perhaps private-sector partnerships can help capitalize SEs that are working on large, local government contracts requiring significant capital investment. It is a sign, too, that SEs can be attractive to the private sector. However, SEs must ensure that any such relationship is based on a shared social mission.

Public-sector partnerships are also important for building capacity in the social enterprise sector. Governments see SEs as a means of modernzing public-sector services. However, the success of SEs in winning public-sector contracts has been patchy across national, regional and local government. This is because they are competing against some large private-sector providers that can deliver economies of scale.

The UK Government has launched a strategy called 'Partnership in public services; an action plan for third sector involvement' (OTS, 2006). The action plan outlines the need to build knowledge of public-sector procurement and commissioning processes within the sector and raise awareness of the value of SEs with central and local government commissioners.

'Procurement' is defined as being the acquisition of goods and services from third-party suppliers under legally binding contractual terms where all the conditions necessary to form a legally binding contract are met. 'Commissioning', however, is different – it is the process of specifying, securing and monitoring services to meet people's needs. Commissioning is done at a strategic level and normally involves elected officers in local government.

The public sector uses procurement to:

- improve services;

- achieve best value;

- make the public sector more efficient;

- encourage innovation.

In the UK, tenders are normally invited when the estimated expenditure or anticipated income is £100,000 or more. Each tender will outline a service specification and the bids will be evaluated against a set of weighted criteria, which will typically include price, management of the service, partnership working, knowledge and experience of working with the client, assessment of needs and support planning and details of the proposed service.

Moves to incorporate well-being and the EU's sustainable procurement agenda into public-sector procurement provide concrete opportunities for SEs. It is important for them to explain fully their experience of working with the client group and so on. Some SEs will have to form consortia with other SEs or private-sector partners to deliver a winning tender, particularly if it needs to be on a national basis. Working with the public sector provides good opportunities for scaling up SEs and such contracts are often solid and long term with timely payments. They provide SEs with opportunities to move their businesses into a city residents' daily lives. However, SEs must guard against contract dependency.

CONCLUSION: THE KEY MANAGEMENT CHALLENGES FOR SEs

Some SEs are set up from the start as SEs, some emerge from the public sector via the modernization of public services agendas, while a sizable number are voluntary organizations that are in transition, becoming SEs. Borzaga and Defourney (2001) highlight the key management challenges facing SEs across Europe:

- developing a supportive regulatory and legislative environment;
- ensuring quality of products and services;
- upgrading skills and jobs;
- securing management expertise;
- financing;
- establishing networks and cooperatives;
- establishing adequate governance structures.

Westall and Chalkley (2007) propose a number of barriers that echo the ones listed above, including problems accessing appropriate forms of finance and advice and support. In addition, a lack of fixed assets and ensuring that public services procured by government at national and local levels are genuinely open to SEs, such as market access (Flockhart, 2005), are mentioned. Also, champions in government need to work with the sector to evaluate the social, environmental and economic contribution made by SEs. Paton (2003) also identified the need for planning and strategic management in the social enterprise sector in order for it to realize its potential.

Bearing in mind these previously published proposals, we also sought the views of a number of opinion leaders on the key management challenges facing the sector.

A number of authors would add that there is a need for the sector to measure the many intangible benefits created by SEs (Aereon-Thomas et al., 2004; Brennan and Ackers, 2004; Darby and Jenkins, 2006). This call is partly driven by the general move towards professionalizing the sector and the need to demonstrate its effectiveness. Arthur et al. (2006) argues that the debate around effectiveness is mainly focused on the enterprise narrative and not the social aspect. They propose that success from a business/enterprise perspective does not naturally lead to the achievement of social aims. The DTI (2002) also highlighted the tensions and conflicts for SEs in meeting both financial *and* social bottom lines. Speckbacher (2003) adds that profit as a single measure of success does not work as it fails to capture other important performance outputs of SEs.

This challenge to measure social performance has been met by a range of methodologies, including:

- social accounting;
- social return on investment;
- social audit (Pearce, 2003);

- local multiplier models, LM2 and LM3 (Sacks, 2001);

- an adapted form of the Balanced Scorecard (Bull, 2006; Somers, 2005).

The Balanced Scorecard, developed in the private-sector literature, is, Kaplan and Norton (1996) suggest, easily transferable to the social sector. The work of Bull (2006) is useful in respect of this tool.

The development of a comprehensive set of indicators that capture the performance and social, economic and environmental value of SEs, represents an opportunity to communicate the added value of SEs with internal and external stakeholders. This could be used to create competitive advantage in public-sector tendering and bidding for contracts with retailers (for example, fair trade organizations). In addition, this focus on performance could lead to more informed strategic decisionmaking (Darby and Jenkins, 2006).

According to Cherry Read, former Head of Policy and Communications at SEC, (interview, 2007):

> Significant numbers of SEs originate from both the voluntary and public sector, which means the need to adopt a performance agenda can be a real challenge. Managers need to develop skills in reporting, measuring impact, entrepreneurship and legal knowledge. Proving what you do should lead to improvements in your performance and will help SEs to both adapt to a rapidly changing environment and create innovation.

George Leahy, who is working for the SEC but has been seconded from the Department of Health (interview, 2007), agrees and proposes that 'measuring impact will put some kind of value on those trust relationships which are an asset of SEs'.

David Brinsford (former Associate Director, Business Development, Charities and Not for Profit Sector, National Westminster Bank, now part of the Royal Bank of Scotland) proposes that:

> SE managers need to be dedicated and business-minded. We look for key competencies within the management team, including financial management, strategic management and human resources. Managers of SEs need to understand the risks. When making assessments we are looking for knowledge of the strategic management process, including market knowledge and understanding of the external environment. This understanding is particularly important in those organizations in transition from the voluntary or public sector.

Greg Walker, Chief Executive at CREATE, the community enterprise that recycles electrical goods discussed earlier, agrees on the importance of understanding the external environment. New EU legislation called the Waste Electrical and Electronic Equipment (WEE) Directive has resulted in CREATE having to redesign its service and supply chain. The new directive means that manufacturers, not retailers or local councils, are responsible for paying for the disposal of electrical goods. CREATE has played a very proactive role in national discussions with government and other key stakeholders in designing how the UK should manage its operations in order to conform with this new legislation. Greg Walker explains, 'we have not only been on top of understanding the environment but we have also taken a proactive role in designing new supply chains with other stakeholders'.

SEs are under pressure to perform in the marketplace and competitive tendering process as well as the subsequent delivery of quality products/services. Hence, there has been a drive within the sector towards professionalization. This has been interpreted as the need to adopt mainstream management practices (Golding and Peattie, 2005). This is not always the case, however. Divine Chocolate Ltd has been successful in main-streaming its fair trade chocolate range in the UK confectionery market. Lowe and Davenport (2005) have warned of the potential for cooption and dilution of the fair trade transformative message when in the mainstream, leading to 'clean-wash' by larger private-sector rivals. However, Divine has managed to maintain its focus on campaign-ing and the transformative message of fair trade. This has been termed 'radical main-streaming' (Doherty and Tranchell, 2007). In fact, being in the mainstream has enabled Divine to speak to more people more often about its social aims and its joint ownership with Kuapa Kokoo farmers cooperative in Ghana than if it had not made such a move.

SUMMARY

Arthur et al. (2006) argue that, currently in SE research, the business narrative is being prioritized over concepts of the social. However, a number of authors propose that the sector is under- researched full stop and call for the gathering of robust evidence to show the value of SEs in society and clarify management aspects (Haugh, 2005; Hines, 2005).

This author would suggest that any research on SEs needs to look at both the social *and* the business considerations. The standard business literature that has accumulated in relation to the profit maximization model (single bottom line) clearly does not pri-oritize these social aspects.

REFERENCES

Interviews

Elizabeth Allen, Operations Manager, ELECT, Liverpool UK, interviewed 21 March 2007.
David Brinsford, Associate Director, Business Development, Charities and Not for Profit Sector, National Westminster Bank, part of Royal Bank Scotland, interviewed 20 June 2007, London.
Julie Court, Deputy Regulator for Community Interest Companies, interviewed 15 November 2006.
George Leahy, Policy Analyst, Department of Health (secondment into Social Enterprise Coalition), interviewed 20 June 2007, London.
John Pearce, Head of Social Auditing network, interviewed 23 October 2007, Birkenhead, UK.
Cherry Read, former Director of Policy, Social Enterprise Coalition, interviewed 20 June 2007, London.
Michael Smith, Director of Business Programmes, Groundwork Trust, North West England, inter-viewed 8 March 2008.
Greg Walker, Chief Executive of CREATE, interviewed 23 July 2007, Liverpool, UK.

Adams, J., Robinson, P. and Vigor, A. (2003) 'A new regional policy for the UK', IPPR, London.

Anheier, H.K. (2000) 'Managing non-profit organizations: towards a new approach', Civil Society Working Paper 1, Centre for Civil Society, London School of Economics, London.

Areon-Thomas, D., Nicholls, J., Forster, S. and Westall, A. (2004) *Social Return on Investment: Valuing what matters.* London: New Economics Foundation.

Arthur, L., Keenoy, T., Scott-Cato, M. (2006) 'Where is the "social" in social enterprise?', Paper presented at the Third Annual Social Enterprise Conference, South Bank University, London, 22–23 June.

Austin, J, Stevenson, H. and Wei-Skillern, J. (2006) 'Social and commercial entrepreneurship: Same, different, of both?', *Entrepreneurship Theory and Practice* 31 (1): 1–22.

Beauchamp, T.L. and Bowie, N.E. (1988) *Ethical Theory and Business* (3rd edn). Englewood Cliffs, NJ: Prentice Hall.

Birch, K. and Whittam, G. (2006) 'The role of the social economy and social enterprise and social entrepreneurship in sustainable regional development', Discussion Paper 12, July, Centre for Public Policy for Regions, Glasgow and Strathclyde 12 July.

Borzaga, C. and Defourney, J. (eds) (2001) *The Emergence of Social Enterprise.* Abingdon: Routledge.

Brennan, S. and Ackers, S. (2004) 'Recycling, best value and social enterprise: assessing the "Liverpool model"', *Local Economy,* 19 (2): 175–80.

Brighton and Hove Business Community Partnership (BCP) (2007) BCP Annual Review 2007, Brighton, UK.

Brown, H. and Murphy, E. (2003) 'The financing of social enterprises: a special report by the Bank of England', Bank of England Domestic Finance Division, London.

Bull, M. (2006) *Balance: Unlocking performance in social enterprises.* Manchester: Centre for Enterprise, Manchester Metropolitan University.

Bunc, M., Kovac. Z. and Kociper, T. (2007) An exhaustive economic, training and educational needs analysis in Slovenia in the sector of social economy and social entrepreneurship. Available at http://www.teses.eu/index.php?id=28 [accessed 29 September 2008].

CLG (2007) 'An action plan for community empowerment: building on success' (community empowerment action plan), CLG, London. Available at: www.communities.gov.uk/communities/ community empowerment/whatweare/action.

Collins, G. and Glossop, C. (2006) *An Introduction to Sustainable Funding: Understanding your options.* NCVO.

Community Action Network (2006) *Match Winners: A guide to commercial collaborations between social enterprise and private sector business.* London: Community Action Network.

Community Interest Companies (2006) 'Community Interest Companies Briefing Pack', Office of the Regulator of Community Interest Companies, Cardiff.

The Co-operative Review, 2007, available at: www.cooperatives-uk.coop/Home/about/the Co-operative Economy/the Co-operative Review

Crane, A. and Matten, D. (2004) *Business Ethics.* Oxford: Oxford University Press.

Darby, L. and Jenkins, H. (2006) 'Applying sustainability indicators to the social enterprise business model', *International Journal of Social Economics,* 33 (5/6): 411–31.

Darby, L. and Jenkins, H. (2005) 'Applying sustainability indicators to the social enterprise', Wastesavers and BRASS, Cardiff.

Dees, J.G. (1998) 'Enterprising nonprofits', *Harvard Business Review,* 76 (1): 54–66.

Dees, J.G. (2001) *The Meaning of Social Entrepreneurship.* Stanford, CA: Stanford Business School.

Defourny, J. and Nysseus, M. (2006) *Defining Social Enterprise: Social enterprise at the crossroads of market, public policies and civil society.* London and New York: Routledge, Taylor and Francis.

DCLG (2007) 'Making assets work: the Quirk review of community management and owenership of public assets', DCLG, London. Available at: www.communities. gov.uk/publications/communities/ making assetswork

Defourny, J. and Nyssens, M. (2008) Social enterprise in Europe: recent trends and developments, *Social Enterprise Journal,* 4 (3).

DOH (2006) 'No excuses. Embrace partnership now. Step towards change! Report of the third sector commissioning task force', DOH, London. Available at: www.dh.gov.uk/en/Publicationsandstatistics/Publications/PublicationsPolicyAndGuidance/DH_4137144

Development Trusts Association (2006) 'Development trusts in 2006: annual membership survey' DTA, London.

Doherty, B. (2004) 'Himalayan inspiration for social enterprise'. *Social Enterprise Bulletin*, 1(1): 8–10, December. http: //cwis.livjm.ac.uk/bus/busrm ccl/me/SEB 1.1.p

Doherty, B. and Meehan, J. (2006) 'Market entry based on social resources: the case of Day Chocolate Company in the UK confectionary sector', *Journal of Strategic Marketing*, 14 (4): 299–313.

Doherty, B. and Thompson, J.L (2006) 'The diverse world of social enterprise: a collection of eight social enterprise stories', *International Journal of Social Economics*, 33 (5/6): 361–375.

Doherty, B. and Tranchell, S. (2005) 'New thinking in international trade?: A case study of the Day Chocolate Company', *Sustainable Development*, 13: 166–76.

Doherty, B. and Tranchell, S. (2007) 'Radical mainstreaming of fairtrade', special edition of *Equal Opportunities International Journal in Culture and Diversity in Marketing*, 26 (7): 693–711.

Drayton, B. (2005) 'Where the real power lies', *Alliance*, 10 (1): 29–30.

DTI (2002) 'Social enterprise: a strategy for success', DTI, London.

Dunn, A. and Riley, C.A. (2004) 'Supporting the not-for-profit sector: the Government's review of charitable and social enterprise', *The Modern Law Review*, 67 (4): 632–57.

ECOTEC (2003) 'Guidance on mapping social enterprise: final report to the DTI Social Enterprise Unit', DTI, London.

ECT (2006) 'ECT Group annual report', ECT, London.

ECT (2007) 'ECT Group annual report: success in partnership', ECT, London.

Flockhart, A. (2005) 'The use of social return on investment (SROI) and investment-ready tools (IRT) to bridge the financial credibility gap', *Social Enterprise Journal*, 1 (1): 29–42.

Golding, K. and Peattie, K. (2005) 'In search of a golden blend: perspectives on the marketing of fair trade coffee', *Sustainable Development*, 13: 154–65.

Harding, R. (2006) *Social Enterprise Monitor*. London: London Business School.

Haugh, H. (2005) 'A research agenda for social entrepreneurship', *Social Enterprise Journal*, 1 (1): 1–12.

Hines, F. (2005) 'Viable social enterprise: an evaluation of business support to social enterprise', *Social Enterprise Journal*, 1 (1): 13–28.

IFF (2005) 'A survey of social enterprises across the UK', research report for the Small Business Service, IFF Research Ltd.

Jones, D. and Keogh, W. (2006) Social Enterprise: A case of terminological ambiguity and complexity, *Social Enterprise Journal*, 2 (1): 11–26.

Jones, D., Keogh, B. and O'Leary, H. (2007) *Developing the Social Economy: Critical review of the literature*. Edinburgh: Social Enterprise Institute.

Kaplan, R.S. and Norton, D.P. (1996) 'Using the Balanced Scorecard as a strategic management system', *Harvard Business Review*, January/February: 75–85.

Kerlin, J. (2006) 'Social enterprise in the United States and Europe: understanding and learning from the differences', *Voluntas: International Journal of Voluntary and Nonprofit Organizations*, 17 (3): 246–62.

Khan, S. (2006) 'What does social enterprise do in London?', Social Enterprise London, London.

Leadbeater, C. (1997) *The Rise of the Social Entrepreneur*. London: Demos.

Letts, C., Ryan, W.P. and Grossman, A. (1999) 'Virtuous capital: what foundations can learn from venture capitalists', *Harvard Business Review*, March/April: 2–7.

Litalien, B.C. (2006) 'Era of the social franchise: where franchising and nonprofits come together', *Franchising World*, 38 (6): 77–80.

Local Government (2007) 'Strong and prosperous communities – the local Government White Paper: one year on', Local Government, London. Available at: www.communities.gov.uk/publications/localgovernment/implementationplanprogress

Lowe, W. and Davenport, E. (2005) 'Has the medium (roast) become the message?: The ethics of marketing fair trade in the mainstream', *International Marketing Review*, 22 (5): 494–511.

Lyon, F. (2008a) 'Mapping the regional social enterprise sector', paper presented at the Social Enterprise Research Conference, London South Bank University, 26–27 June

Lyon, F. (2008b) Mapping the regional Social Enterprise sector, paper presented at Social Enterprise Research Conference, London South Bank University, 26–27 June.

Lyon, F. and Ramsden, M. (2006) 'Developing fledgling social enterprise: A study of the support required and means of delivering it', *Social Enterprise Journal*, 2 (1): 27–41.

Miliband, E. (2007) 'Foreword by the Minister of the Third Sector', *Social Enterprise Journal*, 3 (1): 4–5.

Mulgan, G. and Landry, L. (1995) *The Other Invisible Hand: Remaking charity for the 21st century.* London: Demos/Comedia.

NCVO (2006) *The UK Voluntary Sector Almanac 2006: The State of the Sector.* Sponsored by Sarasin Chiswell, London.

NCVO (2008) 'Real-life tales of earning – the Trojans scheme', NCVO, London. Available at: www.ncvo-vol.org.uk/sfp/inpractice/?id=2174&terms=intra

Nicholls, A. (2006) 'Playing the field: a new approach to the meaning of social entrepreneurship', *Social Enterprise Journal*, 2 (1): Editorial.

Nicholls, A. and Opal, C. (2004) *Fair Trade: Market-driven ethical consumption.* London: Sage

NWDA (2003a) 'Greater Manchester social enterprise survey', NWDA, Warrington, May.

NWDA (2003b) 'Lancashire social enterprise survey', Northwest Development Agency, May.

OECD (2006) 'The social enterprise sector and a conceptual framework', OECD, Paris.

Office of the Third Sector (OTS) (2007) *Third Sector Review.* London: OTS.

Office of the Regulator (2005) 'Community interest company report', Office of the Regulator Cardiff.

OTS (2006) 'Partnership in public services: an action plan for third sector involvement ', OTS, London. Available at: www.cabinetoffice.gov.uk/third_sector/public_services/public_service_delivery.aspx

Parkinson, C. and Howorth, C. (2007) 'The language of social entrepreneurs', Lancaster University Management School working paper.

Paton, Rob (2003) *Managing and Measuring Social Enterprise.* London: Sage.

Pearce, J. (2003) *Social Enterprise in Anytown.* London: Calouste Gulbenkian Foundation.

Peattie, K. and Morley, A. (2008) 'Social enterprises: diversity and dynamics, contexts and contributions – a research monograph, ESRC Centre for BRASS, Cardiff.

HM Treasury (2005) 'Pre-Budget report: Britain meeting the global challenge: enterprise, fairness and responsibility', HM Treasury, December.

Prudential Insurance (2004) 'Guide to downshifting: Group press release', Prudential Insurance' London.

Reid, K. and Griffith, J. (2006) 'Social enterprise mythology: critiquing some assumptions', *Social Enterprise Journal*, 2 (1): 1–10.

Reynolds, Sally (2007a) 'Caring commerce', *The Grapevine Magazine*, December: 1–3.

Reynolds, Sally (2007b), 'Another way into work', *Society Guardian*, 18 December. Available at: www.social firms.co.uk/document/format_uploaded/download.php/doc738.html

Sacks, J. (2001) *The Money Trail: measuring your impact on the local economy using* LM3. London: New Economics Foundation.

Seanor, P. and Meaton, J. (2008) 'Learning from failure, ambiguity and trust in social enterprise', *Social Enterprise Journal*, 4 (1): 24–40.

Shaw, E. and Carter, S. (2007) 'Social entrepreneurship: theoretical antecedents and empirical analysis of entrepreneurial processes and outcomes', *Journal of Small Business and Enterprise Development*, 14 (3): 418–34.

Shigetomi, S. (2002) *The State and NGOs: Perspective from Asia* Singapore: Institute of South East Asia Studies.

Social Enterprise Coalition (2008) 'There's more to business than you think: a guide for social enterprise', Social Enterprise Coalition, London.

Social Enterprise Magazine (2008), 'Crisis of confidence as CICS caps criticized for curbing investment', *Social Enterprise Magazine*, 68, June: 4.

Hampson, Gemma (2008), 'Sale or sell out?', *Social Enterprise Magazine*, 69, July: 12–16.

Somers, A. (2005) 'Shaping the Balanced Scorecard for use in UK social enterprises', *Social Enterprise Journal*, 1 (1): 43–56.

Spear, R. (2006) Social entrepreneurship; a different model?, *International Journal of Social Economics*, 33 (5/6): 399–410.

Speckbacher, G. (2003) 'The economics of performance management in nonprofit organizations', *Nonprofit Management and Leadership*, 13 (3), Spring: 267–81.

Thompson, L.J. (2008) 'Social enterprise and social entrepreneurship: where have we reached?', *Social Enterprise Journal*, 4 (2): 149–161.

Tiffen, P. (2002) 'A chocolate-coated case for alternative international business models', *Development in Practice*, 12 (3 & 4): 383–97.

Triodos Bank (2007) 'Saving money, saving the planet: a Triodos Bank report into the environmental practices of social enterprise across Scotland', Triodos, Bristol.

United Nations (2003) 'Investment promotion and enterprise development bulletin for Asia and the Pacific, Number 2', Economic and Social Commission for Asia and the Pacific, Bangkok, Thailand.

Vega, G. and Kidwell, R.E. (2007) 'Towards a typology of new venture creators: similarities and contrasts between business and social entrepreneurs', *New England Journal of Entrepreneurship*, 10 (2): 15–28.

Westall, A. (2001) *Value Led Market Driven: Social enterprise solutions to public policy goals*. London. Institute of Public Policy Research.

Westall, A. and Chalkley, D. (2007) *Social Enterprise Futures*. London: The Smith Institute.

Young, D. (1999) 'Non-profit management studies in the United States: current development and future prospects', *Journal of Public Affairs Education*, 5 (1): 13–24.

Young, R.D. (2003) 'Nonprofit management in Europe and Asia', *Nonprofit Management and Leadership*, 14 (2 Winter): 227–32.

Building Societies Association: www.bsa.org.uk

Community Interest Companies (CICs): www.cicregulator.gov.uk

Co-operatives/UK: www.cooperatives-uk.coop

Communities and Local Government: www.communities.gov.uk

Community Interest Company Forum: www.socialenterprise.org.uk/pages/cic-forum.html

Employee Ownership Association (EOA): www.employeeownership.co.uk/

Local Government (2006) 'Strong and prosperous communities – the Local Government White Paper': www.communities.gov.uk/publications/localgovernment/strongprosperous

National Affordable Homes Agency: www.housingcorp.gov.uk

NCVO (2006) *The UK Voluntary Sector Almanac 2006: The State of the Sector*: www.ncvo-vol.org.uk/uploadedFiles/NCVO/Research/AlmanacSummary2006.pdf

OTS, 'Social enterprise action plan': www.cabinetoffice.gov.uk/third_sector/social_enterprise/action_plan.asp

OTS: www.cabinetoffice.gov.uk/third_sector

OTS, funding, finance and support section of website at: www.cabinetoffice.gov.uk/third_sector/funding_finance_support.aspx

Sporta (Social enterprises within culture and leisure): www.sporta.org

Social Enterprise Coalition: www.socialenterprise.org.uk

3

STRATEGIC MANAGEMENT FOR SOCIAL ENTERPRISES

In the day-to-day running of an organization it is easy to lose focus on the bigger picture. Strategy is about the bigger picture: the context you work in, the needs of your users, the passion of your staff and volunteers and your desire for things to be different.

Sharp et al., 2007: 17

INTRODUCTION

While academics continue to debate the meaning of 'social enterprise' (SE) (Johnson, 2000; Kerlin, 2006; Young, 2001), there is an emerging consensus that it is broadly along the lines of a double bottom-line focus on social mission and money (revenue), an entrepreneurial culture and a greater utilization of for-profit approaches to management and markets. As Dart (2004: 415) has famously observed, SEs 'differ from traditional non-profits in that they blur boundaries between non-profit and for-profit and that they enact hybrid non-profit and for-profit activities.'

The increasing adoption of holistic missions, financial performance indicators, change-orientated cultures (entrepreneurialism), managerialist techniques and a market orientation are symptomatic of the growing use of strategic management among SEs. While the available research data does not enable us to accurately map the extent of its use, a picture is emerging of the ways in which it is being used and the reasons for its adoption (Bull and Crompton, 2006; Courtney et al., 2005).

SE organizations operating without a formal strategic plan are increasingly rare (Courtney et al., 2005). Competition for funds and customers has led instrumentally rational managers to develop strategic plans clarifying what they are trying to achieve and how they intend to achieve it. In addition, the sector is subject to institutional pressures from commissioners (for greater accountability) and governments, as well as the promotion of strategic management by consultants and network organizations (Chetkovich and Frumkin, 2003; Paton, 2003). The combination of these rational and institutional pressures has made strategic management much more prevalent than it was 20 years ago.

The *legitimating* value of the artefacts of a formal strategic planning process (such as mission statements, objectives, plans, measurement and control processes and so on) is widely acknowledged (Dart, 2004; Reid and Griffith, 2006). However, our focus in this chapter will be on the practical value of strategic management. It will be argued that, as a process and toolkit, to facilitate a proactive approach to ensuring long-term survival and growth, strategic management can enable SEs to better achieve desired social and economic outcomes. However, the causal links between a formal approach to strategic management and organizational performance are not straightforward. Indeed, as will be discussed, the benefits of formal strategic planning may not derive from the plan at all, but from the process of planning.

The aim of strategic management is to articulate a desired future state for the organization and be proactive in implementing actions to bring it about. In other words, strategic management is an attempt to take control of the organization's destiny by developing a rigorous and legitimate strategy for the survival and growth of the organization. Exhibit 3.1 contains some widely used definitions of strategic management.

Exhibit 3.1   Definitions of strategic management

The determination of the long-run goals and objectives of an enterprise, and the adoption of courses of action and the allocation of resources necessary for carrying out these goals.

> Chandler, *Strategy and Structure*, 1962,
> quoted in Grant, 2004: 21

Strategic planning is the process of developing realistic medium- to long-term plans, identifying clear priorities that will help the organization deliver its mission.

> National Council for Voluntary Organizations, 2007: 2

Corporate strategy is the pattern of decisions in a company that determines and reveals its objectives, purposes, or goals, produces the principal policies and plans for achieving those goals, and defines the range of business the company is to pursue, the kind of economic and human organization it is or intends to be, and the nature of the economic and non-economic contribution it intends to make to its shareholders, employees, customers, and communities.

> Andrews, *The Concept of Corporate Strategy*, 1980,
> quoted in Nickols, 2000: 18–19

Strategy is the direction and scope of an organization over the long term which achieves advantage for the organization through its configuration of resources within a changing environment and to fulfil stakeholder expectations.

> Johnson and Scholes, 2005: 9

In emphasizing that the strategies should be rigorous and legitimate, we are drawing attention to two key issues – namely, the strategy process and strategy content. The former refers to the way in which the strategy is developed by the organization, while the latter refers to the validity of the chosen strategy (or strategies). The rigour and legitimacy of the strategy process and content are critical to achieving acceptance by stakeholders and ensuring that it is appropriate to the organization's development needs. Stakeholder acceptance depends in large part on an open and inclusive strategy development process and decisionmaking that is firmly grounded in well-researched evidence, guided by widely accepted values. The appropriateness of the strategy is dependent on an objective appraisal of the organization's current capability to take advantage of the emerging opportunities presented by its evolving external context. By 'objective', we again mean grounded in well-researched evidence rather than simply based on the subjective opinions of internal stakeholders.

Consistent with the majority of writing on strategic management, this chapter offers a prescriptive model of how to implement strategic management. However, rather than an uncritical transfer of techniques, the importance of selecting the appropriate methodologies and tools and, where appropriate, adapting them for the SEs context will be stressed.

This chapter is structured to reflect the six stages of a strategy process model:

1. designing a bespoke strategy development process;
2. the organization's vision and mission;
3. determining the current strategic position;
4. producing effective objectives, strategies and plans;
5. implementation of strategy;
6. performance measurement.

In the remainder of this chapter we will outline a process and supporting tools by which third-sector organizations can develop rigorous and legitimate strategies. To achieve this, we will now systematically explore each of the six elements identified above.

THE NATURE OF THE STRATEGY DEVELOPMENT PROCESS

An organization's strategy is the result of a process embedded in a context.

Pettigrew, 2003: 301

Research into strategy development in SEs has predominantly concerned itself with a narrow conception of it as being formal strategic planning. This focus reflects the influence of funders on SEs to adopt bureaucratic managerial practices, as well as a preference for this model among consultants serving the sector (Siciliano, 1997). While concern persists about the comparability of studies regarding the link between adoption of formal planning and consequent performance – largely due to differences in the definition of both of these constructs – a consensus exists that strategic planners perform better than non-planners (Griggs, 2000; Siciliano, 1997; Stone, 1989). However, many authors have suggested that the take-up of formal strategic planning may not be as widespread as research into the subject would imply (Bull and Crompton, 2006; Stone and Brusch, 1996), adoption being seen as positively related to organization size, board composition and funders' demands.

Reflecting on the incompatibility of the overly rational strategic planning approach with the operating conditions of many third-sector organizations has led several authors to explore alternative models (Courtney, 2002; Rhodes and Keogan, 2005). Consequently, researchers have sought out models that better fit the multi-stakeholder, multi-bottom line, democratic governance conditions characteristic of many third-sector organizations. In other words, models that reflect the social conditions in which such organizations exist in the real world.

As Courtney (2002) argues, there is no one best way to devise a strategy. The appropriate process for developing strategies is the one that is matched to the realities of the organization's context. Some of the key dimensions of the 'context' of SEs are captured in Exhibit 3.2. Acknowledging these dimensions, Sharp et al. (2007: 6) argue that strategy development in SEs 'works best when it is appreciative, reflective, participatory and outcomes-focused.'

Strategy 'context' refers to the external environment, too. As we have seen, most writers acknowledge the influence of institutional pressures on the adoption of formal strategic planning by third-sector organizations in general (Courtney, 2002; Rhodes and Keogan, 2005; Stone, 1989; Stone and Brusch, 1996; Stone et al., 1999). However, some have suggested that it is more appropriate when there is a stability and clarity in the external environment. Where the environment is characterized by greater ambiguity, complexity and dynamism, a more 'emergent' model based on practical learning and an inclusive process may be preferable (Courtney, 2002; Stone and Brusch, 1996).

Strategic management has been described as 'the most managerialist of the management specialities' (Levy, Alvesson and Willmott, 2003). Therefore, in designing the process, to bring forth agreement on strategic direction and action, it is important to heed Paton's (2003: 167) warning that 'managerialism – elevating as it does particular roles, perspectives, terminology, and techniques – can so easily become a liability by making dialogue more difficult.' Consequently, the overriding aim is to design a process that effectively engages the whole organization in a dialogue about direction. This dialogue extends to key external stakeholders as well as internal groups (staff, managers and the board). The product of this dialogue is a consensus about ends (strategic objectives) and means for their achievement (strategies).

Paton's warning above reflects a tendency to view strategic management narrowly as a technical process for producing long-term strategic plans. Mintzberg, Ahlstrand and Lampel (1998) labelled this approach, disparagingly, the 'design school' of strategy making. Courtney (2002: 6) suggests, 'In the voluntary non-profit sector there is perhaps a tendency to create a simple caricature of strategic planning or strategic management in the private sector in order to refute its relevance for the voluntary nonprofit sector.' By contrast, Hudson (2004) stresses the more social and experimental nature of the process that is found in many organizations. He draws attention to three dimensions of the strategy development process, each of which is highly context-specific.

- The process is evolutionary and involves small incremental steps. It follows that experimentation and learning over time are as important as periodic formal planning.

- It is a political process whereby powerful individuals and/or groups negotiate and bargain their way to a consensus about the most suitable strategy.

- It involves an analytical process to produce strategic plans based on rigorous reviews of the organization's strategic position in relation to its current environmental situation.

The capacity for experimentation and learning is dependent on the organization's culture and people. Political activity depends on the organization's power structure and modes of interaction between senior staff. Finally, the analytical rigour of the planning process depends on the sophistication of the organization's formal planning procedures, the skills of the people involved and the management information system and market intelligence-gathering processes in use. For many SEs, these analytical capabilities are underdeveloped, under-resourced and, consequently, partial and ad hoc. Thus, different organizations will exhibit their own unique mix of these three interwoven processes, which reflect their particular management style.

While each organization will differ in the relative influence of the factors noted in Exhibit 3.2, it is clear that strategymaking in the SEs' context is likely to be characterized by two features that distinguish it from strategymaking in the private sector. First, the process is likely to be informed by inputs from a wider range of stakeholders and is, consequently, based more on consensus-building than rational choice (the latter being a dominant theme in mainstream strategy literature). Second, strategic choices are driven more by underlying values and subjective judgements about social need than by concern for market forces (although intensifying competitive conditions are altering the balance between these concerns in some areas).

Exhibit 3.2 Defining characteristics of SEs

Values are of greater significance in the management of third-sector organizations (Hudson, 2004; Waddock, 2004) than conventional companies. Values are ethical and moral codes of conduct shaped by the social, religious, cultural and historical contexts in which we live. Their central importance is illustrated in the description of SEs as being 'value-led, market-driven' (Westall, 2001).

The number of volunteers in SEs is often very high. However, unlike paid workers who, at the limit, will comply with the demands of managerial strategies, volunteers are free to withdraw their labour if they disapprove of the strategic direction the organization is pursuing.

Most third-sector organizations are coalitions of interest groups, each with their own – often divergent – priorities, constraints and power to influence negotiated strategies. In practice, this means that the strategy development process will involve greater time and effort being devoted to networking, communicating, politicking and negotiating in a bid to fashion consensus among the key stakeholders.

Unlike their private-sector counterparts, third-sector organizations are often in a position of resource dependence when their revenue streams derive from fees, grants and donations (Stone et al., 1999). This means that the ability of their managers to develop strategies is constrained by the demands of their existing contracts and the pressing need to replace them to ensure survival. In this situation, strategic choices are often, in fact, 'enforced choices'.

SEs usually exhibit democratic governance structures, whereby their members can meaningfully influence strategymaking (and other types of decisionmaking). However, Pearce (2003: 38) observes: 'Having a democratic structure through which members can exercise control over the organization is seemingly one of the most contentious of the defining characteristics and the one most likely to cause concern to some people.'

Central to understanding the nature of third-sector organizations is the notion of a social mission. A social mission is an organizational commitment to address human needs that are either unmet by state and market providers or arise because of their efforts to satisfy other needs.

The social orientation of third-sector organizations means that, in practice, they are often seeking to achieve a broader set of strategic objectives than are their public and, especially, private-sector counterparts. SEs are more inclined to embrace a double or triple bottom line management philosophy and, therefore, seek to balance economic, environmental and social impacts (Elkington, 2004).

Another contextual determinant is the stage of development of the organization (Stone et al., 1999). Lumpkin and Dess (1995: 1391) note that, 'as organizations grow and mature and face more complex and multifaceted environments, more complex decision-making processes are required.' Stone et al. (1999) point out that the increase in formalization of the planning process is driven by greater availability of resources and the need for internal coordination. The challenge here involves maintaining the integrity of the dialogue about direction as processes for its management formalize – that is, there is a need to guard against excluding some stakeholders or disadvantaging their ability to give voice to their legitimate concerns due to the techniques and language managers use to 'facilitate' dialogue.

Whatever the dominant influences on the nature of the process, it is possible to identify the products of any bespoke system in use. Principally, the process will guide the organization to address the following:

- determining the organization's mission and/or vision;
- evaluating the organization's current strategic position;
- specifying realistic but challenging strategic objectives;
- identifying and screening possible strategies for attaining the agreed objectives;

- strategic plans for translating strategy into actions;
- devising an implementation strategy to manage the organizational change process;
- performance evaluation processes and mechanisms.

Figure 3.1 shows a schematic of these key outputs arranged in a logical process. In practice, 'developing strategy is not a linear process' (Hudson, 2004: 125), but recursive and iterative. Regular reviews are required based on the feedback data and new information from changing circumstances – that is the evolutionary nature of the process noted earlier.

While it is important to be committed to implementing the agreed strategy, it is equally important to retain an open mind about the desirability of adapting the intended strategy in the face of changing circumstances. In effect, the realized (or implemented) strategy is invariably a mix of planned and emergent (or adaptations) elements (Mintzberg and Waters, 1985).

A favoured approach to developing strategy is the 'strategy workshop', whereby the great and the good spend one or more days in intensive exploration and discussion to craft a strategic agenda for implementation. Such workshops can often be exciting and invigorating and produce a lot of creative ideas. However, the detached and ritualized nature of these singular events often means their insights are not carried over into practice back in the real world of the organization. Indeed, Johnson (2008: 3) observes

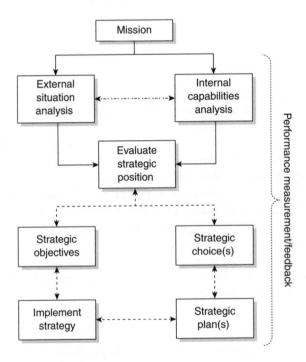

Figure 3.1 The strategy development process

that, after the excitement of the workshop, managers 're-enter their everyday world where things are different. They face the pressures of the immediate; the routines of daily life; the sceptical comments and questions of colleagues who were not at the workshop; the politics of preservation and status. So often the insights from the away day get compromised or simply shelved.'

It follows that, rather than orchestrated ritualized events, what is needed is a series of events that progressively develop the content of the strategy and programme its implementation into the organization. In other words, the process of strategy development and implementation becomes an ongoing activity with successive attention being given to the questions 'What should we be doing?' and 'How do we make it happen?'

Another important consideration for the ultimate success of a strategy is who is involved in its development. Given a reliance on volunteers, more democratic governance structures and the need to address a wider range of stakeholder interests, SEs typically favour inclusive processes of strategy development. This needs to be more than consultation at the analysis stage. It is vital to the wider acceptability of the strategy – and, hence, commitment to making it work – that staff at all levels are represented at all stages of development and implementation. Sharp et al. (2007: 10) note that, 'Some organizations manage the process by assigning responsibility to a single person, small group or external consultant; there is then little wider ownership of the plan, so that even if a plan is produced it may not be implemented and disillusion may result.' An inclusive process is also vital to ensure that the strategy does not fall victim to a dichotomy between development and implementation (Piercy, 2002). This can occur when a strategy primarily developed by senior staff (or external consultants) is perceived by the wider members as inadequately reflecting organizational realities.

Depending on the structure of the organization, and its degree of diversification, the strategy development process may have to produce strategies for different levels within the organization. For example, in larger organizations, strategies will be needed at the corporate, divisional and service delivery levels. Each of these strategies will be concerned with a different set of issues, but be interconnected in a mutually reinforcing hierarchy.

First, corporate strategy is concerned with developing the mission, diversification strategy and portfolio management for the organization. Essentially, 'What activities should we be involved in?' and how the different divisions should be coordinated and supported by the corporate centre (that is, a corporate parenting style).

Second, divisional strategy should focus on developing the resource capabilities needed to deliver a group of services and devising and implementing projects to improve service quality and efficiency.

Finally, service-level strategy is concerned with managing individual services to achieve set objectives for target numbers within budget constraints and other performance indicators.

In the sections that follow, we will examine each of the major outputs from this process in detail. While the exposition may suggest an elaborate series of processes based on a range of detailed systematic analyses, the truth is that informational inputs are often incomplete, out of date, ad hoc, subjective and anecdotal. It is nonetheless desirable to make every effort (within time and other resource constraints) to compile as much relevant evidence as possible to inform the strategy development process. As Pfeffer and Sutton (2006: 41) observe:

> Evidence-based management requires a mind-set with two critical components: first, willingness to put aside belief and conventional wisdom – the dangerous half-truths that many embrace – and instead hear and act on the facts; second, an unrelenting commitment to gather the facts and information necessary to make more informed and intelligent decisions, and to keep pace with new evidence and use the new facts to update practices.

Having said this, we must acknowledge that, despite widespread belief to the contrary, 'facts' rarely speak for themselves. Their meaning is subject to interpretation by management teams, the members of which bring varying analytical skills, experience, preconceptions, biases, political beliefs and blind spots to bear on the process. Consequently, much of our understanding of the social world is socially constructed as a result of our interactions with others. As Paton (2003) puts it:

> The world is not just 'out there,' something that imprints on us as passive perceivers. This active constructing of the world is a social business, undertaken in and through communities of one sort or another, communities that share and evolve their common language in responding to the issues they face.

DEVELOPING A VISION AND MISSION

According to Young (2001: 143) the terms 'vision' and 'mission' refer to 'operational statements deriving from a deeper notion of identity. Organizations struggle with these statements in their strategic planning, especially if they are unclear about identity.' However, it is not just in the development of strategies that failure to understand identity will cause problems. Margolis and Hansen (2002: 279) suggest that, 'Without understanding the underlying assumptions … that are the essence of the organization and the core of the culture, organizational change will be met with resistance and difficulty.' It is therefore appropriate to consider this foundational concept prior to exploring the more 'operational' concepts of mission and vision.

The term 'organizational identity' refers to members' shared perceptions of 'who we are as an organization' (Whetten, 2006). More specifically, Albert and Whetten (1985) define it as member's perceptions of the central, enduring and distinctive (CED) features of the organization. These so called CED features are what make an organization unique in character. They emerge over time as the organization goes through difficult periods, during which it is challenged to make fundamental choices that reveal its value commitments. Because such decisions invariably involve key stakeholders, Young (2001: 142) suggests that, 'Individual leadership, particularly by a charismatic entrepreneurial founder, can be important in forming an organizational identity, but it is not sufficient unless other key stakeholders are ultimately committed to sustain it.'

As these fundamental value commitments become accepted as the defining traits of the organization, its identity crystallizes in the collective mind of members as the basic character of the organization.

Without a collective sense of its own identity, an organization will struggle to develop a workable mission due to the lack of consensus about the organization's fundamental commitments. For Young (2001: 142), these concepts are so interrelated that he suggests identity 'may even be described in terms of what an organization does or "what business it is in."' This view is supported by the empirical work of Margolis and Hansen (2002), who identified organizational purpose and philosophy as being two 'core attributes' of organizational identity. It follows that, where an organization does not have a strong shared identity or is experiencing an identity crisis, preliminary work will be required to build a consensus on it. This is not a trivial task, but, once established, organizational members will often internalize the espoused identity by using it as a reference point in their daily work and relations with external stakeholders (Young, 2001). The same is true for major internal decisions about strategic direction. Perceptions of identity will influence decisions about what is a legitimate direction for the organization's development and what constitutes acceptable strategic behaviour for its pursuance.

The relationship between vision and mission

In seeking to develop an organizational mission, it is inevitable that the notion of 'vision' crops up. While there is widespread agreement on the concept of mission, there is no such general consensus regarding vision. Among authors specializing in third-sector management, a more utopian approach is common, as befits organizations with strong social commitments. In contrast, the mainstream strategy literature – built on observations of large-scale private-sector organizations – favours a more pragmatic approach. We will briefly examine both perspectives.

First, there are those authors who take a utopian view of vision as an idealized state of affairs that the organization is striving towards achieving in society (Courtney, 2002; Sharp et al., 2007; Hudson, 2004). Though unachievable, such utopian visions are usually based on notions of 'fairness' and 'justice' and working towards their achievement is seen as a moral imperative. According to this approach, the vision serves as a commitment to transformational social change (Alvord et al., 2004). For example, the Skoll Foundation (www.skoll.com) is dedicated to the promotion of social entrepreneurship and has as its vision:

> **Our vision is to live in a world of peace and prosperity where all people, regardless of geography, background or economic status, enjoy and employ the full range of their talents and abilities.**

With the utopian approach, the vision emphasizes what the organization stands for (for example, 'a fairer world', 'justice for all', 'education for all') and the mission will clarify what the organization will actually do to further that vision (for example, 'improve the livelihoods of smallholder cocoa producers in West Africa by establishing their own dynamic branded proposition in the UK chocolate market, thus putting them higher up the value chain', as at Divine, (www.divinechocolate.com).

In contrast, the mainstream strategy literature often treats vision more pragmatically. Rather than a utopian ideal or 'higher purpose', the vision is treated as an achievable, though significant, change that the organization can set itself as an overriding objective. Typically, such visions are medium-term and another challenge will be set when the first is achieved. In this way, the vision is a rhetorical tool, used to unleash energy and enthusiasm in pursuit of a meaningful goal. For example, Social Firms UK has a more pragmatic vision statement that is achievable in a reasonably short timescale: 'To be the voice for Social Firms, encouraging, supporting and facilitating growth in the sector' (www.socialfirms.co.uk).

The pragmatic approach uses successive visions as milestone achievements (for example, 'to create a national network of safe houses for victims of domestic violence', 'to bring about a change in legal protection for victims of domestic violence') in its pursuit of its underlying purpose or mission (such as 'to eradicate domestic violence from UK households').

While the former approach to vision is more prevalent in the third sector, the preferred approach should be guided by how the organization wants to use the vision to support its work. The utopian approach is a values-based 'call to arms'; the pragmatic approach uses the vision as a rhetorical device to generate and direct effort. However, these aspects are not mutually exclusive and are a matter of managerial choice in how the vision is communicated and used.

Developing the social mission

When we use the word 'mission' we are referring to a widely accepted understanding of what the organization stands for (its values) and why it exists (its purpose). Clearly, this is intimately bound up with the organization's sense of itself (identity) and its vision of a better world that it wants to work towards. The mission may, or may not, be communicated by means of a mission statement. It is not the making of such a formalized statement that is important, but developing a sense of mission in the hearts and minds of the members (Campbell and Yeung, 1991). The value that comes from having a written mission statement derives from its use in communicating to stakeholders inside and outside the organization just what it stands for and is trying to achieve. It therefore has more utility in a large organization. The primary aim, though, is to develop a collective sense of purpose and underpinning values. Once established, the mission acts as a guide so that appropriate strategy choices can be made.

Developing the required sense of mission extends beyond the consultative processes for identifying common values and fashioning a statement of purpose reflecting them. It is important that the core values and purpose are embedded internally and in relations with external stakeholders. This can be achieved by using devices such as communication, policy guidelines, recruitment and selection, training and development, reward systems, decisionmaking, resource allocations, codes of conduct and so on. In this way, the mission becomes enacted in the day-to-day behaviours of the organization. In terms of decisionmaking, the key decisions regarding mission centre on the choice of strategy – that is, what the organization will actually do to realize its mission.

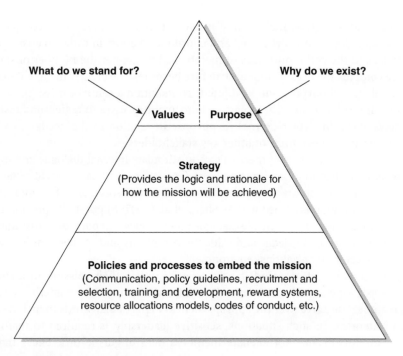

Figure 3.2   The mission pyramid

The basic approach of stating a purpose with clarity, articulating core values and translating these into an organizationwide strategy are illustrated in the mission pyramid shown in Figure 3.2.

In relation to all start-up organizations (not just SEs), Ireland and Hitt (1992: 37) argue that, 'failure to articulate a firm's focus through a mission statement may partially account for the fact that approximately 50 per cent of start-ups fail in the first year of operation, whereas 75 to 80 per cent fail within their first three to five years.'

For a small organization with a single focus, developing its mission can be relatively straightforward (at least internally). The initial reasons for starting the organization are often still fresh in people's minds and the ability of such organizations to communicate effectively with members ensures clarity and consistency of purpose without resort to formalized processes for generating and disseminating the mission. What is required is proactivity by managers to reinforce the mission through communication and use it as a guide to managerial decisionmaking, both internally and in relation to client groups. One of the surest ways to devalue the mission is for senior managers to make decisions that are inconsistent with the mission. Staff will judge the importance of the mission according to what managers *do* about the mission, not what they *say* about its importance. In smaller SEs where 'senior' managers have a more hands-on involvement in operational delivery, the opportunity to embed the mission is more direct than in larger organizations where the available tools comprise the making of broad strategic decisions and supporting resource allocations, guiding policies and communication.

As organizations grow, maintaining mission focus becomes more complex and, therefore, requires a more structured and coordinated effort in order to ensure clarity of purpose and the common values of members. The greater the number of staff and the more complex the organizational structure becomes, the greater the likelihood that the core values and purpose will be diluted. To maintain a sense of mission, the organization will need, periodically, to engage in formal processes to review and restate its core values and refine (or redefine) its purpose in relation to the needs of its target client groups and expectations of other key stakeholders.

This implies the existence of mechanisms to stimulate internal dialogue and external stakeholder consultation on an ongoing basis. The latter is critical to establishing legitimacy. The aim is to capture viewpoints across the entire spectrum of relationships in which the organization is embedded. As Sharp et al. (2007: 6) put it, the process 'should bring stakeholders together to enable dialogue about values and purpose across the wider organization and to acknowledge and value the complexity and connections across each TSO's [third-sector organization's] environment.'

Organizations sometimes find it hard to encapsulate their mission in a succinct form of words for external communication. Attempts to do so can sometimes be divisive as members disagree over the appropriateness of particular words to include in the mission statement. In such situations, sensitive leadership is required to maintain a shared commitment and not alienate members over linguistic differences that will likely be lost on external readers not sensitized to such nuanced interpretations. Ultimately, it is better for the strategic needs of the organization to take precedence over the beliefs of a few individuals lest the majority become alienated.

The advantages of a well-conceived sense of mission are well known. These include:

- providing a context for strategic decisionmaking by senior management;
- providing guidance about resource allocation priorities;
- generating commitment and motivation of the organization's members;
- communicating the organization's purpose and values to external stakeholders;
- acting as a moral compass to guide decisionmaking and behaviour.

However, there are also occasions when a strong sense of mission can be a hindrance. This typically occurs when the management of a growing organization wishes to revise the mission to reflect the changing character and scope of activities of a developing organization. For example, when an organization diversifies through new contracts, merges with another organization, experiences a change of leader or simply following a major strategic review. In such circumstances, the members of the organization (and its trustees) are challenged to revise their understanding of the organization's essential purpose and identity. This involves enacting the process outlined above but with the added need to build a consensus around the need for change and manage the resulting friction (perhaps conflict) that may emerge in the face of the proposed change. The friction arises when some organization members (and trustees) view the proposed changes as being a departure from the existing mission and perceive this as compromising the organization's prior social commitments.

DETERMINING THE CURRENT STRATEGIC POSITION OF THE ORGANIZATION

Evaluation of an organization's current strategic position provides the foundation for informed debate about how to grow and develop the organization. This is made possible because the evaluation consists of two interrelated analyses. Specifically, it involves analysis of the external operating environment and the internal resources and capabilities of the organization. Assessment of the strategic position is the result of comparing the requirements for successful operation in the present environment with the current resources and capabilities of the organization. In this way, we arrive at an understanding of the 'strategic fit' between the environment and the organization.

The aim is to not only determine the current fit between environmental demands and internal resources but also identify and evaluate future opportunities and the changes in organizational resources and capabilities needed to be able to exploit them. This is a critical point because the aim of a strategic approach to management in third-sector organizations is to build capabilities to better meet the needs of target client groups and serve more of those clients. To the extent that changes in client needs can be anticipated, investments can be made ahead of time to ensure that service changes come on stream when needed and so avoid clients experiencing a lack of service provision.

However, several studies of strategic planning in non-profitmaking organizations have highlighted that strategic analysis tends to focus more on the requirements to satisfy funders than clients' needs. For example, Stone et al. (1999: 409), in a major review of literature on strategic planning in non-profitmaking organizations, observed 'little evidence that nonprofit organizations took changing client demands into account during the strategy formulation phase.' This led them to question if many non-profitmaking organizations view funders and not clients as their actual customers, with the consequence that organizations are 'tempted to shift away from their original mission and goals to the extent that plans had to reflect actual or perceived funder priorities' (Stone et al., 1999: 390).

This concern is reflected in the use of strategic analysis tools by SEs. Of the 12 most commonly used strategic analysis tools identified in a survey by Jackson and Irwin (2007 – see also Exhibit 3.3), none relates directly to determining clients' needs (and the discussion suggests none is being applied to this issue). The overriding focus of the tools and discussions confirms Stone et al.'s (1999) conclusion that securing resources from funders and understanding how to compete for these funds dominates. While slightly at odds with the prevailing discourse of SE as a solution to meeting social needs, this focus is understandable. In an emerging sector with large numbers of start-up organizations, conforming to the expectations of funders to achieve legitimacy is a rational intermediate tactic.

Exhibit 3.3   The 12 most commonly used strategic analysis tools according to Jackson and Irwin (2007)

- PEST.
- SWOT.
- Stakeholder analysis.
- Core competencies.
- Cost–benefit analysis.
- Market share and competitor analysis.
- Scenario planning.
- Risk analysis.
- Mind mapping.
- Balanced Scorecard.
- Strategy mapping.
- Project or outcome evaluation.

A further key component is a review of the current mission, objectives and strategies to determine their current relevance and effectiveness. However, Stone et al. (1999) point out that the effectiveness of a strategy's content is often judged in relation to its success in securing resources from funders, rather than how well it meets clients' needs. They suggest that this is in part pragmatic, as determining causal links between particular strategies and outcomes for clients is difficult – a problem exacerbated when the outcomes are the result of multi-agency collaborations.

In relation to the internal component of the analysis, reference has been made several times to 'resources' and 'capabilities'.

By resources is meant the quantity and quality of resources available to the organization – that is, financial position, human resources, physical assets and equipment and intangible assets, such as brands, social capital assets, stakeholder relationships and so on. These need not be limited to resources that the organization owns or controls directly, but may also include those the organization can access through service delivery partnerships, support networks and government-sponsored schemes.

In addition, the analysis need to focus on 'strategic capabilities', by which is meant the accumulated management skills, organizational processes and systems that enable one organization to perform better than another (given similar resource endowments). These are generally the result of conscious efforts to invest in capacity-building activities. In simple terms, the former is concerned with the question 'What resources are available?' while the latter is concerned with the question ' … are the resources are used?'

Exhibit 3.3 has highlighted some of the many frameworks available in the strategic management literature for facilitating analysis of an organization's strategic position. This is a very small selection of the available tools. In general, each of these tools focuses on a specific set of strategically relevant issues. The sheer number of tools and the skills and information needed to utilize them effectively makes the task of analysis seem unduly daunting. Many organizations opt for the simplicity of the familiar SWOT framework (SWOT standing for strengths, weaknesses, opportunities and threats analysis) as an intuitive and manageable tool to structure the internal and external analysis. This may be supplemented by selective use of specific tools to build a richer picture of the dynamics of the wider institutional environment for the purposes of understanding emerging policy and funding priorities.

Smith (2003: 291) notes that, though widely used, in practice, SWOT analysis 'is usually reduced to a "subjective listing exercise", identifying none of the key issues that are the intended output of the technique.' This misapplication of the tool often occurs because of the following issues.

- The acronym SWOT (and its representation as a 2 × 2 matrix) leads managers to consider strengths and weaknesses before opportunities and threats. This encourages a subjective brainstorming approach rather than one given perspective and empirical grounding in the reality of the external operating environment.

- Producing lists of strengths, weaknesses, opportunities and threats without any prioritization of their importance or impact lessens the value of the SWOT technique in shaping the key issues into a strategic agenda.

- As anyone who has used the technique knows, classifying issues as strengths/weaknesses and opportunities/threats is problematic. The process is often subjective, reflecting the prevailing managerial culture (that is, whether the members of the management team are honest with themselves and entrepreneurial or complacent and risk averse) as much as the 'objective' properties of the issue itself.

Johnson et al. (2008: 120) suggest that 'SWOT analysis is not a substitute for more rigorous, insightful analysis.' The challenge, then, is to combine the rigour of detailed, focused analysis with the usability of SWOT analysis. To this end, Figure 3.3 shows a reformulated SWOT framework that addresses the above weaknesses and grounds the analysis in a more detailed empirical evaluation of the underpinning issues. The SWOT framework now becomes an interpretive tool, facilitating a review and debate rather than being a simplistic brainstorming tool.

This reformulated SWOT framework offers a number of important advantages in terms of rigour and validity. First, by starting with analysis of the external operating environment, when managers move on to consider the internal resources and capabilities of their organization they are driven to ask the central question 'Do we have the appropriate resources and capabilities to survive and prosper in our sector?' This is a central question for strategic management.

Second, this revised SWOT framework requires the prioritization of identified issues in terms of their relevance (for example, minor opportunity or major opportunity and so on) and scale of impact (high, medium, low). This avoids the unstructured 'laundry lists' generated by the simple 2 × 2 matrix and moves the management team towards a structured agenda of key strategic issues, with those being classified as major/high used as the primary drivers of decisionmaking about strategy choices.

Finally, in addition to these improvements in rigour, the validity of the exercise is greatly enhanced because it requires managers to support their analysis by reference to empirical evidence wherever possible.

External issues	Evidence	Major opportunity	Minor opportunity	Neutral*	Minor threat	Major threat	Impact High	Impact Medium	Impact Low
PEST factors 1, 2, 3, 4, etc.									
Market/client issues 1, 2, 3, 4, etc.									
Competitor issues 1, 2, 3, 4, etc.									
Other stakeholder issues 1, 2, 3, 4, etc.									
Internal issues	**Evidence**	**Major weakness**	**Minor opportunity**	**Neutral***	**Minor threat**	**Major threat**	**High**	**Medium**	**Low**
Financial issues 1, 2, 3, 4, etc.									
People issues 1, 2, 3, 4, etc.									
Operations issues 1, 2, 3, 4, etc.									
Intangible resource issues 1, 2, 3, 4, etc.									

Figure 3.3 An enhanced SWOT analysis framework

* 'Neutral' would imply that it is currently unclear whether the identified issue represents a threat or an opportunity

The need for the methods that are chosen to determine the organization's strategic position to generate a prioritized list of key strategic issues is paramount given the desire to achieve maximum social impact with constrained resources. However, a prioritized list of key issues needs to be translated into a set of measurable objectives, strategies and plans if the organization is to maintain and develop its abilities to meet the needs of its target client/customer groups. This is the focus of the next section.

DEVELOPING OBJECTIVES, STRATEGIES AND PLANS

Developing objectives, strategies and plans is the means by which the insights from the strategic position analysis are translated into an agenda for change and a set of guidelines detailing how this can be achieved. Our earlier emphasis on the importance of contextual influences in shaping the nature of the strategy process holds true here where we are discussing strategy content. The defining characteristics of the SE form, the unique identity of the organization and its internal dynamics all influence what are deemed to be appropriate, feasible and acceptable objectives, strategies and plans.

Strategic objectives in SEs

One of the major challenges facing SEs seeking to employ strategic management is how to reconcile their multiple commitments (to stakeholders and values) with a desire to give focus and direction to their activities.

Functionalist explanations of how strategic objectives are determined and used fail to account for the multiple, often conflicting, objectives adopted by SEs. This is because they overemphasize rational choice at the expense of acknowledging the social embeddedness of the process for determining and deploying such objectives (Baruch and Ramalho, 2006; Granovetter, 1985).

The apparent incoherence in strategic objectives may reflect the diversity of stakeholder relationships and the greater priority given to democratically acknowledging stakeholders' interests over a managerialist commitment to having coherent objectives. This in turn is a reflection of the fact that meeting clients' needs depends on multi-stakeholder coordination (to mobilize resources and/or deliver services) as well as the practical difficulty of measuring performance to determine the causal links between stated objectives and actual achievements (Stone et al., 1999). In other words, the strategic objectives may have greater symbolic than practical value.

Furthermore, being value-driven leads most SEs to adopt a double, or even triple, bottom line focus. Such an orientation inevitably leads to trade-offs as organizations seek to balance their economic, social and environmental commitments. Through the lens of a managerialist emphasis on efficiency, such a stance inevitably looks irrational because it favours balance over maximization. According to Granovetter (1985) this stance is locally rational if viewed through the norms and values of the SE's context. Frumkin and Andre-Clarke (2000) argue strongly that values are a neglected source of differentiation which can underpin viable competitive strategies for SEs. This implies that there are more important strategic benefits to be derived from a values-based strategic orientation than a technicist overemphasis on the logical coherence of objective setting would suggest.

Several authors have noted that strategic objectives are a prerequisite for effective strategic planning rather than a product of such activity (Bryson, 1995; Stone et al., 1999). This seemingly paradoxical view implies, for many organizations, that formal strategic planning is a process for codifying and testing pre-existing views about strategic direction and the appropriate strategies for its pursuance. The planning process will be viewed as legitimate to the extent that it is underpinned by a prior consensus among key stakeholders about how it should be conducted and what outcomes it will yield (Bryson, 1995; Hudson, 2004).

Competitive and institutional pressures are pushing more SEs from grant dependence to earned income autonomy. It is a move likely to be accompanied by a shift of emphasis from stakeholders towards performance as they then have to meet the exacting demands of the commissioners of fee-based services or consumers of traded goods.

To the extent that SEs become more independent financially they will likely adopt more market-orientated and challenging strategic objectives. These will challenge the organization to change in fundamental ways (for example, through diversification, merger, greater formalization of management and structures and so on), raising questions about identity and social missions.

Strategic choices and plans

According to Chetkovich and Frumkin (2003: 565), 'the discussion of strategic choice has remained tethered fairly tightly to ideas from the for-profit world. Two basic approaches are offered, one emphasizing efficiency and the other differentiation.' In the prescriptive strategy literature, both approaches take survival for granted. For SEs, struggling with the issue of survival, differentiation and efficiency is more significant later in their development. Thus, we can view the strategic choices of SEs (and for-profit organizations) as initially addressing the issue of survival by securing resources, then differentiating themselves to build reputation and legitimacy (as a platform for growth), then focusing on greater efficiency as they increasingly compete with larger-scale competitors. The challenge throughout is to maintain focus on the social mission while securing and administering enabling resources, achieving a 'blended value' proposition (Emerson, 2003).

Mintzberg and Waters (1985) pointed to the discrepancy that often exists between intended and realized strategies of an organization. That is to say, between what their plans *say* they are going to do and what their actions reveal they are *actually* doing. When ongoing appraisal of a changing environment leads to an organization selecting alternative means (strategies) to achieve its stated aims (mission), the discrepancy between plan and action is legitimate. However, to the extent that SEs are exposed to competition with for-profit providers, they are faced with pressures that may lead to mission or goal displacement (Chetkovich and Frumkin, 2003; Dart, 2004; Foster and Bradach, 2005; Stone et al., 1999). These pressures are briefly reviewed below.

First, as has been noted, the adoption of strategic planning has been driven partly by the demands of external funders. To the extent that the priorities of commissioners diverge from those of SEs, whose survival depends on securing contracts from said funders, the latter may experience 'mission creep'. Where one stakeholder's interests become dominant and that stakeholder is a major source of resources, financial considerations are likely to compromise the organization's social goals (Westall, 2001).

Second, SEs seeking to operate in competitive markets that are targeted by large, for-profit companies will generally find that competitive strategies based on efficiency are unattractive simply due to relative scale effects. Larger, private-sector providers are often better able to absorb risk, offer a complete package of services, invest in large-scale infrastructure and do so at attractive prices (Chetkovich and Frumkin, 2003; Reeves and Ford, 2004). This exacerbates the inherent tensions in double bottom line missions by focusing attention on cost control and financial performance and its associated trade-offs as opposed to the desired social impact (Bull and Crompton, 2006). Reeves and Ford's (2004) review of empirical studies of healthcare in the USA found overwhelming evidence that service quality in non-profitmaking organizations exceed that of their for-profit competitors, supporting the view that pursuit of efficiency compromises provision eventually.

Third, the growing professionalization of third-sector management practices entails a degree of homogenization. As standardized best practices proliferate in the sector, early adopters gain a competitive advantage. However, as these practices become widespread, they then become standard operating procedures and any differential advantage is lost. Competing on efficiency, though important, is a zero sum game that draws organizations away from what they are able to offer as a unique or differentiated product/service (Porter, 1996).

Finally, exposure to the first two pressures is often resolved by embracing managerialist practices in the interests of greater efficiency and (external) legitimacy. This exerts pressure on the organization's culture. Specifically, it may have the effect of changing the organization's culture with respect to its democratic and inclusive nature, as managerialist techniques favour control over consultation (Chetkovich and Frumkin, 2003; Foster and Bradach, 2005; Stone, 1989).

Another key strand in the growing body of literature on non-profitmaking strategic choices focuses on the internal and external drivers of growth, or, 'scaling' (Dees et al., 2002; Foster and Fine, 2007; Rhodes and Keogan, 2005; Toepler, 2004).

Growth is most frequently measured as rising annual revenues or members (Stone, 1989). In one sense, growth is a reflection of an organization's success in habituating its practices to the demands of funders, as noted above – that is, they are rewarded with contracts – but it can be much more, too (Performance Hub, 2007: 4):

> In the third sector the concept of growth is not limited to just income and expenditure, as it tends to be in the public or private sectors. An organization's growth is obvious when it is taking on more staff, developing new projects or expanding its area of work, but other kinds of growth may include an organization having more impact, increasing its advocacy or learning, or extending its quality improvement.

A number of authors have suggested a differentiation strategy as being the best route to growth for third-sector organizations. Their unique identity and pro-social values are often advocated as the basis for this differentiation (Emerson, 2003; Nicholls, 2006). This is stated most forcefully by Frumkin and Andre-Clarke (2000: 159):

> it is all but certain that values may be the right starting point for either aggressive growth or product differentiation strategies. No matter how this translation is made from values to specific strategy, thinking about the relationship between values and an organiza- tion's ultimate ability to perform is an important task. It is this fun- damental tension that frames both strategy and identity within the nonprofit sector.

The benefits of seeking to focus on differentiation around pro-social values and the organization's social mission are twofold. In the first instance, the strategic posture of the organization creates a counterweight to the internal and external pressures to adopt managerialist practices that would foster greater emphasis on financial perfor- mance over its social impact, as noted above. In effect, it helps to promote a balance between the economic and social aspects of the double bottom line. Second, it offers a distinctive competitive position that emphasizes how the organization, uniquely, cre- ates value to meet clients' needs and does so in a way that offers a greater likelihood of sustainability as rivals cannot easily replicate the unique values and culture of another organization. Nicholls (2006) views the centrality of pro-social values to strategy as a defining feature of SEs: 'real values are at the heart of all strategic planning within the genuine social venture.'

If strategy is to be based on an organization's unique pro-social values and social mission, it follows that these must be widely recognized as legitimate, both inside and, perhaps more importantly from a competitive point of view, externally. Legitimacy, in turn, depends on their appropriateness and relevance to the needs of identified client groups.

Based on the forgoing review, it is clear SEs face the simultaneous challenge of devising strategies to improve efficiency and build capacity while positioning themselves externally to reflect their unique blended value proposition. In other words, they need both inward-facing and market-facing strategies to build capac- ity and present this capability as a viable, innovative solution to an identified social need.

Dees et al. (2002: 2) observe that 'social entrepreneurs frequently fail to consider all of their scaling options systematically.' One of the reasons for this is the narrow conception of growth as equating to market presence rather than also including internal capacity-building activities, such as innovation and learning, quality enhancement and social impact. This narrow conception is reflected in the promi- nence of the Ansoff matrix as the preferred tool for examining strategic options. It is the most commonly featured tool in prescriptive strategic management and fre- quently identified as appropriate for use by SEs (Jackson and Irwin, 2007). For the purpose of comparison, the Ansoff matrix is illustrated in Figure 3.4 and briefly dis- cussed below.

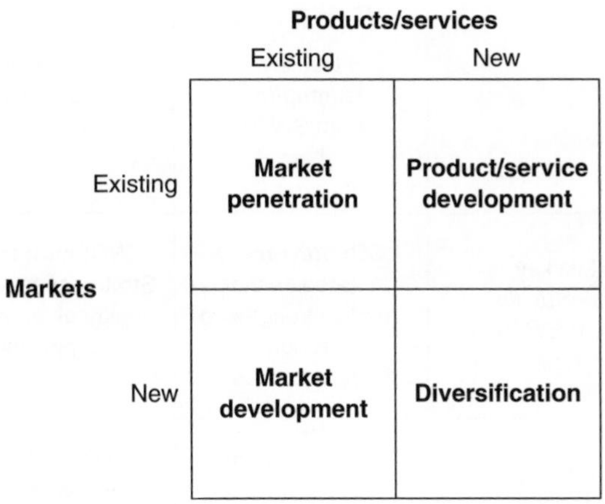

Products/services

Existing   New

	Existing	New
Existing	**Market penetration**	**Product/service development**
New	**Market development**	**Diversification**

Markets

Figure 3.4   The Ansoff matrix

The four strategies given in the matrix all focus on different methods of developing an organization's activities.

- *Market penetration* involves building on existing success to widen the client/customer base to increase its share of the market. Methods involve increased promotional activity, refining the brand strategy, improving customer/client retention rates and developing the distribution infrastructure.

- *Product/service development* involves building on existing customer relationships as a basis for launching new product/service offers to meet additional needs of these groups.

- *Market development* this strategy involves finding new markets for existing successful product/service offers. It could involve finding new geographical locations to operate in, segmenting existing markets into new customer/client groups (with differentiated needs) or seeking to grow the existing market through education and networking.

- *Diversification* combining the previous two strategies involves higher levels of risk, but is often appropriate when current areas of operation are in decline or offer no growth potential (perhaps due to funding restrictions). A key issue is the extent to which existing resources and capabilities are relevant to the new area of operation.

In practice, the Ansoff matrix is often used as a creative brainstorming technique, detached from the insights of the strategic analysis. While creativity is central to strategy development, it needs to be set against the reality of the organization's operating environment and internal capabilities (Stevenson, 1976).

In order to emphasize the link between strategic analysis and strategy choice, Weihrich (1982) developed the TOWS matrix. This tool is a more rigorous approach than the Ansoff matrix, not only linking analysis and choice but also focusing attention on the need for strategies to build capacity. It is therefore

	List key *strengths* from SWOT here	List key *weaknesses* from SWOT here
List key *opportunities* from SWOT here	**SO: maxi-maxi** Strategies that bundle strengths to exploit opportunities	**WO: mini-maxi** Strategies to reduce weaknesses relevant to opportunities
List key *threats* from SWOT here	**ST: maxi-mini** Strategies that use strengths to nullify threats	**WT: mini-mini** Strategies that reduce susceptibility to threats

Figure 3.5   The TOWS matrix (adapted from Weihrich, 1982)

particularly appropriate for SEs. The model is illustrated in Figure 3.5 and discussed in detail below.

The TOWS (threats, opportunities, weaknesses and strengths) matrix adapts SWOT analysis, providing a framework for considering a range of responses to deal with the identified strategic issues in an integrated way (that is to say, it avoids the reductionism of the traditional SWOT, which views identified issues in isolation rather than as interacting elements of a complex reality). As noted, the TOWS matrix integrates consideration of both capacity-building and market positions. It is thus an appropriately complementary tool to use alongside the augmented SWOT framework discussed earlier.

By integrating both internal and external perspectives, the TOWS matrix serves to maintain a focus on the realities of the organization's strategic position, thus increasing the likelihood of developing strategies that are matched to identified social needs and the specific development needs of the organization. It therefore offers the potential for maintaining a better balance between market perspectives and the unique pro-social values and mission by which the organization is able to differentiate itself in a competitive marketplace.

Here is a brief explanation of each of the four sets of strategies shown in the TOWS matrix:

- *SO strategies*   seek to leverage internal capabilities and resources to provide a solid platform for exploiting identified opportunities. This encourages debate about the feasibility of pursuing particular opportunities.

- *WO strategies*   focus on capacity-building to improve the organization's ability to pursue available opportunities. A key advantage of this approach is that these capacity-building efforts will be targeted at areas of strategic priority.

- *ST strategies* encourage a proactive stance to external threats by considering how existing strengths can be used to offset risk. One obvious area is the development of multiple revenue streams via related diversification – that is, diversification which applies existing skills in new contexts.

- *WT strategies* are defensive strategies appropriate to an organization facing the threat of extinction. These might include mergers, diversification out of a very competitive sector or subcontracting.

As Figure 3.5 illustrates, the TOWS matrix integrates strategic analysis and strategic choice, thus providing a rigorous and logical integration of the stages of strategy development. In so doing, the validity and legitimacy of the resulting strategy proposals are enhanced due to their clear basis in the realities of the organization's internal and external conditions (including their stakeholder networks, pro-social values and social mission).

The aim of applying the model is to produce a coherent set of proposals that address most of the major issues identified through the strategic analysis. Some of these proposals will be market-facing, intended to grow activities, while others will be enabling strategies, designed to build the capacity needed to support growth. Getting to this point is often an iterative process that involves consideration of each of the four strategy types and then their interdependence to develop coherence between the differing proposals.

Application of the TOWS matrix is a more intensive and challenging task than is the case with the simpler Ansoff matrix. Proposals have to be continuously validated by reference to market conditions and internal capabilities as well as their interactions with other proposed actions. This complexity can be a weakness of the model in practice if care is not taken to avoid getting bogged down in detail. It is therefore important to bear in mind that the aim is to develop the essential elements of the strategy proposals, not consider all the operational details of their implementation (these details are addressed when planning the implementation phase).

The generation of strategy proposals generally results in multiple incompatible ideas for each situation. The appropriateness, feasibility and acceptability of each proposal should therefore be subjected to a screening process to determine its relative merits when compared to agreed criteria and other competing proposals. The precise criteria will depend on the specific organizational context, but several guidelines are offered in the literature. Rumelt (2000) suggests four broad filters for screening proposed options:

- *consistency* the proposed strategy must be consistent with the organization's mission, existing strategies, policies and values;

- *consonance* the proposal must represent an appropriate adaptive response to evolving external conditions;

- *advantage* the proposal must create or reinforce competitive advantage in line with the critical success factors of the prevailing environment;

- *feasibility* the proposal must be achievable given the resources and capabilities that the organization can mobilize.

A variation on the same issues is offered by Thompson (1998), who draws attention to the importance of achieving a balance between environmental concerns (arising from the external analysis), resource issues (strengths and weaknesses) and the values (associated with the social mission, identity and culture) of the organization. He refers to this 'balance' as environment–values–resources congruence (EVR congruence).

The above discussion has highlighted the dominance of for-profit management approaches in discussions about SEs' choice of strategy. Specifically, there is an emphasis on either efficiency- *or* differentiation-based strategies. This approach suffers from several flaws with regard to the context in which many SEs find themselves operating. Survival is taken for granted (a reflection of the large organization origins of much strategic management thinking) and growth is narrowly conceptualized as market position (size or market share). The narrow conception of growth is particularly troubling as it excludes issues of learning and development related to the internal capacity-building activities so critical to small- to medium-sized SEs.

As an alternative to the familiar (market-focused) Ansoff matrix, the more holistic TOWS matrix was presented. This model offers a more holistic approach by integrating internal and external perspectives. Additionally, the TOWS matrix grounds the consideration of future actions in the reality of prevailing organizational and market conditions. The richness of the TOWS matrix is accompanied by the risk of getting bogged down in too much detail, however, so care is needed in its application to keep everyone's attention focused on broad proposals, not operational detail.

Whatever tools are used to generate strategic options, it is important that time is taken to compare and contrast resulting ideas with some organization-specific decision selection criteria. The aim of this period of reflection is to test the appropriateness, feasibility and acceptability of the proposals.

In the following section, our attention turns to the thorny issues associated with the implementation of agreed strategies.

IMPLEMENTING THE STRATEGY

Implementing a strategy involves making efforts to bring about changes in organizational behaviour that will result in the achievement of the long-term performance objectives of SEs. The question of the extent to which managers can exert control over such behaviour and, consequently, the efficacy of particular approaches and tools for managing change has received much attention in the mainstream literature, but very little in that specifically relating to third-sector organizations. It is beyond the scope of this chapter to review the complex debates on the relative influences of 'structure' and 'agency' in determining the extent of managerial discretion in the control of organizations. It is, however, helpful to understand the essential elements of the two main schools of thought regarding the management of change before looking in more detail at the process of implementation and measurement of strategic performance.

In the mainstream management literature, two schools of thought on how change should be managed are commonly identified. These are termed the 'planned approach' and the 'emergent approach' (Burnes, 1996; Wilson, 1992). The former, built on the pioneering work of Kurt Lewin, acknowledges the need for meaningful dialogue between members to shape the content of change projects but, critically, gives priority to the role of managers in proactively controlling phased change interventions with the aim of achieving rationally determined outcomes.

In contrast, the latter views change as more of a bottom-up process, shaped organically by the interactions between the competing agendas of individuals, groups and organizations (in wider networks), the success of which in asserting their claims depends on their relative power and political skills.

Though theoretically distinct, in practice, elements of each of these approaches will feature in pragmatic change projects so as to match the contextual situation of a given SE.

The implementation process

As with all other aspects of strategic management, managing implementation is highly context-specific. The design and implementation of any change project is dependent on the specific conditions inside and outside of the organization. It is therefore appropriate to be cautious about overly prescriptive or 'best practice' approaches to change management (Balogun and Hope-Hailey, 1998).

Many factors influence the chances of the successful implementation of a chosen strategy (or strategies). Among these is the readiness of the organization to accept change. This is influenced by a number of factors, which are briefly summarized below.

First, the extent to which members have been persuaded of the need for change and reassured about the personal risks associated with the process is critical. Schein (1985) has pointed out that, where proposed changes challenge collective and personal identity, members are likely to resist them. The strength of this resistance is, in turn, likely to reflect the quality of the prior dialogue about direction and sensitivity when selecting strategies in terms of how well they reflect the needs and identity of the organization and, therefore, the degree to which members can judge the strategy to be legitimate.

Second, as 'SEs are widely viewed as stakeholder organizations' (Low, 2006: 379), it is vital that internal and external stakeholders have reached a consensus on the desirability of change and the way it ought to be managed (Bryson, 1995). Where wide stakeholder engagement has characterized the strategy development process, this consensus may be implicit in the resulting strategy selections. Where resource constraints didn't allow for widespread consultation, internal marketing may be needed to convince stakeholders of the appropriateness of the proposals.

Third, readiness depends on current capacity and ability to change. Has the organization got the resources and skills in place to support the process? These would include management overheads, funds, systems, structures and processes that will enable the change to happen. One survey (Executives Online, 2002) notes that, 'Almost a third of those questioned bring in interim managers or change specialists to help them progress a major change initiative ... Indeed 75 per cent of the senior managers and directors interviewed view change management as a specialist skill in its own right.'

Collectively, the above factors have a significant bearing on the timing of any intervention. The design of the change process, by means of which the intervention is managed, is another key factor and it is to this that we now turn.

Given its long and close association with managerialism, it is not surprising that the strategic planning literature tends to emphasize the structural elements of change interventions. That is to say, the stages, roles, budgets, timing and other planned or designed elements. However, Siegal et al. (1996) remind us that process elements, emphasized by the behavioural sciences, are often the causes of failure when

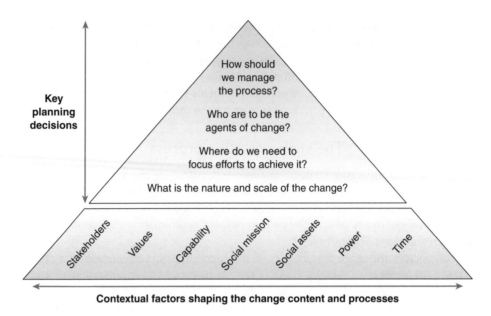

Figure 3.6   An embedded model of change management

implementing strategic change. They cite two key issues that they claim often result in the failure of change interventions – namely, resistance by members of the organization and poor implementation skills on the part of the change agents. Both of these points are particularly relevant to SEs as change challenges existing identities and cultures and the nascent nature of such organizations means that managers are relatively inexperienced and unskilled when it comes to the sector's challenges.

In the model outlined in Figure 3.6, therefore, attention is paid to both structural and processual elements in the interests of contextualization relating to the unique features of the SE sector (as far as such features can be generalized).

Figure 3.6 outlines a model designed to encourage a dialectical approach to change management. A series of interlinked questions foster dialogue between internal and external stakeholders so that they can fashion the change programme. While higher-level managers should address major outcomes, broad changes and required resources, detailed 'activity planning' (Beckhard and Harris, 1987, quoted in Siegal, 1996) should be left to those affected by the specific phases of the change programme in conjunction with relevant change agents. In this way, the model reflects the democratic nature of many SEs and allows a degree of flexibility to ensure that the planned activities adequately reflect the realities of the local contexts and capture lessons from prior interventions and progress. This, then, should be an unfolding conversation about change.

The variables shown at the base of the pyramid represent the situational factors on which the legitimacy of any proposed change project depends. These variables may be augmented to reflect the unique operating conditions of an organization. The legitimacy of any plans will be judged by the organization's members and wider stakeholders in terms of their appropriateness ('Will these changes achieve what we want?'), feasibility ('Are we convinced that the changes can be implemented effectively?') and acceptability ('Do the process and outcomes reflect our mission and preferred modes of operation?').

The identified planning questions are a starting point to direct attention towards some of the key issues and roughly sequential, for reasons discussed below. Each is now briefly elaborated on to clarify its particular purpose.

What is the nature and scale of the change?

It is generally accepted that the design and scale of the change intervention should be commensurate with the type and extent of change the organization is seeking to effect (Balogun and Hope-Hailey, 1998; Burnes, 1996; Wilson, 1992). The rationale is that change is disruptive and provokes conflict so should, therefore, be just sufficient to achieve the desired outcomes. Change is often characterized as a continuum from incremental adaptation through to transformation – that is, from a specific capacity-building initiative through to a radical reorientation of the organization (for example, following a merger, significant change of direction, significant jump in scale and so on).

Where do we need to focus efforts to achieve it?

Clarifying the nature and scale of the change will direct attention to the *site* where the change effort needs to be focused and the *variables* that might be altered to effect the change. In terms of the 'site' this may be an organizational unit such as a team, a department (or series of them if several interact with a process being changed), a division, a programme, the whole organization, or a network of collaborating organizations. *Strategic change* may involve several of these as part of a large scale project. The variables are the factors which are seen to affect performance such as team composition, skills sets, structures, systems, processes, policies, resources, and relationships, etc.

Who are to be the agents of change?

Consideration of the first two questions will provide insight into what outcomes are required (the nature and scale of change), where the effort is to be applied (site) and what changes are needed to effect the outcomes (variables). This in turn should lead to a consideration of what skills and experience are required to manage the changes and who (internally or externally) may possess them.

Many writers stress the importance of assembling transition management teams (TMT) to coordinate and support (project sponsors) and actually manage the transition phases (process champions; Bryson, 1995; Piercy, 2002; Siegal et al., 1996). It is particularly important that external change agents don't impose formulaic solutions on SEs, irrespective of the unique identity and context of each SE. The aim should be to guide and coach, not direct and lead, if the people who are involved in the change are to own the process and shape its content as a necessary condition of their embracing responsibility for the intended performance.

How should we manage the process?

The widely reported preference of SEs for democratic governance gives priority to stakeholder consultation and treating people with respect and dignity. It therefore

Table 3.1   Contextual factors explained

Factor	Explanation
Stakeholders	Different approaches to implementing an agreed strategy will require different levels of engagement by particular stakeholders and result in differential impacts on them. Consequently, the dialogue about direction in which they were engaged during strategy development must be maintained with regard to how it should be implemented
Values	Values are important in terms of both outcomes and processes. Implementation involves a series of trade-offs as resources are reallocated to new priorities. Judgement of the desirability (benefits) of such trade-offs against their acceptability (costs) will depend on prevailing values. Similarly, the acceptability of processes by which reallocation occurs, and particularly the empathy shown towards those adversely affected, will again depend on values in place. Where change challenges values, resistance will result
Capability	'Capability' refers to the available resources the organization is able to mobilize to effect the change. This covers the staff (numbers and expertise), finances and physical assets available, but also the levels of expertise and skills available through support networks
Social mission	Since advancement of the social mission is the raison d'être of a SE, the relative impacts of different approaches to implementation on its furtherance will be a critical decision criteria
Social assets	It is vital to ensure that the implementation of change does not come at the price of unwarranted damage to key social assets. The role of values as a basis for differentiation has already been noted and so it is important not to change them too radically where such a strategy is involved. However, there are other social assets, such as brand, reputation, legitimacy, relationships and staff relations, that it will be desirable to protect in the face of change
Power	Change has the effect of reordering power structures in organizations according to the approach taken. Powerful individuals and groups will therefore assert their power to shape the change content and process in ways they deem acceptable. Consequently, the agreed change content and processes will be influenced by politicking and compromise to secure agreement
Time	Time is a key factor from the obvious standpoint of planning horizons, project time scales, deadlines, etc. However, more subtle aspects of rhythm, cycles and pace, relative to the organizational environment, are important to the perceived experience of change (Wilson, 1992). Is the pace too fast leading to stress, or too slow and lacking urgency?

follows that a bottom-up process, characterized by inclusivity and dialogue, will be appropriate, as opposed to a top-down (imposed) change process.

This has the advantage of basing the process design in the social aspects of organization (for example, relationships, politics, power structure, values, sub-cultures and individual and group concerns), as advocated by Carnall (1986), Kotter (1995) and Siegal et al. (1996), among many others. Thus, rather than simply consulting members about the process, it is preferable that they are fully engaged in determining and implementing the agreed changes rather than having changes done to them. In this way, support for, and commitment to, the process can be encouraged as a counter to the inertial forces that tend to make organizations cling to founding values, strategies and modes of operation (Boeker, 1989).

The model outlined in Table 3.1 intentionally avoids glib checklists of action sequences in favour of drawing attention to contingency variables and a series of related points that focus attention on the issues that will support development of a socially embedded, and well-supported, change process.

All change involves structural adaptation, changed roles and working practices for members, as well as, often, changes in the level or application of technology. Where change is pervasive, the culture might need to change also in a bid to align it with the requirements of the new strategy. It is likely to be changed anyway as a by-product of the new modes of operation even if it has not been intentionally pushed in particular directions.

MEASURING PERFORMANCE

Measuring the effectiveness of the implementation process in bringing about the improvements in performance set out in the organization's strategy is clearly desirable. However, performance measurement is a particularly difficult challenge for third-sector organizations, as many authors have noted (Bull, 2007; Bull and Crompton, 2006; Rhodes and Keogan, 2005; Rotheroe and Richards, 2007; Somers, 2005; Stone, et al., 1999). The difficulty stems, principally, from three areas.

First, there is the problem of plurality. As discussed earlier, there are often conflicting and incoherent objectives in third-sector organizations that arise from their attempts to balance performance across multiple constituencies and bottom lines and this makes evaluating their performance problematic (Herman and Renz, 1998). According to Somers (2005: 47), 'SE managers continuously make trade-offs between increasing productivity for financial gain versus increasing productivity for social gain', making objective evaluation difficult using the maximization principal fostered by the neoclassical economics of the for-profit sector. A more appropriate approach for understanding goal-directed behaviour in relation to espoused objectives is that of 'satisficing', derived from managerial models of firms' behaviour. Nonetheless, the problem of evaluating performance is compounded by the constantly changing environments in which SEs operate (Bull, 2007).

Second, many writers have noted the problem of causality. Evidence of causal links between the adoption of strategic management and performance is often ambiguous at best and is inclined to suggest that indirect links are at work (Siciliano, 1997). For example, Stone et al. (1999: 409) note that it is 'not clear how formal planning is related to strategy content and to implementation nor is it clear why planning by itself would improve performance.' Reasons for this causal ambiguity may lie in the problems of isolating the links between a single organization's adopted strategies and its performance where it is involved in multi-agency work. Some have suggested that the causal link between adoption of strategic management and performance stems not from the strategies applied, but from the higher levels of control and coordination accompanying more systematic practices (Siciliano, 1997; Stone et al., 1999). In such circumstances, it is understandable that strategy is viewed as a 'language game' that is of more symbolic than practical value (Stone, 1989).

Finally, there is the problem of measurement. Tools available from the corporate world are often inappropriate for measuring the performance outcomes targeted by SEs – social impact and sustainability reporting being two key areas in this regard (Rotheroe and Richards, 2007). Inhibiting the development of appropriate tools is the fact that small- to medium-sized SEs have often not developed the levels of formalization in their management systems that yield the data on which to base measurement. Where progress has been made by individual organizations, that learning and knowledge is often not transferable to other contexts (Bull, 2007).

In spite of the above difficulties, the increasing demand for SEs to be accountable and demonstrate their impacts is leading practitioners and academics to develop tools to measure economic and non-economic dimensions of performance (Griggs, 2000). One such tool that is seen as being particularly useful to strategic management in third-sector organizations is the Balanced Scorecard (BSC). The BSC is briefly reviewed below in relation to the strategic control of SEs.

The Balanced Scorecard

Pioneered by Kaplan and Norton (1992, 1996), the BSC is a holistic performance management tool that is intended to support the pursuance of an organization's mission by focusing management attention on controlling the performance of internal activities perceived as causally related to achieving the stated goals or objectives derived from it.

The original model, designed for the for-profit world, is holistic in so far as it advocates managing performance in four interrelated domains (or 'perspectives' in the language of the BSC) – namely the financial perspective, customer perspective, internal process perspective and a learning and growth perspective. In Kaplan and Norton (1996), the financial performance is given priority with performance in the other domains acting as lead indicators of superior financial performance. However, all four perspectives are to be populated by contextually relevant measures directly related to the organization's mission.

Several authors specializing in third-sector management have noted the need to amend the model to better serve the needs of SEs (Bull, 2007; Ronchetti, 2006; Somers, 2005). The

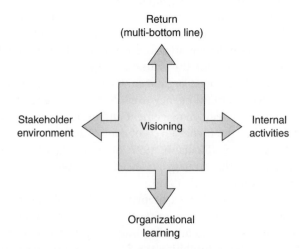

Figure 3.7   Bull's balance model (based on Bull, 2007)

proposed amendments are invariably designed to address the problem of plurality noted above. Thus, Bull (2007) offers the revised model illustrated in Figure 3.7.

Bull's model broadens the scope of each of the four perspectives of the BSC to better reflect the operating conditions and social missions of third-sector organizations. By expanding the financial perspective to include social and environmental returns, the predominance of economic returns is downgraded in favour of a more balanced consideration of the contributions of the four domains. Somers (2005) developed a model on behalf of SE London with very similar adaptations in the financial and customer perspectives.

Both Ronchetti (2006) and Somers (2005) stress that the BSC can also offer a way to overcome the problem of causality in so far as it requires managers to identify cause and effect links between performed activities and strategic objectives in the process of specifying the measures to be included in the organization's BSC.

The BSC approach is thus still seen to offer a number of benefits to SEs.

- Reducing strategic control to the four performance domains 'meets managerial needs by distilling varied unrelated measures from multiple areas within the company into a single report and ensuring that managers are looking at all measures across the operation' (Ronchetti, 2006: 28).
- Strategy decisions are grounded in actual performance data rather than subjective opinion (Ronchetti, 2006).
- The BSC has the advantage of 'simultaneously taking into account both financial and intangible resources that can determine success or failure' (Somers, 2005: 44).
- 'Whilst having the structure of an assessment, the tool benefits from offering managers self-diagnosis, a qualitative approach to business analysis and space for critical refection, without the time-consuming need for quantitative assessment through financial inputting and in-depth statistical analysis' (Bull, 2007: 57).
- 'By connecting financial to non-financial objectives, external to internal processes, and current to future performance, corporate strategy will be mapped more cohesively, and employees at all levels of the organization work towards the same goal' (Somers, 2005: 45).
- The BSC can ensure 'SE managers make decisions that are strategy-led rather than reactions to short-term conditions in the marketplace' (Somers, 2005: 47).

However, studies of the use of the BSC in third-sector organizations also note several barriers to the use of such a modified tool due in large part to the emergent stage of development of many SEs. Issues raised include that:

- most performance management tools are designed for use in large organizations that possess the systems required to gather and analyse the data needed to operate the BSC (Bull, 2007; Ronchetti, 2006);
- SEs lack the managerial resources needed to operate such a complex performance measurement system (Bull, 2007; Ronchetti, 2006);
- cynicism may be a factor, as Bull (2007: 51) notes that 'many SEs see impact measurement as a burden, rather than a source of competitive advantage or a useful management tool.'

Overall, the BSC seems to offer potential as a viable integrative approach for performance measurement given its promotion of a bespoke set of measures and amenability to stakeholder engagement. It is certainly capable of complementing the aims of strategic management by encouraging a focus on mission and the means to its achievement through the noted stress on cause and effect relationships between activities and performance. However, just how SEs are to identify and map such relationships is not addressed by the authors advocating BSC models for the third sector.

CONCLUSION

This chapter has sought to offer a review of strategic management in SEs. The giving of precise definitions of the concepts 'social enterprise' and 'strategic management' has been set aside so as not to diminish the usefulness of the content for particular readers. Inevitably this entails a less strict adherence to our central theme of contextualization with regard to the practice of strategy formulation and implementation in particular organizations.

Central to our exposition has been a model of strategic management that is centred on the organization's unique identity, as expressed in its social mission and modes of operation. A processual model of strategy development was then outlined with an emphasis on the social embeddedness of the process and the importance of consensus-based outcomes so as to maintain legitimacy and, hence, the commitment of the stakeholders. This democratic and discursive approach was carried through the whole process, from determining the mission, evaluating the organization's strategic position and debating and selecting strategies to follow to designing a bespoke implementation process.

Throughout this chapter, we have sought to stress the real-world complexity and contested nature of strategy in the academic and organizational realms. Strategy is strongly promoted in the third sector despite conflicting evidence regarding its usefulness in achieving its stated aims of improving the strategic fit between internal capabilities and operating environments. Instead, we have noted that improvements in performance may be associated with the greater levels of control and coordination that accompany the increase in structure that adoption of strategic management (in the form of strategic planning) occasions.

Many obstacles to the uptake of for-profit management practices exist in third-sector organizations. Of these, resource constraints, lack of skills, inadequate systems, ideological resistance and changing environments play their part. Nonetheless, the professionalization of the sector is happening through the combined efforts of organizations themselves, supporting networks, consultants, university programmes and the sharing of knowledge and experience. Strategic management is one of the lead disciplines in this transformation as organizations faced with institutional pressures to demonstrate their legitimacy and competence recognize its utility in bringing direction and coherence to their projects to alleviate an increasing range of social needs and the results of other market failures.

REFERENCES

Albert, S., and Whetten, D.A. (1985) 'Organizational identity', *Research in Organizational Behaviour*, 7: 263–95.

Alvord, S.H., Brown, L.D. and Letts, C.W. (2004) 'Social entrepreneurship and societal transformation: an exploratory study', *The Journal of Applied Behavioural Science*, 40 (3): 260–82.

Balogun, J. and Hope-Hailey, V. (1998) *Exploring Strategic Change*. London: FT Prentice Hall.

Baruch, Y. and Ramalho, N. (2006) 'Communalities and distinctions in the measurement of organizational performance and effectiveness across for-profit and nonprofit sectors', *Nonprofit and Voluntary Sector Quarterly*, 35 (1): 39–65.

Boeker, W. (1989) 'Strategic change: the effects of founding and history', *The Academy of Management Journal*, 32 (3): 489–515.

Bryson, J.M. (1995) *Strategic Planning for Public and Nonprofit Organizations*. San Francisco, CA: Jossey-Bass.

Bull, M. (2007) '"Balance": the development of a social enterprise business performance analysis tool', *Social Enterprise Journal*, 3 (1): 49–66.

Bull, M. and Crompton, H. (2006) 'Business practices in social enterprises', *Social Enterprise Journal*, 2 (1): 42–60.

Burnes, B. (1996) *Managing Change* (2nd edn). London: Pitman.

Campbell, A. and Yeung, S. (1991) 'Creating a sense of mission', *Long Range Planning*, 24 (4): 10–20.

Carnall, C.A. (1986) 'Managing strategic change: an integrated approach', *Long Range Planning*, 19 (6): 105–15.

Chetkovich, C. and Frumkin, P. (2003) 'Balancing margin and mission: nonprofit competition in charitable gaming versus fee-based programs', *Administration and Society*, 35 (5): 564–96.

Courtney, R. (2002) *Strategic Management for Voluntary Nonprofit Organizations*. New York: Routledge.

Courtney, R., Marnoch, G. and Williamson, A. (2005) 'The adoption of strategic management by third sector organizations: findings from a census of third sector organizations in Northern Ireland and further behavioural questions', Third Sector Study Group, EGPA, Bern, 31 August–September 2005.

Dart, R. (2004) 'The legitimacy of social enterprise', *Nonprofit Management and Leadership*, 14 (4): 411–24.

Dees, J.G., Anderson, B.B., and Wei-Skillern, J. (2002) 'Pathways to social impact: strategies for scaling out successful social innovations', Case Working Paper, Series No. 3, August, Centre for the Advancement of Social Entrepreneurship, The Fuqua School of Business, Duke University, Durham, NC.

Elkington, J. (2004) 'Enter the triple bottom line', Chapter 1 in A. Henriques and J. Richardson, *The Triple Bottom Line: Does it all add up?*. London: Earthscan.

Emerson, J. (2003) 'The blended value proposition: integrating social and financial returns', *California Management Review*, 45 (4): 35–51.

Executives Online (2002) 'Challenge of Change', Executives Online, Winchester. Available at: www.executives online.co.uk

Foster, W. and Bradach, J. (2005) 'Should nonprofits seek profits?', *Harvard Business Review*, February: 92–100.

Foster, W. and Fine, G. (2007) 'How nonprofits get really big', *Stanford Innovation Review*, spring: 46–55.

Frumkin, P. and Andre-Clarke, A. (2000) 'When missions, markets, and politics collide: values and strategy in the nonprofit human services', *Nonprofit and Voluntary Sector Quarterly*, 29 (1): 141–63.

Granovetter, M. (1985) 'Economic action and social structure: the problem of embeddedness', *The American Journal of Sociology*, 91 (3): 481–510.

Grant, R.M. (2004) *Contemporary Strategy Analysis*, (5th edn). Oxford: Blackwell.

Griggs, H.E. (2000) Corporatisation of the nonprofit sector: strategic planning and organisational performance in disability based organisations, University of Tasmania, School of Management, working paper series no. 20–03. Available at: http://www.utas.edu.au/mgmt/wps/wps_2000.htm

Herman, R.D. and Renz, D.O. (1998) 'Nonprofit organizational effectiveness: contrasts between especially effective and less effective organizations', *Nonprofit Management and Leadership*, 9 (1): 23–38.

Hudson, M. (2004) *Managing without Profit: The art of managing third-sector organizations*. London: Directory of Social Change.

Ireland, R.D. and Hitt, M.A. (1992) 'Mission statements: importance, challenge, and recommendations for development', *Business Horizons*, May–June: 34–42.

Jackson, A. and Irwin, D. (2007) 'Tools for strategic planning: what works best', Performance Hub. Available at: www.performancehub.org.uk

Johnson, G. (2008) 'Ritualizing strategic thinking: the effectiveness of the strategic away day', *Strategic Direction*, 24 (1): 3–5.

Johnson, G. and Scholes, K. (2005) *Exploring Corporate Strategy* (7th edn). Harlow: Prentice Hall.

Johnson, G., Scholes, K. and Whittington, R. (2008) *Exploring Corporate Strategy*, (8th edn). Harlow: Prentice Hall.

Johnson, S. (2000) 'Literature review on social entrepreneurship', Canadian Centre for Social Entrepreneurship, University of Alberta.

Kaplan, R.S. and Norton, D.P. (1992) 'The Balanced Scorecard: measures that drive performance', *Harvard Business Review*, January–Febuary: 71–80.

Kaplan, R.S. and Norton, D.P. (1996) 'Using the Balanced Scorecard as a strategic management system', *Harvard Business Review*, January–February: 75–85.

Kerlin, J. (2006) 'Social enterprise in the United States and Europe: understanding and learning from differences', *Voluntas: International Journal of Voluntary and Nonprofit Organizations*, 17 (3): 246–62.

Kotter, J. (1995) 'Why transformation efforts fail', *Harvard Business Review*, March–April: 59–67.

Levy, D.L., Alvesson, M. and Willmott, H. (2003) 'Critical approaches to strategic management', in M. Alvesson and H. Willmott, *Studying Management Critically*. London: Sage.

Low, C. (2006) 'A framework for the governance of social enterprise', *International Journal of Social Economics*, 33: 376–85.

Lumpkin, G.T. and Dess, G.G. (1995) 'Simplicity as a strategy-making process: the effects of stage of organizational development and environment on performance', *The Academy of Management Journal*, 38 (5): 1386–407.

Margolis, S.L. and Hansen, C.D. (2002) 'A model for organizational identity: exploring the path to sustainability during change', *Human Resource Development Review*, 1 (3): 277–303.

Mintzberg, H., Ahlstrand, B. and Lampel, J. (1998) *Strategy Safari*. New York: The Free Press.

Mintzberg, H. and Waters, J.A. (1985) 'Of strategies, deliberate and emergent', *Strategic Management Journal*, 16 (3): 257–72.

National Council for Voluntary Organizations (2007) 'Adventures in strategy 1: renewing your strategy', National Council for Voluntary Organizations. Available at: www.askncvo.org.uk

Nicholls, A. (2006) 'Playing the field: a new approach to the meaning of social entrepreneurship', *Social Enterprise Journal*, 2 (1): 1–5.

Nickols, F. (2000) 'Strategy: definitions and meaning', Distance Consulting. Available at: http://home.att.net/~nickols/strategy_definition.htm

Paton, R. (2003) *Managing and Measuring Social Enterprises*. London: Sage.

Pearce, J. (2003) *Social Enterprise in Anytown*. London: Calouste Gulbenkian Foundation.

Pettigrew, A. (2003) 'Strategy as process, power and change', Chapter 10 in S. Cummings and D. Wilson, *Images of Strategy*. Oxford: Blackwell.

Pfeffer, J. and Sutton, I. (2006) 'Profiting from evidence-based management', *Strategy and Leadership*, 34 (2): 35–42.

Piercy, N.F. (2002) *Market-led Strategic Change* (3rd edn). Oxford: Butterworth-Heinemann.

Porter, M.E. (1996) 'What is strategy?', *Harvard Business Review*, November/December: 61–78.

Reeves, T.C. and Ford, E.W. (2004) 'Strategic management and performance differences: nonprofit versus for-profit health organizations', *Health Care Management Review*, 29 (4): 298–308.

Reid, K. and Griffith, J. (2006) 'Social enterprise mythology: critiquing some assumptions', *Social Enterprise Journal*, 2 (1): 1–10.

Rhodes, M.L. and Keogan, J.F. (2005) 'Strategic choice in the non-profit sector: modelling the dimensions of strategy', *The Irish Journal of Management*, 26 (1): 122–35.

Ronchetti, J.L. (2006) 'An integrated Balanced Scorecard strategic planning model for nonprofit organizations', *Journal of Practical Consulting*, 1 (1): 25–35.

Rotheroe, N.C. and Richards, A. (2007) 'Social return on investment and social enterprise: transparent accountability for sustainable development', *Social Enterprise Journal*, 3 (1): 31–48.

Rumelt, R.P. (2000) 'Note on strategy evaluation', available at www.anderson.ucla.edu/faculty/dick.rumelt/Docs/Notes/StratEvaluation1999.pdf

Schein, E.H. (1985) *Organizational Culture and Leadership*. San Francisco: Jossey-Bass.

Sharp, C., Bitel, M., Gross, T. and Jones, J. (2007) 'Successful strategies: real learning from real experiences', Performance Hub. Available at: www.performancehub.org.uk

Siciliano, J. (1997) 'The relationship between formal planning and performance in nonprofit organizations', *Nonprofit Management and Leadership*, 7 (4): 387–403.

Siegel, W., Church, A.H., Javitch, M., Waclawski, J., Burd, S., Bazigos, M., Yan, T.F., Anderson-Rudolph, K. and Warner Burke, W. (1996) 'Understanding the management of change', *Journal of Organizational Change Management*, 9 (6): 54–80.

Smith, B. (2003) 'Success and failure in marketing strategy making: results of an empirical study across medical markets', *International Journal of Medical Marketing*, 3 (4): 287–315.

Somers, A.B. (2005) 'Shaping the Balanced Scorecard for use in UK social enterprises', *Social Enterprise Journal*, 1 (1): 43–56.

Stevenson, H. (1976) 'Defining corporate strengths and weaknesses', *Sloan Management Review*, 17 (3): 51–68.

Stone, M.M. (1989) 'Planning as strategy in nonprofit organizations: an exploratory study', *Nonprofit and Voluntary Quarterly*, 18 (4): 297–315.

Stone, M.M. Bigelow, B. and Crittenden, W. (1999) 'Research on strategic management in nonprofit organizations: synthesis, analysis and future directions', *Administration and Society*, 31 (3): 378–423.

Stone, M.M. and Brusch, C.G. (1996) 'Planning in ambiguous contexts: the dilemma of meeting needs for commitment and demands for legitimacy', *Strategic Management Journal*, 17 (8): 633–52.

Thompson, J.L. (1998) *Strategic Management: Awareness and change* (2nd edn). Stamford, CT: Thomson Learning.

Toepler, S. (2004) 'Conceptualising nonprofit commercialism: a case study', *Public Administration and Management: An Interactive Journal*, 9 (4): 1–19.

Waddock, S. (2004) 'Parallel universes: companies, academics and the progress of corporate citizenship', *Business and Society Review*, 109 (1): 5–42.

Weihrich, H. (1982) 'The TOWS Matrix: a tool for situational analysis', *Long Range Planning*, 15 (2): 54–66.

Westall, A. (2001) *Value-led Market-driven: Social enterprise solutions to public policy goals*. London: Institute for Public Policy Research.

Whetten, D.A. (2006) 'Albert and Whetten revisited: strengthening the concept of organizational identity', *Journal of Management Inquiry*, 15 (3): 216–34.

Wilson, D.C. (1992) *A Strategy of Change*. London: Routledge.

Young, D.R. (2001) 'Social enterprise in the United States: alternate identities and forms', paper prepared for the EMEA Conference, 13–15 December, Tento, Italy.

ACKNOWLEDGEMENT

Exhibit 3.1, page 55, NCVO quote from National Council for Voluntary Organisations (NCVO), Adventures in Strategy 1, p2. www.askncvo.org.uk

Andrews quote Copyright 1980 by McGraw-Hill Companies, Inc.- Books. Reproduced with permission of McGraw-Hill Companies, Inc - Books in the format Textbook via Copyright Clearance Center. Johnson and Scholes quote, Johnson, Gerry; Scholes, Kevan; Whittington, Richard, *Exploring Corporate Strategy*: Text & Cases, 7th edition, © 2005, Pg. 9. Reprinted by permission of Pearson Education, Inc., Upper Saddle River, NJ.

4

MANAGING PEOPLE IN A SOCIAL ENTERPRISE ENVIRONMENT

LEARNING OBJECTIVES

- Understanding the nature of human resource management (HRM), its role in managing people and its relevance to SEs.
- Identification of the elements of HRM strategies and integrating these with enterprise strategies.
- Analysis of HRM support in capacity-building within SEs – the skills required to manage people in the social economy sector.

HRM AS A SUPPORT TOOL FOR THE SECTOR

In considering the challenges facing SE organizations, Borzaga and Solari (2004) highlight corporate governance and HRM as the two critical issues facing the sector overall. HRM has been defined by Torrington et al. (2005) as a distinctive philosophy regarding carrying out people-orientated organizational activities. More simply expressed, HRM is about managing people in an organizational context. The history of HRM reveals a social justice theme with origins in the work of social reformers and paternalist Quaker family firms, such as Rowntree, Cadbury and Lever Brothers. Such firms held a business as well as an ethical view concerning the welfare of their workers.

Traditionally, HRM has been restricted to a functional level of coping with the 'downstream' consequences of earlier high-level policy decisions or resolving short-term people issues that threatened the long-term success of a particular business-level strategy. More recently, a strategic approach to the management of people is seen by Sissons and Storey (2000) and Leopold et al. (2005) as embracing the following key issues:

- perceiving people as a strategic resource for achieving competitive advantage;

- making use of planning;

- adopting a coherent approach to employment policies and practices;

- integrating employment policies and practices with business strategy;

- reacting proactively to managerial issues, not reactively;

- taking action on employment matters at the most senior management levels.

Beardwell and Holden (2001) state that a major assumption behind much of the recent literature in this area is that HRM is essentially a strategically driven activity that plays a major role in determining and influencing business strategies. Current mainstream thinking in HRM supports the view of Borzaga and Solari, that these internal management challenges constitute the key competitive advantages of SEs.

Storey (2007) believes that two forms of alignment with strategy are desirable. The first is horizontal integration between the consistency and fit of the various strands of HR strategy. The second is the alignment of those HR strategies with business strategy. Indeed, HRM is seen by writers in the field as essentially strategic (Leopold et al., 2005). While functional, operational or line mangers focus on local or functional performance, HRM must consider the needs of the whole organization and preferably take a longer-term view.

Storey (2007) defines two strategic approaches to managing people in organizations. The first is a cost-based approach that views employees as being a cost to the organization and is primarily concerned with minimizing the cost and controlling the performance of those employed. This is known as a 'hard' strategic approach. The alternative, a 'soft' approach, views employees as assets who contribute to the competitive advantage of the organization. In reality, organizations may employ a mixture of hard and soft behaviours across skill levels and in differing market conditions. The requirement of SEs to manage a commercial and a social mission would suggest the possibility of a hybrid approach, possibly a middle view somewhere between hard and soft. Alternatively, the SE might be transformed by something in its environment so that it could be hard in some conditions, soft in other environmental situations.

One 'soft' model, the Harvard model of HRM proposed by Beere et al. (1984), is that HRM strategy is formed once stakeholder and situational conditions have been understood and that these conditions influence the strategy choices. This particular model of HRM regards individual and societal well-being as the outcomes of a coherent HRM strategy and, as such, links directly with the strategic aspirations of many SEs. The focus on stakeholders when shaping HRM strategy can be seen in the governance structures of such organizations, but simply having that stakeholder link does not guarantee that strategic decisions will be made, nor clarity, as research by Chapman et al. (2007) discovered.

Chapman et al. (2007) asked public-sector stakeholders about their views of SEs and, while broadly applauding the social aims and community context, there was frustration about a lack of focused objectives and evaluation. Chapman identified a perception among those in the stakeholder group that, for some SEs, a feeling that simply to be doing something recognized as 'good' was enough. The stakeholders from the public sector also felt that a more focused approach was needed to gain funding or representation, win contracts or secure other forms of support.

The need for such clarity from the leaders of SEs adds a further dimension to the development of strategy and the HR requirements of the SEs. SEs must balance short-term, objective-driven funding regimes with the desire to provide job security, progression and creativity in the work environment. Additionally, the need to manage a board of trustees with variable levels of skill and ability to commit time and reach out to volunteers who may be highly skilled or unskilled with low confidence creates the need for a strong communication culture that will be diverse and inclusive. As the sector moves towards sustainability and funding bodies demand detailed reporting of project management, so the pressure is on the sector to respond with professional and sensitive HRM policies that, while conforming to a legal framework and established good practice will also be focused directly on the differing needs of SEs. In trying to achieve the balance between the social and the entrepreneurial, SEs must face the inevitable changes in culture and values arising from either moving from a not-for-profit or voluntary sector ethos to also giving consideration to the commercial dimension or from a more conventional business that seeks to add a social mission dimension to its objectives and operations. Either way, these organizations need to address the issues of fit for purpose governance, people to resource the organizations, whether paid workers or volunteers, and the creation of a performance culture capable of delivering on both their commercial and social objectives.

Managing people is a complex business in any organization. The challenge of being enterprising while focused on social objectives creates an even more complex environment for those managing people in this sector. Traditional HRM processes may seem to offer little to an organization staffed predominantly by volunteers or those wishing to support a vulnerable workforce or work with those excluded from the mainstream. However, there are common strands linking the HRM agenda to that of SEs:

- need to establish clarity about staffing levels and patterns of work;
- culture-fair recruitment and selection processes;
- motivational performance and reward options;
- an energizing work relationship;
- progressive development policies.

The achievement of coherent and capacity-building people management policies and procedures require SE managers to count strategic thinking, interpersonal skills and comfort with cultural diversity among the many skills to be found in their personal kit bags. SEs, state Borzaga and Solari (2004: 340), 'must find suitable ways to manage their key assets including their social mission and efficiency constraints, committed volunteers and employees and enlarged governance structures'. Within their own cultural context, SEs will need to make choices about their approach to managing people and these choices will, as suggested by the Harvard model (Beere et al., 1984), have consequences for the individuals who work within the organization, the achievement of organizational objectives and possibly the well-being of communities with stakeholder ties to the organization.

HRM increasingly recognizes, through work–life balance initiatives and individualized responses to performance, reward and development issues, that a 'one size fits all' approach is unlikely to lead to either high standards of performance or enhanced employee satisfaction. The growing diversity of traditional organizations demands an environment more responsive to individuality and creative employment solutions. In this more responsive climate, there is possibly a degree of transferability from the traditional profit-making sector organization to the SE organization. SE writers, however, warn that SEs are essentially different from the for-profit, public and traditional not-for-profit sectors and, the ultimately, models and good practice must be contextualized to recognize the SEs' culture (Borzaga and Defourny, 2004; Borzaga and Solari, 2004).

While accepting the need for contextualization of models and practice, managers of SEs find themselves, in common with frontline managers in other sectors, having to understand and take ownership of recruitment, performance, pay, attendance, training and welfare issues. Some of these complex skill areas take time to evolve and may not be part of the skills the manager of a SE project or organization was recruited for. Indeed, the diverse nature of SEs can make it hard to define their culture and requirements, which will impact significantly on their ability to make focused decisions when appointing staff, volunteers or board members.

In recognizing that the sector has a global identity, Salamon et al. (2003) identify key challenges of legitimacy that infer the requirement for strong governance, sustainability, which demands independence in terms of skills and ability to develop in the chosen market, and the forging of working partnerships with other sectors, requiring communication skills and strategic vision.

We need to consider the role that HRM can play in meeting the challenges laid down by Salamon et al. (2003). In preparing SEs to harness the resources of both paid staff and volunteers, there is a role for strategic HRM.

Storey (2007) outlines complementary pathways to developing an HRM strategy:

- good practices;
- best fit;
- response to analysis of trends;
- building on and exploiting the resource base.

While being well-intentioned in terms of good practice, funding limitations and shortfall, as well as the unpredictability of commercial contracts, can lead to organizational decisions about best fit (short-term contracts, low-level security) that do not coincide with good practice or, indeed, sector perceptions of how SEs should behave towards their volunteers and employees.

Responsiveness to trends and situational and environmental information are strategic functions that should be part of board-level planning. This can only happen if the board and senior management team is free from having to make bureaucratic decisions and be involved in day-to-day supervisory management issues. However, volatile market conditions and the environment in which SEs operate increase the importance of making effective use of the available resource base. Phrased in businessspeak, it feels very 'hard', but building skill capacity in individuals and organizations is at the heart of many SEs. Also, this maximization of talent and regarding individuals as assets embodies the 'soft' approach discussed previously. The ability to make the most of resources and stakeholder involvement may well be crucial to the survival of SEs and it is the importance of the role of stakeholders that makes a consideration of the Harvard model of HRM useful to social entrepreneurs.

The Harvard model (Beere et al., 1984) recognizes the importance of situational, environmental factors to the development of HR strategies. Social missions within SEs often involve working with marginalized communities, but within those marginalized communities there is a very real danger that they may not be able to provide a marketplace for the new commercial activity. The old voluntary sector provided services in communities that were unattractive to more commercialized, better-resourced organizations. By moving towards commercialization, therefore, the risk is that market-driven sustainability is being expected to thrive in an environment that would have challenged stronger, better-resourced organizations. In choosing the areas of the enterprise suitable for commercialization, the leadership and local knowledge of the senior management and board must be able to recognize where market sustainability is and may fail to be achievable. This very practical consequence of the decisionmaking ability of the board and senior management is illustrated in Exhibit 4.1 in an example from Pakistan quoted by zia Ul Islam (2007) in research on sustainability within SEs.

Exhibit 4.1 Understanding situational factors in SEs – learning from HRM

Islam's (2007) research tells the story of a search for sustainable skill-building projects and a review of the potential viability of a stitching and sewing industry for local women.

The feasibility study showed that most poor women made simple clothes for themselves and their families in the home and did not buy clothes made by others and on sale in local markets. Charitable institutions in the area were already offering sewing skills training and even donating sewing machines to those completing the training. Despite this, as there was no market for their clothes, the participating women remained poor and unempowered.

Islam, very graphically through this example, reminds us that generalized social goals in terms of upskilling or providing resources will not necessarily achieve the other social goals of alleviating poverty or creating economic inclusion.

> Within SEs, the skills to recognize the wider economic and market forces and their impact on the social mission need to be understood. There is good integration between HRM-related strategies in raising skill levels and recruiting participants excluded from the economy, but the situational factors here are so strong that they dominate the outcome. Strategic awareness in senior decisionmakers is crucial to success (2007).

The example given in Exhibit 4.1 shows the importance of HRM-related skills as a way of achieving cultural change. McBrearty (2007) suggests that culture change is critical to commercialization. The organization must, she suggests, place internal cost values on its activities, which represents a major cultural shift if an organization is moving from the voluntary sector to a SE footing.

McBrearty points us towards research on Housing Associations by Manzi and Smith Bowers, suggesting that, as SEs, housing associations put enterprise before the delivery of social capital and, as such, behave rather like private landlords. The development of the commercial objectives at the expense of the social worry writers such as McBrearty who believe that the development ventures are expensive in terms of senior management time – the inference being that this time is then lost to the maintenance of stakeholder and social aspects of the organization.

Culture change may lie at the very heart of the communities the SEs wish to serve. Zia Ul Islam (2007) points to the cultural barriers preventing relatively affluent individuals investing in SEs because they prefer to make personal donations to charities on an individual basis, creating a dependency mentality and making it difficult for entrepreneurial models based on sustainability and self-reliance to thrive.

The importance of recognizing cultural constraints and perceptions in SEs has been recognized by Imamura (2007), who considers that the Japanese model of linking human and social capital needs closely to private organizations and paid work creates a gap if private enterprise is unable, through adverse economic conditions, to continue to meet those needs. At this point, Imamura argues, SEs provide a community and family link to meet these human and social capital needs.

RESOURCING SEs – RELATIONSHIP WITH THE LABOUR MARKET

Within HRM research, the relationship organizations have with the labour market, whether it be local or global is discussed under the heading of human resource planning.

Price (2004) defines human resource planning as a process that anticipates and maps out the consequences of business strategy on an organization's human resource requirements. The resultant planning reflects skill and competence needs as well as total headcount, although the harder the approach to human resources, the more the focus will be on the acquisition of forecasted requirements rather than on capabilities and skills.

Human resource planning requires organizations to map the demand for labour within them against the available supply. Balance is achieved when demand equals supply. That the social sector might be experiencing difficulties in achieving such balance becomes understandable in the light of research from the Hopkins Institute (Salamon et al., 2003) carried out by Salamon et al. that confirms the number and variety of organizations in the social economy has grown in every region of the world. The attractiveness of a third sector, a third way to remedy some of the perceived ills of government-controlled or private-sector services and initiatives, can act to boost supply as those with skills look for a way to combine their skills with bringing about social good. However, the growth and speed at which the sector has grown globally suggests that it would be difficult for sector-specific skills in leadership, project and people management to have developed at the same pace.

For SEs, the supply of labour may be in the form of volunteers (see Exhibit 4.2) or secondments (interns), as well as more traditional contracted or project-based staff. A human resource planning strategy therefore aims to match supply to demand and it becomes more complex to balance these two things when demand fluctuates or the resources used to maintain the supply of people are subject to changes occurring in the environment. In order to meet the demand for labour, an assessment of the potential supply is made, both internally (within the organization) and externally (within the labour market). Internally, information is gathered on numbers, skills, levels of performance, potential, length of service, time in a job role, attendance, aspirations – all the factors that build a picture of the internal capabilities and potential existing within the staff and volunteer framework of the organization.

Exhibit 4.2   Volunteers around the globe

Salamon et al. (2003) found that volunteers comprised 43 per cent of the social economy's workforce across the globe, but the level of reliance on volunteers varied significantly in different countries. At the extreme ends of the spectrum, they reported Egypt as having under 10 per cent volunteer participation whereas Sweden and Tanzania had 75 per cent volunteer participation.

The Salamon research in 2003 found that the level of volunteering tended to be higher in developed countries than in developing ones, with 2.7 per cent of the economically active population in developed countries and 0.7 per cent in developing and transitional countries.

The results of their research led Salamon et al. to think about the nature of volunteering compared to paid work in the sector and they concluded that the presence of paid employees does not displace volunteers. Volunteers were shown to be more involved in service functions in developing and transitional economies where public funding was at a lower level than in developed countries.

Externally, the demographics, local national and international availability and the competition for required skills and competences are assessed with a view to identifying potential sources of people for the organization.

The Canadian Centre for Philanthropy (1998) has identified the changing environment in which SEs must operate. Focusing on the demand for services and those with the capacity to deliver these, the Centre's research has identified three areas of demand fuelling the need to supply staff to SEs:

- changing needs resulting from changing populations, exposing gaps in services provided by the public sector;

- changes in public perception in relation to the not-for-profit sector;

- political encouragement given to SEs as an alternative and cost-effective delivery mode.

In viewing the relationship with the labour market, the changing landscape for SEs will be a major consideration, both in terms of the range of skills and services requiring people and in the ability of the sector to be attractive to those able to drive forward the strategy to match demand and supply.

CLARITY ABOUT STAFFING AND PATTERNS OF WORK

Human resource planning decisions for SEs may be linked to their very existence. For example, Brothers of St Lawrence Canada, exists to create employment opportunities for those marginalized and excluded from the traditional labour market.

Where it may be difficult to compete in the external market due to pay levels or perceptions regarding career development or because of the short- to medium-term aspects of funding regimes, then organizations may find that an internally focused, grow your own approach enables the supply of people with an understanding of the sector. Internal progression and the development of transferable skills may also fulfil the strategic objectives of the organization, but, while their may be motivational and morale advantages to using the internal market, there are also potentially less favourable outcomes in terms of development and training time, costs and a risk of a lack of diversity if there is only limited engagement with the wider labour market.

Research carried out annually in the UK by the CIPD Recruitment and Retention Survey (2006, 2007) suggests that there is a real shortage of sector-specific skills within the social economy. The consequences of such a shortage have been discussed by Lepak and Snell (1995, 2007) who see rarity in the marketplace and the value placed on individuals by organizations as the two driving forces of organizational behaviour in relation to the marketplace.

Lepak and Snell have adapted their architecture of human resource planning model to show how these twin considerations of rarity and value impact on SEs. Where skills are considered rare and the approach to people in the organization has been one of showing that they are valued, then the Lepak and Snell model shows how organizations will move to protect workers, paid or volunteers, and try to retain their skills through development, progression and participative HRM practice. Where skills are more readily available in the marketplace, there will be less emphasis on protection, but value may be represented in the form of working conditions and contractual terms. As part of their social mission, SEs will *intend* to value staff and volunteers, but uncertainty within the market may lead to low-value behaviour, typified by insecurity, a lack of personal development and poor contractual terms.

One strategy that reflects the value organizations put on volunteers and workers is flexibility at work. Flexibility can be organizationally driven to meet business requirements, individually driven and focused on the work–life balance or mutually flexible, representing the middle ground. Since the 1980s, there has been recognition that numerical flexibility (Atkinson, 1984) can support organizations as they respond to uncertain environmental conditions. Using a balance of permanent core workers who have key company-specific skills supported by a range of less secure peripheral and outsourced workers, organizations are able to create numerical flexibility to fit with their demand or funding requirements. Excessive use of numerically flexible, insecure positions, though, is seen as taking a 'harder' HRM position and writers such as Torrington and Price believe that organizations then also become vulnerable to negative consequences, such as higher labour turnover, lower performance, reduced emphasis on quality.

The commercial and funding position of SEs mean that even their core workers may be insecure in the longer term. This lack of security may damage the relationships between individuals and organizations and may lead to assumptions being made about the extent to which those individuals are valued. The challenge for SEs is to maintain flexibility while building employment relationships and performance levels synonymous with core rather than peripheral employees. Storey (2007) stresses the importance of building agility into the interactions organizations have with their labour market.

LEADING SEs – HR SUPPORT FOR STRATEGIC DECISIONS

Fowler (2000) recognizes that SEs call for a specific type of capability to manage a profitable enterprise in a not-for-profit organization. Entrepreneurial leaders in SEs are often able to mobilize effort from both paid and unpaid workers that are disproportionate to their resources (Young, 2006). The ability to relate to such entrepreneurial drive may be a struggle for members of a board of directors or trustees who come from a voluntary sector or a commercial business background. This can lead to a lack of focus on the combined social and entrepreneurial goals of SEs and prevent them from truly reaching their potential.

The reported lack of HRM skills in the sector (Borzaga and Solari, 2004) suggests that organizations may struggle with accessing the expertise that will help them resolve their difficulties in appointing key members of the board. Indeed, the only HRM advice available may be via voluntary board members recruited to fill the skills gap in this area. Acquiring appropriate skills and resources may be a concern at board level as well as at the point of delivery.

It follows, therefore, that the progression and development of individuals at board level is linked directly to the progress of the organization (Sisson and Storey, 2000). Organizational objectives seek quality, productivity and high levels of service and, to meet these objectives, organizations require skilled human resources, capable of performing effectively in the environment in which they operate. The management and measurement of performance capability at board level remains under-researched, although SEs have recognized that board skills and development are essential for their future well-being. Having boards that are fit for purpose requires people who have the HRM skills to identify core competences and gaps and select and develop board members with the capacity to balance the complex requirements of an effective business agenda with social and environmental priorities.

The rapidly changing landscape of SE provides further challenges to a board's capacity to perform. Boards may become stagnant over time, depriving the SE of much-needed skills and advice. Low (2006) suggests that board membership may only change when board members have proved themselves unable to manage the situations developing within the organization. The extent to which skills development in board members, staff and volunteers has been evaluated within the social economy sector is poorly reported as yet, but it is an area that may prove to have a profound influence on the ability of SEs to be effective and sustainable.

To increase the effectiveness of the organization, there will need to be a sufficient balance of expertise among the members of the board in order for if to grow. Therefore a trade-off will have to be made between enabling stakeholder democracy and adapting to the demands of the market, forcing a change in philosophy at board level. In turn, this has implications for the legitimacy of the SE.

SEs are likely to evolve to a much narrower business focus than public-sector companies (Dart, 2004). Narrower business focus – needing to focus on outcomes rather than being satisfied with the social good – actually means there is a need for broader skills rather than just for the good of the community interest. In turn, this moves away from the inclusive representation at board level of a range of key stakeholders regardless of their strategic instrumentality, towards a skills set that can more effectively manage the entire operation. In practical terms, the key aim is to ensure that the composition of the board is both representative and sufficiently skilled to be fit for purpose and provide strategic direction for successful tendering in the short term and sustainability in the longer term.

The relevance of a board's composition and skills has been highlighted in case study and questionnaire data (Royce, 2006). The issue of skills at board level is central to this discussion. Though 'skills' are clearly of importance, more attention must be paid to the types of skills required. We must examine how SEs identify the skills that they require at board level and how they respond to board changes and 'upskilling' of members to enhance their performance. Also, consideration must be given to the appropriate mix of board-level skills. Understanding the nature of this mix will be crucial in determining the resourcing requirement of SEs at board level and then through the rest of the organizational layers.

CULTURE-FAIR RECRUITMENT AND SELECTION PRACTICES

Resourcing is a critical element in the sustainability of SEs, but, in identifying the success factors associated with management in this sector, it is useful from the start to be aware of the difficulty identified by Fowler (2000) in Lowe (2006) of having the human capability to manage 'the interplay between potentially competing sets of values – social action set against the demands of market behaviour'. Contradictions can be seen where the greater need of the community competes with the need for regular, sustainable income. Such contradictions add a layer of complexity to the recruitment and selection of social entrepreneurs and those who support them.

Faced with increasing demand and a shortage of skills, the social economy sector has looked to develop its entrepreneurs through a varied and sometimes fractured support structure, including educational establishments, funded networks, volunteer board members and so on. Dees (1998) suggested that, to balance the requirements in an SE, an individual would need to be able to create and sustain social value, recognize and peruse opportunities to sustain the mission, act boldly without being limited to the resources at hand and be conscious of stakeholder accountability and the impacts of initiatives.

Traditional models of recruitment and selection (CIPD Recruitment Factsheet, 2008, www.cipd.co.uk) show a sequence of events something like this: job analysis leading to the preparation of a job description explaining the content of a job role and a person specification identifying the characteristics an individual would need to have in order to carry out the job role successfully. Authors such as McKenna and Beech (2008) and organizations such as London Transport (an example given in McKenna and Beech) have also looked to the identification of competences as a way in which to describe and ultimately find the skills required by an organization.

McKenna and Beech (2008) define competences as the underlying individual characteristics needed to be successful in the job role and give as examples communication and problem-solving ability, delegation or the ability to work in a team. These characteristics can be broken down into further detail. For example, Tesco, also cited by McKenna and Beech, break down people skills into communication, teamworking and interpersonal skills. These competences are related to on-the-job performance job and business needs and may intuitively appeal to SEs as they reflect the skills needed to do a job role rather than the more traditional list of qualifications or experience. Non-traditional and non-standard acquisition of competences in job-related skill areas may also be easier to identify using the term competences rather than taking a more traditional approach to job descriptions and person specifications.

Traditional models, such as the CIPD model, tend to take a practitioner approach and not focus on the wider perspective or the interests of multiple, possibly competing, stakeholders (Illes, 2000).

CIPD has been collecting data for the UK voluntary, community and not-for-profit sector since 2005 and, from this data, we can see that organizations in this sector reported themselves as experiencing difficulties in recruiting for one or more categories of vacancy. While some of the difficulties reported had some commonality with other business sectors, the 'social' sector organizations more frequently expressed concern about a lack of experience in the sector, an absence of interest in advertised positions and concern that the image of the sector might be an issue in attracting candidates.

Experience in the sector is shown by this data to be the main concern of recruiting organizations, suggesting that the sector overall may need to work harder at developing and growing staff into the new roles being sought. Additional data from the survey suggests that voluntary, community and not-for-profit organizations undertake very limited succession planning compared with those in the rest of the economy. Only 5 per cent of the sector reported undertaking planning on a formal and regular basis. Although 48 per cent reported succession planning as happening on an ad hoc basis, this was lower than the overall survey average of 61 per cent. Also, 46 per cent of organizations in the sector claimed that they did not undertake succession planning, whereas 20 per cent of the other survey respondents did so. This would suggest the need to engage more directly with medium- term and longer-term planning, but highlights the dangers of short-term responses to funding and initiative requirements.

Price (2004) looks at the culture and organizational strategy as well as labour market considerations when defining recruitment and selection strategies. He outlines three distinctive strategic approaches to recruitment and selection.

Evidence of a suitability strategy can be seen where an organization clearly and specifically identifies fixed job roles and recruits directly into those roles, selecting those with the best skills-match to the job. This works well when market conditions are favourable to the organization and there is ample availability of suitable staff, but, with increasing rarity (Lepak and Snell, 1995, 2007), the organization may find itself unable to recruit those with a skills-match or be priced out of the available market and, in such conditions, a different approach may need to be taken.

Price offers two such alternatives as recruitment and selection strategies – malleability and flexibility. A malleability strategy fixes on the culture of the organization and the fit of the individual to that culture rather than job-specific skills. Malleable organizations will tend to have a small core and variable periphery with an emphasis on job-related training once in post.

A flexibility strategy focuses on potential and the ability to adapt skills and performance to the challenges of the future. Such a strategy suits organizations that are competitive and they tend to be lean in terms of core employees with an emphasis on project-based performance.

Iles (2000) uses a similar analysis to describe the strategic approach organizations take to recruitment and selection. Iles uses the term psychometric objective to describe the search for the 'right' individual with the 'right' set of talents and recognizes the use of predictive selection methods to assist organizations in their search.

Iles offers an alternative to this more traditional route – the social process model. The model views selection as a learning process, with the participant as an active player in the process. It is more of a two-way event than more traditional methods and allows both the organization and the individual to learn about and from each other. Different strategies will suit recruitment and selection at different points in the organizational lifecycle and when dealing with different skill levels. The length of the relationship envisaged (core, peripheral, outsourced) will also influence the nature of the selection strategy, which will apply equally to volunteer and paid workers. Whichever strategy is used (Storey, 2007), what talents an individual is required to have must be clear and accurate.

A strong and easily identifiable brand image that reflects the core values of the organization is often asserted as a requirement for attracting talented staff. Also, employee branding, where the cultural prerequisites of an organization are clear, will support the ability of the organization to attract those most likely to share the mission and goals of the organization.

DIVERSITY IN SEs

One of the consequences of sector-specific recruitment in SEs is that there is a danger of creating a workforce that is somewhat lacking in diversity. Price (2005) calls this 'elective homogeneity' – people like us recruiting people like us – and there is a danger of the malleable, culture-driven approach taking over.

Difficulties in achieving diversity in SEs' selection process come also from matching to characteristics previously seen as being successful. The inclusive nature of the SE culture carries with it a suggestion that SEs' HRM strategies will be rooted in equality, but the very specific nature of some SEs, equally, suggests that, while striving to be equal, the organizations may struggle to also be diverse.

Kandola and Fullerton (2004) give some clear guidance on the differences between equality and diversity, seeing equality as legislation-driven and focusing on the differences between perceived minority groups. Diversity, however, is identified as being business-focused, inclusive and focused on the individuality of all those within an organization.

Diversity is sometimes portrayed as a potentially soft option as, by claiming inclusivity for all, it is possible to avoid some of the more challenging questions posed by the equality statistics. However, in producing action plans for diversity, organizations such as the Bluecoat Arts Centre in Liverpool (see Exhibit 4.3) have built in milestones and measurement mechanisms that go beyond the legal requirements to evaluate the progress being made to develop diversity at board, staff, volunteer and client base levels.

Exhibit 4.3   Diversity at the Bluecoat Arts Centre, Liverpool

In 2004, the Bluecoat Arts Centre reviewed all staff policies in preparation for a major refurbishment. One key decision was made: to move away from traditional equal opportunities statements towards a more holistic diversity policy – one that would encompass paid staff and volunteers but also the arts programming, construction and maintenance decisions and operations so that diversity in audience, participation and staffing was to be a primary objective.

Diversity was designated a core value in 2007 and has become one of the key indicators by which personal and organizational performance is measured. The progression of diversity as a core value at the Bluecoat Arts Centre has been supported by board recruitment, to bring in and recognize diversity, diversity training and diversity awareness in all areas of the organization's operations. Within the performance management process, both board and staff reflect on the extent to which diversity objectives have been achieved and consider any lost opportunities to extend diversity and how these might be captured in the time ahead.

Although mainstreaming diversity can risk avoidance of responsibility, where there is genuine engagement at the most senior level and follow-up through HRM processes, including recruitment, performance management, training and development, then a real opportunity exists to embed diversity in the life and development of the organization.

MANAGING TALENT – INDUCTION AND RETENTION

Resourcing the enterprise does not end with recruitment. The placing, supporting and retention of those who have been selected as having the required talent and skills present an additional set of challenges to a sector that is itself in need of support.

Wilson (2007) recognizes the need for a range of support to be given to SEs from outreach and specific skills tutoring to high-end business consultancy. In considering the enhancement of professionalism in SEs, he also calls for a diagnosis of the individual in receipt of that support, emphasizing, in this sector, individual focus rather than one size fits all training may hold the key to success.

McBrearty (2007), researching the transformation of voluntary-sector organizations into SEs, identified a lack of business perspective and management skills within the sector. McBrearty's research (2007) also suggests that there is a need for SEs to be better equipped to deal with the tensions arising from the commercialization of not-for-profit activities.

Developing talent is about raising the performance level of both the individual and the organization and Pfeffer (2001) argues that the environment and organizational structures and systems play a critical role in performance issues. Pfeffer (2001) believes that people can perform above or below their natural ability levels depending on the situation, including matters of leadership and gaining help from others in the environment.

Induction creates early impressions on the new employee of expectations of working standards and the support available. HRM resources will start with the induction as the first step to building competence and knowledge: 'The purpose of induction is to help new employees to adjust to their new jobs and organizational environment' (Cornelius, 2002). Fowler (2000) also acknowledges the role of induction in helping new recruits to become fully integrated into their work teams and prevent a high incidence of early leavers.

The risk of leaving has been shown to be at its highest in the first six weeks of employment (Cornelius, 2002) and one of the causes of early leaving can be a difference between the expectations of the organization and the expectations of the employee. To further complicate matters, there is often a difference between the organization's formal or official expectations and the informal and unofficial expectations set by those involved with the new recruits in those first few weeks. Cornelius calls this the induction dilemma and, to avoid confusion, organizations need to be systematic and organized in introducing new recruits and volunteers to their working environment.

Newell and Scarbrough (2002) argue that, as organizations shift their focus from short-term cost-reduction to long-term innovation strategies, employees' knowledge and skills will be viewed as the key to success. The focus would be on building and retaining organizationally focused skills. For some organizations, this will represent their standard induction format. Others will see in induction an opportunity to help new starters 'adjust emotionally to the new workplace' (Torrington et al., 2005). The induction period should allow new employees to understand where things are and what their role is in a safe and supported environment. Induction can also be used to 'convey to new employees important cultural messages' about expectations and organizational style.

The induction period having been successfully navigated, Torrington et al. (2005) discuss the application of a model of training and learning that recognizes the organizational environment. Iles (2000 via Sisson) suggests that talented people are likely to stay with an organization only if they feel it has the right culture and provides them with self-fulfillment, in the sense of accomplishment and emotional attachment or engagement. Given the social mission of organizations working within the social economy sector, the importance of development as a potential lever for engagement and fulfillment, in the needs recognition.

Overall business and HRM strategy choices directly influence the extent to which there will be investment in the design and implementation of training and development activities. Bones (2005 via Storey) asserts that the achievement of commitment of individuals to organizational cultural aspirations can be met through the development of individuals who already share the attitudes and beliefs the organization is built on.

The question mark over the effectiveness of development interventions remains, particularly if the evaluation of changes in behaviour and performance are not investigated. The investigation itself is resource-intensive and explains why many organizations are unable to give a full account of wider changes resulting from the training or development initiative. In attempting to capture the nature of learning and the contribution of learning to the organization, writers such as Pedlar and Burgogne developed the concept of the learning organization.

Beardwell and Holden (2001) view learning organizations as being ones that look beyond mere survival. These are companies that learn from their people. Pedlar et al. (1991) described learning organizations as ones that have a climate in which individual members are encouraged to learn and develop their full potential. Learning organizations will extend the boundaries of the learning to include customers, suppliers and other stakeholders, have a culture of continuous improvement and foster a 'safe' environment in which mistakes are learning points, not matters for blame. Learning organizations will invest heavily in a learning environment that will be integrated with reward and progression strategies.

Perhaps unsurprisingly, some writers question the realism of such an environment. Price (2004) wonders if such idealistic objectives can be met in a competitive business environment and points to criticism that the learning organization is unrealistic and of theoretical use only. In an environment where the measurement of organizational success may be in terms of how it is contributing to an individual organizational community and societal learning, the concept of the learning organization in the social economy may seem more pragmatic than Price imagines.

Developing competency frameworks that enable opportunities to be extended to a more diverse range of potential employees and volunteers is a strategy that would support SEs in planning to meet resourcing skills and shortages.

ENERGIZING THE WORK RELATIONSHIP – INVOLVEMENT AND INFLUENCE

Earlier in this chapter, the Harvard model of HRM with its stakeholder perspective and recognition of societal outcomes was considered to be of relevance to management practice in SEs. The design and administration of mechanisms for encouraging employee influence has been considered by Beere et al. (1998) to be crucial to the involvement of individuals within mainstream organisational structures. Beere et al.

(1998); considered it to be critical that 'managers design and administer mechanisms for employee influence.'

The importance of employment relationship issues in retention cannot be overlooked. Where sector-specific skills are rare, retention becomes part of the fabric of survival and requires the development of a formalized strategy to retain the skills of the volunteer and paid worker alike.

The nature and extent of employee involvement will be dependant on the strategic response of the organization to its employees. Marchington (in Storey, 1995: 542) considers that, where a hard HRM approach exists, the involvement is likely to be of a limited, marginalized nature, designed to convey and convince employees of the appropriateness of the organizational strategy. If the softer HRM approach is apparent, then the mechanisms for creating involvement need consideration.

Marchington (1995) divide EI schemes into four categories. The first of these is downward communication, including online and paper news journals, reports and briefings. A second category is upward problemsolving, where mechanisms are designed to tap into employees' knowledge and opinion, examples of which would include attitude surveys, quality management systems and customer care programmes. Marchington et al. identify financial involvement as a third possible mechanism, linking rewards to individuals with the performance of the organization, such as a bonus for winning a public-sector contract or establishing an income-generating service. The fourth mechanism is representative participation, in the form of trade union membership and works councils. Capelli (2001) considers that human capital is becoming the most important issue for businesses in that no employer can afford to see valuable knowledge and skills lost.

MOTIVATIONAL PERFORMANCE AND REWARD OPTIONS

As Torrington et al. (2005: 267) point out, 'On the basis that we have sufficient evidence to claim that HR policies and practices do affect company performance ..., we need to understand better the processes which link these HR practices to business performance.'

Applebaum et al. (2000) identify three practices that are critical to business' performance: skill-enhancing practices, motivational practices and involvement practices. The relevance to SE organizations of such practices has been considered. Gennard and Judge (2005) identify one of the keys to linking people and performance as being the existence of a unifying 'big idea' – a concept that may be easier to apply in a mission-driven SE context than in some more conventional organizations. They recognize it is not just the big idea that will bring rewards in terms of linking people and performance, however – there needs to be a transformation process that will turn HRM policies and practices into business and performance outputs. Purcell (2003) suggest that there is a 'Black Box', which delivers this transformation from policy to active outputs and the Black Box transformation is dependent on the abilities of line managers to engage and motivate employees to work above the level of minimum expected practices. For SEs, the unlocking of the Black Box may well be linked to the motivation to achieve the social mission of the organization, but, with growth, it is harder to maintain the strength of individual focus on the mission, so the skills and understanding of line managers and their ability to gain commitment to higher levels of performance will become increasingly important.

Motivating employees to achieve performance and show commitment has been researched widely. Extrinsic motivators are pay, benefits and working conditions and examples of intrinsic motivators include respect, praise, challenge of the job, developing skills or knowledge. There is extensive HRM literature reviewing the relative merits of each of these and the benefits of a combined approach to rewarding employees.

The theories of Porter and Lawler (1968) are useful in the design of reward management as they recognize a link between the value employees place on the reward received (whether intrinsic or extrinsic) and the behaviour of the employees in terms of work performance. Porter and Lawler (1968) recognize the importance of employees' expectations. If there is an expectation that good work effort will be rewarded and the reward is one that will be valued, then Porter and Lawler believe better motivation and performance will result. If employees cannot see the link between their effort and the reward or if the reward offered is not valued by the employees, then the power of the reward to motivate will be reduced.

Understanding the nature of individual views on the value of reward and creating structures whereby the result of effort can be seen and applauded in some way is an attractive proposition to SEs as they may not be able to offer top salaries by way of extrinsic motivation but do have a wealth of intrinsic possibilities on offer in terms of job satisfaction and community impact, for example.

Putting this into practice, Bloisi (2007) suggests that all employees are aware of the total rewards accumulated by the job role rather than a one-dimensional view of the direct compensation in terms of basic salary and paid extras. Bloisi's model of total reward clearly identifies the importance of non-monetary rewards in the form of both social and career rewards. Indirect rewards, in the form of pensions, insurance, training, sick pay, childcare and so on, are included in the model. The model is helpful to SEs because it recognizes the importance of the social capital to be gained and assists individuals in being able to assess what they might stand to benefit from in a paid or volunteering position within the organization in addition to or instead of direct pay.

An understanding of the total reward structure can support the ability of SEs to take their place in the employment market and help attract and retain those with the skills required. Royce (2002) suggested a conceptual model linking value to retention and questioned the ability of organizations to recognize what their employees and volunteers truly valued. One of the strategies organizations develop to assist with retention is reward, but, in February 2002, the CIPD Annual Reward Survey suggested that reward packages meet business objectives, but not people's needs. Given the increasing focus on achieving a work–life balance, it is unsurprising that rewards are relegated to a 'hygiene' role and fail to act as a positive motivational tool. If we accept that the work–life balance *is* a motivating factor, then organizations appear to be failing to achieve horizontal integration of reward and retention strategies.

A recognition of the role of flexibility in developing a work–life balance as understood by diversity theorists could increase the potential of reward systems to contribute more positively to retention and performance.

Pay and reward strategies play a major part in most theoretical models of HRM and Bratton and Gold (1999) consider rewards to be central to the regulation of the employment relationship. Both HRM practitioners and academics recognize the difficulty of evaluating the success of reward strategies as a lever to achieve HRM goals such as commitment or flexibility. Beere et al. (1984) consider that the design and management of reward systems are among the most difficult HRM tasks. Bratton and Gold (1999) define rewards as 'all forms of financial returns and tangible service and benefits employees receive a part of an employment relationship'. Rewards then are the centrepiece of the employment relationship.

WHAT CONSTITUTES GOOD PERFORMANCE IN A SE?

Bull (2007) reflects on the fact that SEs may see impact measurement as a burden rather than a tool and potential source of competitive advantage. The transferability of performance management models, often designed, as Bull says 'through the lens of a large organization', may not work as intended if parachuted into an SE's context. The measurement of social value (Bull, 2007 and Somers, 2005) presents problems with articulating and measuring social objectives and social capital that may (Dees and Anderson, 2003) be intangible and difficult to quantify. Bull and Somers both present the potential of using the Balanced Scorecard approach. Originally a manufacturing tool designed by Kaplan and Norton (1996), both writers believe that the multi-bottom line, stakeholder and social capital and impact requirements for measuring performance in SE can be supported by this multi-criteria model.

An interesting example of the way in which the criteria impacts on our belief and assessment of performance can be seen in Exhibit 4.4, which contemplates measures of success and failure in SEs in Kenya.

Exhibit 4.4   Developing social capital – a study of faith-based enterprises in Kenya

Ndemo (2006) undertook a study of faith-based organizations in Kenya and asked crucial questions about measuring success.

Ndemo found that, in terms of community impact and income earned, the enterprises could be said to have succeeded. The question of sustainability was more difficult to answer. The training to make, market and sell products and services while sheltered by the SE enabled them to measure individual and organizational performance in terms of impact and income positively. However, longer-term sustainability was dependent on tools, market access and understanding and without these there would be a return to earlier levels of dependency. Given the longer-term measure, the performance assessment would be negative.

Ndemo concludes that, while positive impacts on the community and initial income can be generated successfully by SEs, their ultimate success is dependent on infrastructure, markets, finance and motivation.

CONCLUSIONS

In recent years, an increasing number of studies and research evidence have highlighted the contributions that HRM can make to organisational performance.

Researchers at Sheffield University's Institute of Work Psychology (Guest, 2000) found in a sample of manufacturing businesses that 18 per cent of variations in productivity and 19 per cent in profitability could be attributed to people management.

An analysis in 2000 of the 1998 'Workplace employment relations survey' by Guest et al., confirmed the link between progressive HR practices and financial performance over a much larger sample of firms.

If these improvements are transferable to the social economy sector, then the application of HRM practices would seem to have much to offer.

McBrearty (2007) argues that, as policies encourage greater levels of commercialization, then the social values and ethos of the organization become vulnerable. Part of the role of HR can be to organize structures to support a culture that is comfortable with integrating both of these objectives.

The social impact culture of SEs fits well with the argument put forward by Sissons (2007) when he quotes Edwards (2005), commenting that it may not be in the interests of a particular employer to promote human resource development and social capital transformation, but it is in the interests of society as a whole.

Salamon et al. (2003) point to the growing interest in social capital acquired through involvement in the sector and go so far as to say that this social capital seems to be crucial to the development of democratic structures and the market economy. Salamon et al. conclude that involvement in the sector 'teaches norms of co-operation' that carry over into political and economic life.

The measurement of the impact of the HRM function and the way in which an organisation's people can be considered to be an asset or 'human capital' is a major area of research in mainstream HRM. This is not an issue for people management specialists alone. As Mayo (2002:) explained:

> It is not just a problem for the HR function – far from it. The pursuit of value for shareholders is not achieved long-term by playing with current profitability. In the knowledge era more value is place on the 'intangible assets' of an organization. For these there are no international accounting standards or established management systems. Establishing such rules and systems for valuing human capital is one of the greatest challenges facing management today.

The infrastructure to support coherent people management systems in SEs would not appear to be sufficiently robust or fit for purpose. Piecemeal support and advice from a raft of well-meaning board members, fragile networks and higher education institutes has not provided a strong framework for growth and sustainability in managing human resources. Understanding of the labour market and relationships, resourcing, skills, leadership and sustainability through focused and evaluated development have been consistent themes. These are all areas in which there is a very real opportunity for HRM tools, knowledge and expertise to support SEs in achieving their social goals.

REFERENCES

Applebaum, T., Bailey, E., Berg, P. and Kallenberg, A. (2000) 'Manufacturing Advantage: Why high performance work systems pay off', in J. Storey (2007) *Human Resource Management: A critical text* (3rd edn). London: Thomson.

Armstrong, M. (2006) *A Handbook of Human Resource Management Practice* (10th edn). London: Kogan Page.

Atkinson, J. (1984) 'Manpower strategies for flexible organisations', *Personnel Management*, 16: 28–31. London: CIPD.

Beardwell, I. and Holden, L. (2001) *Human Resource Management – A Contemporary Approach*. London: Prentice Hall.

Beere, M., Spector, B., Lawrence, P.R., Mills, Q.N. and Walton, R.E. (1984) *Managing Human Assets*. New York: Free Press.

Bloisi, W. (2007) *An Introduction to Human Resource Management*. London: McGraw Hill.

Bones, C. (2005) The talent management paradox, CIPD, Reflections on the 2006 Learning and Development survey. London: CIPD.

Borzaga, C. and Defourny, J. (2001) *The Emergence of Social Enterprise*. London: Routledge.

Borzaga, C. and Solari, L. (2004) 'Management challenges for social enterprises', in C. Borzaga, J. Defourny, S. Adam and J. Callaghan (eds), *The Emergence of Social Enterprise*. London: Routledge.

Bratton, J. and Gold, J. (1999) *Human Resource Management Theory and Practice* (2nd edn). London: Palgrave.

Brothers of St Lawrence, Canada (1998) The voluntary sector Canada – literature review and strategic considerations for a HR sector study. Toronto, Canada.

Bull, M. (2007) 'Balance: The development of a social enterprise business development tool', *Social Enterprise Journal*, 3: 49–66.

Canadian Centre of Philanthropy (1998) 'The voluntary sector in Canada', Canadian Policy Research Network, Toronto, Canada.

Capelli, P. and Newmark, D. (2001) 'Do high performance work practices improve establishment level outcomes?', *Industrial and Labor Relations Review*.

Chapman, T., Forbes, D. and Brown, J. (2007) 'They have God on their side . The impact of public sector attitudes on the development of social enterprise', *Social Enterprise Journal*, 3(1).

CIPD Recruitment and Retention Survey 2006 and 2007, CIPD www.cipd.co.uk

CIPD Recruitment Factsheet , CIPD, www.cipd.co.uk

CIPD Reward Survey 2006/2007, CIPD, www.cipd.co.uk

Cornelius, N. (2002) *Building Workplace Equality – ethics, diversity and inclusion*. London: Thomson.

Dart, R. (2004) 'The legitimacy of social enterprise', *Nonprofit Management & Leadership*, 14: 411–24.

Dees, J. (1998) *The Meaning of Social Entrepreneurship*. Stanford, CA: Graduate School of Business, Stanford University.

Dees, J.G. and Battle Anderson, B. (2003) 'Sector-bending: Blurring lines between nonprofit and for-profit', *Society*, 40 (4): 16–27.

Edwards, P. (2005) Workplace Justice: Why a New Public Policy Initiative is needed. Available from paul.edwards@wbs.ac.uk

Fowler, A. (2000) 'NGDOs as a moment in history: beyond aid to social entrepreneurship or civic innovation?', *Third World Quarterly*, 21, 637–54.

Gennard, J. and Judge, G. (2005) *Employment Relations*. London: CIPD.

Guest, D. (2000) Human Resource Management, employee wellbeing and organisational performance. Paper presented to the CIPD Professional Standards Conference, University of Warwick.

Iles, P.A. (2000) 'Employee Resourcing and talent management' (2007) in J. Storey (2007) *Human Resource Management: A critical text* (3rd edn). London: Thomson.

Imamura, H. (2007) Social capital formation for supplying local community services through coordination of social economy, local government and for profit enterprises in Japan 1st International CIRIEC Research Conference on the Social Economy, October 2007, Canada.

Kandola, R. and Fullerton, J. (2004) *Managing the Mosaic.* London: CIPD.

Kaplan, R.S. and Norton D.P. (2006) *The Strategy Focused Organisation.* Boston: Harvard Business School Press.

Leopold, J. Harris, L. and Watson, T. (2005) *The Strategic Managing of Human Resources.* London: Prentice Hall.

Lepak, D.P. and Snell, S.P. (1999) 'The strategic management of human capital: determinants and implications of different relationships', *Academy of Management Review.*

Lowe, C. (2006) 'A framework for the governance of social enterprise', *International Journal of Social Economics*, 33: 376–85.

Marchington, M. (1995) 'Involvement and participation', in J. Storey (ed.), *Human Resource Management – A critical text.* London: Routledge. pp. 280–305.

Martin, G. (2005) *Technology and People Management: Transforming the HR function or the function of HR.* London: CIPD.

Manzi, T. and Smith Blowers, B. (2004) 'So many managers, so little vision: Registered Social Landlords and consortium schemes in the UK', *European Journal of Social Housing Policy*, 4: 57–75.

Mayo, A. (2002) *A Thorough Evaluation, People Management.* London: CIPD.

McBrearty, S. (2007) 'Social enterprise – a solution for the voluntary sector', *Social Enterprise Journal*, 3 (1).

McKenna, E. and Beech, N. (2008) *Human Resource Management – A Concise Analysis* (2nd edn). London: FT Prentice Hall.

Newell, H. and Scarborough, H. (2002) *Human Resource Management in Context – A Case Study Approach.* London: McMillan.

Ndemo, E. (2006) 'Assessing sustainability of faith-based enterprises in Kenya', *International Journal of Economics*, 33 (5/6).

Pedlar, M., Burgogne, J. and Boydell, T. (1991) *The Learning Company: A strategy for sustainable development.* Maidenhead: McGraw Hill.

Pfeffer, J. (2001) 'Fighting the war for talent is hazardous for your organisation's health', *Organisational Dynamics*, 29: 248–59.

Porter, L.W. and Lawler, E.E. (1968) 'Managerial attitudes and performance', in D. Rollinson (2002) *Organisational Behaviour and Analysis.* New York: Pearson.

Price, A. (2004) *Human Resource Management in a Business Context* (2nd edn). London: Thomson.

Purcell, J. (2003) 'Business strategies and hr management: Uneasy bedfellows or strategic partners', in J. Storey (2007) *Human Resource Management: A critical text* (3rd edn). London: Thomson.

Royce, M. (2006) Managing Reward and Performance in a diversity centred environment, paper to Performance and Reward Conference, MMU, Manchester 2002.

Salamon, G., Storey, J. and Billsbury, J. (2003) *Strategic Human Resource Management.* London: Sage.

Salamon, L., Wojciech Sokolowski, S., List, R. (2003) *Global Civil Society – An Overview.* The John Hopkins University, Institute for Policy Studies.

Sisson, K. and Storey, J. (2000) *The Realities of Human Resource Management: Managing the Employment Relationship.* London: Open University Press.

Sissons, K. (2007) 'Facing up to the challenges of success: putting governance at the heart of HRM' in J. Storey (2007) *Human Resource Management: A critical text* (3rd edn). London: Thomson.

Storey, J. (2007) *Human Resource Management: A critical text* (3rd edn). London: Thomson.

Somers, A. (2005) 'Shaping the balanced scorecard for use in UK social enterprises', *Social Enterprise Journal*, 1: 43–56.

Torrington, D., Hall, L. and Taylor, S. (2005) *Human Resource Management.* London: FT Prentice Hall.

Ul Islam, Zia., (2007) 'A new model for supporting social enterprise through sustainable investment', *Social Enterprise Journal*, 3: 1–10.

Watson, T. (2005) 'Organisations, strategies and human resourcing', in J. Leopold, L. Harris and T. Watson, *The Strategic Managing of Human Resources.* London: FT Prentice Hall.

Wilson, A. (2007) *Social Enterprise Futures, School for Social Entrepreneurs.* Social Enterprise Coalition, Smith Institute, UK.

Young, C. (2006) 'Have you faced the leadership challenge?', *Social Enterprise*, May 2006, Social Enterprise Coalition. London.

SOCIAL ENTERPRISES AND FINANCIAL MANAGEMENT

INTRODUCTION

SEs make a significant contribution to the economies of many developed countries worldwide: 'In many ways they represent a new or renewed expression of civil society against a background of economic crisis, the weakening of social bonds and the difficulties of the welfare state' (Borzaga and Defourrey, 2001). Their impact across Europe can be gauged by the following examples in relation to the social economy.

In Austria, the success of Aktion 8000 in the early 1980s and its later evolution into the Public Integration Allowance (GEB) has brought 50,000 jobs in the area of social welfare services and cultural and environmental activities to long-term unemployed. In Belgium, it is estimated that 350,000 people are employed in the social economy that has flourished post World War II and over 100,000 volunteers are involved.

Such statistics can be repeated for many European and other countries across the world. For a number of reasons – historical, cultural, social and economic – SEs play a significant part in the financial and social economies of many countries.

The financial management of both profitmaking and non-profitmaking organizations has changed considerably in the recent past. In many ways, the financial management of SEs differs little from any other organization – profitmaking or not – in terms of the core content of the financial management process. Non-profitmaking organizations (and, increasingly, profitmaking ones) often produce additional information to demonstrate to various stakeholders that they have achieved their aims and objectives in a social sense as well as a financial sense. Corporate social responsibility (CSR) is heavily influenced by the notion of the triple bottom line (Elkingon, 1998), which is when bodies move beyond reporting only their financial 'bottom line' to assessing and reporting on the three spheres of sustainability: economic, social and environmental.

Most organizations have been influenced by the changes in the business and social environment of Western Europe and elsewhere in the last two decades and their impact on the quality, scope and content of the financial management of all organizations.

The world prior to the 1980s afforded many organizations a protected competitive environment. Barriers to competition included limited communication and geographical

Table 5.1 Social economy funding from statutory sources in the UK

Year	Income from public sector (£ million)	Annual % change	Total income (£ million)	Annual % change
1991	3,365.5		12,708.9	
1994/95	4,251.6	6.2	15,068.3	4.3
1997	4,481.7	2.7	15,302.0	0.8
1999	4,594.3	1.2	16,068.1	2.5
2000/01	7,857.3	30.8	22,769.8	19.0
2001/02	8,267.2	5.2	22,309.5	−2.0
2003/04	10,246.7	11.3	26,907.5	9.8
2004/05	10,650.4	3.9	27,653.7	2.8

Source: NCVO, 2007

distance, along with sometimes protected markets and limited competition in many others, particularly manufacturing. However, in the 1980s many of these barriers began to be dismantled. By establishing global networks for acquiring raw materials and distributing goods overseas, competitors were able to gain access to domestic markets throughout the world. Competition became international rather than national and, to be successful, organizations had to compete against others worldwide. Knowledge and understanding of costs and cost behaviour became an essential part of the financial management process (Drury, 2006).

Many service industries also faced equally major changes in their competitive environment. Prior to this time, numerous service organizations, including airlines, utilities and financial services were either state-owned monopolies or operated in a highly regulated, protected and non-competitive environment. In such an environment, little attention was paid to quality and efficiency. Price increases were merely passed on to the customer/client in the main.

The privatization of UK government-controlled companies and deregulation in the 1980s completely changed the competitive environment in which service companies operated. Pricing and competitive restrictions were virtually eliminated. The deregulation, intensive competition and an expanding product range created the need for service organizations to focus on cost management and develop management accounting systems that enabled them to understand their cost base more intelligently and, hence, improve the quality of the financial management of their organizations. To be able to survive and compete it was clear that manufacturing and service organizations had to develop knowledge and systems regarding their costs and prices to ensure economy and efficiency in their activities.

SEs and the not-for-profit sector generally were not isolated from these requirements and, for them, they came at a time when government support for the sector, certainly in the UK, was gaining significant momentum. This can be clearly identified from an analysis of income for the UK voluntary sector that identifies income from the public sector separately, as shown in Table 5.1. The figures in Table 5.1 show an increase in income from the UK government of 217 per cent over 14 years. That is an increase of over three times and equivalent to a year-on-year increase of

8.6 per cent. This can be compared with an increase of 118 per cent for all income sources, equivalent to a year-on-year increase of 5.7 per cent. These figures under-pin the UK government's commitment to the development of the voluntary and community sector, in which SEs play a significant part.

The increased support for SEs has its genesis in a number of UK government policies including:

- *localism* a government policy that numerous and appropriate local issues are to be determined by local people;

- *marketization and choice* the monopoly provision of many public services being challenged by changes in service architecture and processes to allow other providers into the public services arena;

- *SE development* these are seen as legitimate vehicles in terms of the potential scope of services provided and philosophically acceptable.

SEs

While the SE is not a legal form, Pearce (2003) argues that SEs share characteristics that define them. SEs are businesses that deliver goods and services, but their primary mission is to deliver social benefit (Lewis et al., 2006). In general terms SEs are organi-zations that seek to address a range of social and environmental issues and any surplus profits are reinvested for that purpose, as opposed to being distributed to shareholders and owners (DTI, 2002). They are diverse organizations, ranging from small, commu-nity-owned village shops to large companies with multi-million pound contracts. It is estimated that there are in the UK at least 55,000 SEs, generating more than £27 billion turnover and contributing more than £8 billion to its GDP a year (DTI, 2006).

Some theorists writing about the social economy believe that SEs should function in the same way as traditional businesses and be treated and supported as such. Pearce (2003) argues that SEs are in fact altogether different from mainstream busi-nesses as they seek to measure the triple bottom line of social and environmental impact as well as the financial impact. However, one thing that SEs have in common with for-profit organizations is that, in order to be effective, they need access to financing and improved financial management and increased understanding of the financial consequences of their managerial actions. They are therefore no less excluded from the demands of good financial information than those organizations in the for-profit sectors.

This requirement for additional and appropriate financial skills has been a consis-tent theme running through a number of more recent UK Government policy docu-ments addressing the financial framework and management of SEs. The July 2002 document 'Social enterprise: a strategy for success' (DTI, 2002) highlighted a number of financial problems facing the sector, including that it is undercapitalized, struggles to access external finance and has a fear of debt and these problems are directly linked to the lack of financial skills in the sector. It is recognized in the document that by addressing the lack of financial skills the other issues will begin to be addressed.

The Bank of England report 'The Financing of Social Enterprises' (2003) found, for example, 'little evidence of demand for, or supply of, conventional venture capital or business angel finance ... not as a result of market failure but instead reflects the specific characteristics of the social enterprise sector.' These comments have been interpreted by many commentators as meaning that the sector is underskilled in pursuing this avenue of financing and a further example of the lack of financial skills throughout the sector.

The DTI's action plan for SEs, 'Social enterprise action plan: scaling new heights' (2006), built on the policy and guidance of the above reports, its recommendations including the following:

- 'the Office of the Third Sector and the DTI's Small Business Service will roll out futher financial awareness training for social enterprises';

- 'the DTI's Small Business Service will include social enterprise within mainstream "access to finance" interventions.'

The plan also recognized that the challenges facing SEs are the same as those facing the wider business community in many cases, but in SEs these challenges are more complex because they deliver both a financial and a social or environmental bottom line. They need additional support to maximize their business performance and, in turn, their social impact. SEs need business management support in a variety of forms to deliver their own complex and difficult agendas. This support will come in a variety of different guises and it is hoped that this chapter will contribute in some small way to the business development of SEs.

FINANCIAL MANAGEMENT

The financial management of any organization is a complex process. It is impossible in one chapter to describe fully all the various components that constitute this process, so the remainder of this chapter is meant to achieve the following aims. First, indicate to managers topics that they should be aware of. Second, indicate financial issues that they may need to consider in some further detail. Third, raise some questions – relating to the financial management process and financial records produced – that managers might need to consider further. The principal purpose of this chapter, though, is to indicate to managers of SEs the areas of financial management that either they should be aware of or regarding which they may need to improve their knowledge. This will improve the management process overall and enable SEs to achieve their mission more effectively.

Costing – the basics

'The basic requirement in the management of the business process is for the provision of information for decision making purposes' (Coombs et al., 2005). The information provided is dependent on the decision that is being made. In a business context, it is essential that costs are attributed to the activities that initiated them. Thus, identifying what activity generates which costs is a fundamental aspect of management accounting.

This information can then be used by the appropriate people, usually managers, to aid them in their decision making processes. It can be argued that the better the quality of the information provided, the better the quality of the decision made is likely to be.

The information provided, to be meaningful, has to be:

- relevant – to the decision that is being made;
- accurate – or at least sufficiently accurate in order to make a reasonable decision;
- timely – provided in time;
- understandable – so the recipient can make use of the information given.

It is a challenge for any accounting system to provide what is required by decisionmakers/ management. This challenge is made even greater by the triple bottom line of many SEs.

In conventional businesses, we need to know the costs of goods and services so that profits can be maximized. In SEs, the purpose of the organization is more than merely the pursuit of profit. However, in relation to costs, cost analysis and cost attribution, it as important as in a conventional company for SEs to understand and manage their costs for the purposes of survival, economy and efficiency and, in many cases, accountability to funders.

Cost classification and decision making go hand in hand in many situations. The more complex the decision, the more complex the probable information requirements of managers are likely to be. However, managers need to be aware of the danger of being overwhelmed by a huge volume of data (Simon, 1953).

This leads us on to a discussion of the various cost classifications there are for data for decisionmaking:

- cost behaviour by volume of activity;
- sunk costs;
- relevant and non-relevant costs;
- avoidable and unavoidable costs;
- opportunity costs;
- marginal costs.

Cost behaviour by volume of activity

At different levels of activity, costs behave differently, which can have important implications for decisionmakers. Thus, managers will often ask the following (or similar) questions:

- 'If I do more, how much will it cost?'
- 'What level do we need to achieve to break even?'
- 'If we buy more, will we save money?'

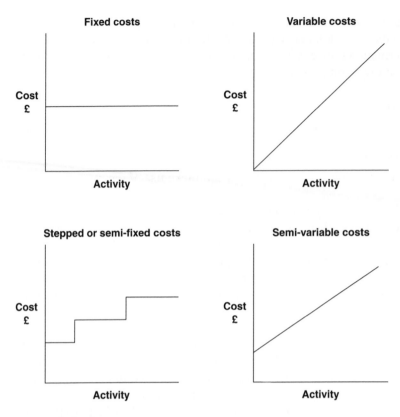

Figure 5.1 Cost behaviour

These questions raise issues about how accountants estimate costs and revenues for different levels of activity and how information is presented to managers.

The classical terms used in this respect are fixed costs, variable costs, semi-variable costs, and stepped or semi-fixed costs. Figure 5.1 illustrates how these categories of cost behave in relation to different levels of activity.

- *Fixed costs*   remain constant for a wide range of activity levels for a specific period of time (normally at least one year) and include, for example, costs such as rent and rates, certain management salaries, depreciation, vehicle tax, insurance premiums. They are costs that have to be incurred regardless of the number or scope of outputs or services delivered.

- *Variable costs*   are costs that vary in direct proportion to activity/output. Costs are assumed to be linear and, thus, are represented by a straight line. Variable costs include fuel for vehicles (the more miles covered, the more fuel is used), heating costs (the colder it is, the more heating is required), ink for a photocopier (the more copies, the more ink is used).

- *Semi-variable costs*   can be illustrated by many service or utility contracts that have two elements – a fixed period rental charge and a charge per unit consumed or used. Most utility bills have a standing period charge and a variable cost according to usage. A telephone bill normally comprises a rental charge (fixed) and a call element – that is, a charge for each call made (variable).

- *Stepped or semi-fixed costs*   remain fixed within a specific band of activity, but, outside of that band, additional costs will be incurred. A nursery is often legally required to have a specific number of qualified staff to look after a specific number of children – for example, one member of staff per three children. If an additional child joins the nursery and it is, for example, the fourth, seventh or tenth child in the nursery, an additional member of staff could be required. That new member of staff could look after up to an extra three infants. Thus, the step costs occur are at four, seven, ten and so on infants.

Sunk costs

These are costs that have already been incurred by the organization and will be unaffected by any future decision. A room, for example, has been furnished as resources were made available. In the subsequent year, the room is used to provide a service for which the organization charges. The cost of the furniture should not feature in any such charge that is made, however, as it was incurred in the past – that is, 'sunk' by the organization.

Relevant and non-relevant costs

In making decisions managers are normally only concerned with those costs and revenues that will change if a decision is made. If costs and revenues will be unchanged by a managerial decision, then these are considered non-relevant costs. If cost and revenues will change if a decision is made, then these are considered relevant.

Avoidable and unavoidable costs

These demonstrate a different perspective on the above analysis of costs. Avoidable costs are those that have to be incurred if a course of action is decided on. Savings cannot be made on unavoidable costs.

Opportunity costs

Such costs represent the sacrifice made when a choice of one course of action precludes the pursuit of an alternative course of action. It is a formal definition of the more often used phrase 'you can only spend money once'. Once it has been spent you cannot spend it again, which is an important consideration in many business situations.

Marginal, or incremental, costs

Additional costs or revenues that arise as a result of following a chosen course of action are called marginal or incremental costs and can include fixed costs depending on the decision made.

METHODS OF COSTING

There are several generally accepted costing methods available to managers, including:

- full costing;
- marginal costing;
- activity-based costing.

Full costing

Managers need full cost information to help them work towards achieving the organization's objectives. There are three particular areas where managers need to know the full cost of the organization's output.

- *Budgetary planning and control* If budgets are to be used as the yardsticks against which actual performance is to be assessed, the information on actual performance must also be expressed in the same full cost terms.
- *General decisionmaking* Having full cost information can enable managers to make decisions about all aspects of the organization.
- *Pricing* When setting a price for a good or service, it is essential to know the cost to ensure that it is covered and, hopefully, some profit is made. If not, then the organization is placing itself at risk by creating a shortfall in its income, which could eventually lead to its demise. In addition, in many instances, funders of services require organizations to adopt the principle of full costing when pricing goods or services to be sold.

What is full costing?

It is the total amount of resources, usually measured in monetary terms, sacrificed to achieve a particular objective. To derive a full cost figure, we must accumulate the costs incurred and then assign them to a particular product or service. See Exhibit 5.1 for an example.

Multi-product businesses

Most organizations produce more than just one type of product or service, however. In such situations, the units of output of the product or service will not be identical, so a different approach is needed to that used above for a single product or service organization.

To provide full cost information for organizations producing multiple products or services, we need to have a systematic approach to accumulating costs and then assigning these costs to particular units of a product or service on some reasonable basis. The starting point is to separate the costs into two categories:

- direct costs

- indirect costs/overheads.

Exhibit 5.1　An example of full costing for a single-product business

Realfruit is a SE that produces one product: a sparkling apple drink that is marketed as RealApple. It produced 73,000 litres of the drink in the last year. The costs it incurred were as follows.

	£
Ingredients	3,900
Premises costs	3,500
Transport	850
Labour	8,800
Depreciation	750

What is the full cost per litre of RealApple? The figure is found by simply adding all the costs incurred and dividing the sum by the number of litres produced:

£3,900 + 3,500 + 850 + 8,800 + 750/73,000 = 0.2438 pence per litre

---

Direct costs can be identified with a specific cost unit. A cost unit is one unit of a product, be it a service or a manufactured item. The classic direct costs are direct materials and labour. These costs can be readily collected in the main by a simple cost recording system.

Indirect costs or overheads are all the costs other than direct ones. The major issue in relation to these costs is how to apportion them to individual cost units or products. For this reason, guidance is often given in many big organizations. for example:

- payroll costs are allocated to departments according to the number of employees in that department;

- heating/air-conditioning costs are allocated per cubic metre;

- building maintenance costs are allocated per square metre.

The process has to be open, transparent and understood by all involved. If the organization achieves its income by means of the sales of products or services, then all its costs have to be recovered via the selling price of the good or service. Thus, the organization has to determine some methodology for apportioning indirect costs to the direct costs to determine a unit cost that will enable all the costs incurred by the organization, at least, to be recovered.

Marginal costing

To use a marginal costing technique, the distinction between fixed and variable costs needs to be understood:

- *fixed costs* do not vary with output – for example, rent needs to be paid regardless of the amount of activity;
- *variable costs* are normally those associated directly with the output, normally referred to as direct labour and direct materials.

The marginal cost is the sum of the variable costs of direct labour, materials and overheads.

The marginal cost equation

$S =$ Sales revenue
$V =$ Variable costs
$C =$ Contribution
$F =$ Fixed costs
$P =$ Profits

$S - V = C$
$C - F = P$

or

$C = F + P$

Therefore, the marginal cost equation is:

$S - V = F + P$

The contribution is an important feature of this equation and to the concept of marginal costing. The contribution is defined as the difference between the sales revenue and total variable cost. Thus it makes a contribution to fixed costs in the first place and then to profits.

The main use of marginal costing is as a basis for providing information to management for short-term planning and decisionmaking. The marginal cost equation given above enables management to cost quickly the implications of any potential short-term changes in volume or activity. This is possible because it can normally be assumed that fixed costs remain constant and are therefore not affected by a particular decision. Also, the contribution can be calculated at any level of sales activity as variable costs are assumed to vary in direct proportion to the sales revenue. The fixed costs can then be deducted.

An example of the application of marginal costing and how it can be used to calculate profit or loss at different levels of activity is given below.

The A.N. Other SE makes garden benches from reclaimed timber:

Output	1,000	2,000	3,000	4,000	5,000
	£	£	£	£	£
Sales	10,000	20,000	30,000	40,000	50,000
Less variable costs	5,000	10,000	15,000	20,000	25,000
Contribution	5,000	10,000	15,000	20,000	25,000
Less fixed costs	10,000	10,000	10,000	10,000	10,000
Profit/(loss)	(5,000)	–	5,000	10,000	15,000

With marginal costing, once all the fixed costs have been covered by total contributions, each extra unit sold results in additional profit/surplus. The point at which the total contribution equals the fixed costs is referred to as the break-even point. Exhibit 5.2 gives you an example to work out for yourself.

Exhibit 5.2 Working out the break-even point

G and M Services is planning to run an introductory course to teach participants the basic techniques of homeopathy. All students will be charged a fee of £125, to include refreshments, lunch and all materials. The maximum number of students that can be accommodated on the course is 20. The estimated running costs are as follows.

Room hire	£150
Lunches	£10 per student
Advertising	£300
Equipment hire	£100
Refreshments	£5 per student
Speakers' fees	£400
Students' materials	£10 per student
Insurance	£50

The question

How many students need to be signed up to break even?

The solution

The first action to take is to identify which costs are fixed and which are variable. You will recall from earlier that fixed costs will be incurred regardless of participants numbers and variable costs will, by definition, vary according to participant numbers.

(Continued)

(Continued)

Cost	Fixed (£)	Variable (£)
Room hire	150	
Lunches		10
Advertising	300	
Equipment hire	100	
Refreshments		5
Speakers' fees	400	
Students' materials		10
Insurance	50	
Totals	1000	25

As G and M Services will be charging each student £125, the contribution for each student is:

Selling price = £125
Less
Variable costs = £25
Contribution = £100 per student

The question to be asked now is how many student contributions will it take to cover the fixed costs of £1000?

Break-even point in sales units = Fixed costs/Contribution per student

Thus £1000/£100 = 10 students

Break-even points can be represented diagrammatically, as follows.

Break-even chart

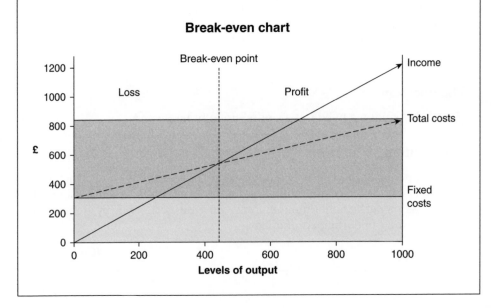

In summary, marginal costing enables us to work out quickly and easily the profit or loss at any level of output if we already know the break-even point and the contribution per unit. That is because, for every unit sold above the break-even point, the profit will equal the contribution (income less variable costs) per unit. If we sell fewer than the break-even number, we will lose the contribution of that shortfall.

Activity-based costing

Activity-based costing (ABC) is one of the main developments in cost accounting in recent years. As the consumption of overhead costs by individual units of output cannot be directly observed and measured, a surrogate measure has to be found to trace the various patterns of usage to products and services. This has traditionally been achieved by means of a time-based measure of production volume – for example, direct labour hours. This approach has assumed that overheads are related closely to production time and output volume. However, it has been felt by many practitioners that this process may mask the true cost-consumption patterns in the organization and, consequently, generate misleading information for managers.

The realization that overheads do not just occur but are caused by activities (such as holding products in a storage area) that 'drive' the costs is at the heart of ABC. It is not always easy to see why or how some overhead costs have arisen. Thus, they have become more difficult to control than some obvious direct costs. However, if cost drivers can be identified, questions can be asked about whether or not the activity driving the costs is necessary and the cost justifies the benefit.

Cost pools

When using ABC, an overhead cost pool is established for each cost driver into which all of the costs caused by that driver are placed. The total costs in that pool are then allocated to the output, using the cost driver identified, according to the extent to which each unit of output 'drove' those costs. See Exhibit 5.3 for an example of how to set up cost pools for ABC.

Exhibit 5.3   Setting up cost pools

Merseyside SE Producers manufacture two products: Product A and Product B. On completion of the production process, the products are stored in a 'finished goods store'. It is estimated that this store costs around £90,000 per year to run.

It is estimated, too, that each Product A will spend, on average, one week in the store. The period for Product B will be four weeks. Both products are of approximately the same size and with similar storage needs. The cost

(Continued)

(Continued)

driver, therefore, is deemed to be the quantity in store and the time they spend in the store (product weeks).

It is estimated that, in the coming year, 50,000 Product As and 25,000 Product Bs will pass through the store. Hence, the 'product weeks' in the store will be:

Product A = 50,000 × 1 week =	50,000
Product B = 25,000 × 4 weeks =	100,000
	150,000

The store's cost for each product week is given by the equation:

£90,000/£150,000 = £0.60

Therefore, each Product A will be charged with £0.60 for storage costs and Product B with £2.40 (£0.60 × 4).

Allocating overhead costs to cost pools, as is necessary with ABC, contrasts with the traditional approach where overheads are normally allocated to production departments (cost centres). In both cases, however, the overheads are then charged to cost units. ABC attempts to represent the extent to which each particular cost unit is believed to cause the particular part of the overheads.

This attempt at greater accuracy in the apportionment of overheads, and thus more accurate costing, is seen as the attraction of ABC.

PRICING GOODS AND SERVICES

Many organizations face two differing situations regarding pricing decisions:

- pricing goods and/or services externally to paying customers
- pricing goods and services provided internally.

The issues facing the organization in these circumstances are different and we shall deal with the pricing for external consumption first.

In the marketplace, prices have a number of important functions. In particular, they signal to the organization how much customers are prepared to pay for a good/service, which influences whether the organization is capable of staying in this particular market or not. When pricing goods or services, the organization needs to consider several factors, including the following.

- The objectives of the organization – is it there to meet a social need alone or a social need plus make a return or merely a return on the capital invested?
- What is the nature of the market the organization wants to operate in? What is the extent of the competition, if any?

- The demand for the organization's services – is there sufficient demand at the price the organization needs to charge? How sensitive is demand to price changes? What is the elasticity of demand?

- The cost of the good/service – what are the expected future marginal and fixed costs?

- Current and future levels of demand and provision – are these compatible? Can demand increase significantly and can the provider fulfil future demand within existing capacity?

- Laws and regulations – does implementing and adhering to them increase costs? Do they do so to such an extent that they will influence price setting?

It is unlikely that *all* these factors will need to be considered when a pricing decision is being made. In particular, information regarding demand for an organization's services/goods is difficult to accurately assess without considerable investment in market knowledge assessment, including surveys, market testing and so on.

There are three general processes that are used when pricing goods/services:

- cost-plus;

- marginal;

- market rate.

Cost-plus pricing

It could be argued that it is not the purpose of SEs to make profits but I would suggest that this is a limited and negative view – it is the nature and use of the profit/surplus that is more meaningful. If an organization exists primarily to make a profit, then it is unlikely to be designated or viewed as a SE. However, if an organization provides a service to a section of the community and that has a social impact plus makes a profit used to develop the organization, it may define itself as a SE. That is because, in the latter case, the profits are likely to be used to widen its impact and effectiveness rather than pay shareholders dividends, for example.

Most organizations in the commercial and not-for-profit sectors use cost-plus pricing methods to establish a selling price. There are two essential questions to be answered when using this methodology.

- What are the relevant costs that need to be included in the price?

- What is the profit margin that must be added to the costs to determine a selling price?

There are two cost-plus methodologies

- full cost pricing;

- rate of return pricing.

Full cost pricing

This is where a percentage mark-up is added to the full cost of the goods/service provided to establish a full cost selling price. Two main difficulties are linked to this method of pricing. First, determining the full cost including indirect costs and overheads.

The second is deciding the level of mark-up. In a private-sector organization, the mark-up may be related to levels of risk and rates of stock turnover or it may be influenced by market conditions. For a SE, however, the mark-up may be influenced by factors such as:

- funders – for example, government – setting a target return in exchange for funding;
- the internal rate of return decided on to show external financiers the efficiency of the organization in order to attract future funding;
- a rate of return being determined by future financial requirements – for example, capital investment, collateral for future borrowing.

Rate of return pricing

This method is adopted by many public-service organizations where the performance measurement used is based on a concept of a rate of return on capital employed (ROCE). Managers will need to know what selling price it will need to charge to achieve a given rate of return on capital employed. See the following formula:

$$\frac{Capital\ employed \times Planned\ rate\ of\ return\ of\ capital\ employed}{Total\ annual\ costs}$$

If the required rate of return on capital was 5 per cent, the amount of capital involved was £2 million and the annual running costs £4 million, the required mark-up on costs would be 2.5 per cent.

$$Mark\ up = \frac{2}{4} \times 5\%$$
$$= 2.5\%$$

Both of these methodologies are, in reality, long-term pricing strategies that, if applied rigidly, lead to a lack of flexibility that is needed to deal with short-term pricing decisions. This flexibility could be of benefit to the organization, particularly when there is spare capacity within the organization and fixed costs still need to be covered.

Marginal pricing

This process is closely linked to the marginal cost equation referred to earlier in this chapter. This method aims to establish prices that cover variable costs and maximize a contribution towards fixed costs and profits. It is more flexible than cost-plus pricing as no fixed mark-up percentage on cost is used to determine a selling price. Let us look at an example.

The variable costs of a service provided are as follows:

	£
Materials	15
Labour	20
Overheads	30
Total variable costs	65

The selling price must therefore be at least £65 to recover the variable costs. Any higher selling price results in a contribution towards fixed costs. Once all fixed costs have been recovered, then any contribution becomes a profit/surplus.

The great attraction of marginal pricing is that it allows organizations to take advantage of any spare capacity that they have to attract new business by offering an initial price that is lower than normal. It also allows organizations to develop and penetrate new markets with new goods or services.

SEs might use marginal pricing to establish social charges for services, charging the client for marginal costs only with fixed costs being covered by other streams of funding/ grants and so on, for example, where the funder is keen to see that the services are provided as part of a policy decision to achieve a social objective.

Market rate

This is simply a rate that the market prepared to pay and has little or no relation to the costs incurred. This method of pricing is not recommended for SE's as they need a degree of certainty in relation to their income and are unlikely to take risks involved in letting the market determine the price.

FORMAL ACCOUNTS

Almost all organizations are required to produce some formal financial statement(s) as an official record of their financial performance. These statements can be a legal requirement, a condition of funding or for stakeholders' information. Formal accounts rarely give the full picture of organizations' achievements or otherwise in the accounting period used to produce the statements. However, if used properly, they can be a useful aide memoire to managers undertaking their duties.

The formal accounts of an organization have one of a number of titles depending on the nature and size of the organization, including income and expenditure account (I+E), profit and loss account (P+L), statement of financial affairs (SOFA) or receipts and payments account. In addition, the accounts are likely to be accompanied by a list of assets and liabilities of the organization, which is commonly known as the balance sheet.

If we concentrate on the profit and loss account and balance sheet statements, these are likely to relate to a significant proportion of SEs currently trading in the UK. The general format of a profit and loss account is as follows;

Sales income
− Cost of sales
= Gross profit
− Expenses
= Net profit

The account, in the main, relates to a period of time – often 12 months. It gives a comparison of the income earned and expenditure in a 12-month period for the principal purpose of ascertaining whether or not the organization has made a profit or loss.

The income and expenditure included in the accounts has to relate to that period. Income is included in the accounts if it has been earned in the period, regardless of whether it has been received or not. Similarly, expenditure is included in the accounts if it has been incurred in the period, regardless of whether it has been paid for or not.

The general format of a balance sheet is as follows:

Assets − Liabilities = Net assets of the organization

Financed by

Trading profits
Stakeholder investment

The balance sheet lists the assets and liabilities of the organization at a point in time – as at 31 December, for example. Remember, this contrasts with the profit and loss account, which is an account of income and expenditure over a 12-month period. The assets are likely to include land, buildings or equipment owned by the organization at the date of the balance sheet. In addition, it will include any money owed to the organization at the balance sheet date, as mentioned in the previous paragraph (debtors). Similarly, the balance sheet liabilities will include any monies owed by the organization at the date of the balance sheet, also as mentioned in the previous paragraph (creditors).

While the accounts in themselves cannot tell the full story of the organization, they can act as an important prompt to managers who may not be financial experts but do need to have a meaningful financial appreciation of the organizations they manage. A number of headings found in a profit and loss account and balance sheet are listed below and some questions a manager might want to think about are included and commented on.

Sales income

Is the income recurring (trading income) or non-recurring (grants)?

Self-generated funds/income give the organization a degree of self-determination that might not be available if it were wholly funded by grants. If the majority of funding is in the form of grants – particularly from a single source – there is a danger that a SE could lose control of its destiny, principal aims and purposes. The funder might consciously or unconsciously use its financial power to move the recipient to a different position from the one that its founders originally intended.

If a combination of both, what is the ideal proportion?

Most organizations see the advantages of recurring income, as described above. However, there are situations in which some income is only available via grant funding. If an organization can balance grant income with earned income, the dependency issues referred to above may be avoided and the journey to sustainability might be more easily achieved.

What is the customer profile?

Is the demand for your goods and services measureable? Are there many customers? Do they know you well? Are there other services that you could provide? The answers to these questions and similar will play a significant role in the way that the organization develops, or not.

Is there any potential growth in the marketplace or are there signs of a contraction of demand? Does the organization need to think of alternative goods or services to meet demand or as alternatives to existing business?

Is income received on an even basis or are there significant peaks and troughs?

Organizations will need to pay particular attention to their cash flow if income is received on an intermittent basis. Overdraft facilities may need to be carefully thought about and possibly negotiated with the bank.

Cash is the lifeblood of any organization and it is recommended that all senior managers as well as finance managers have a general understanding of the nature and frequency of its flow in and out of the organization. Organizations can be successful, achieving their aims and objectives, but be brought down by a lack of cash flow.

Cash is needed, for example, when staff need to be paid. Cash is needed to pay suppliers of goods and services on the due date. If cash is not available to pay these debts, the survival of the organization could quickly be brought into question.

Cost of sales

The cost of sales means those costs directly related to the goods or services offered by the organization. It excludes indirect costs/overheads (see above) and its particular importance lies in the simple fact that organizations cannot sell or provide goods or services for less than the cost of those services to the organization if they want to survive. The cost to the organization is the net cost – that is, what it costs the organization to provide the goods or services *less* any grants or subsidies received to enable the service to be provided.

Gross profit

The figure for sales income less the cost of sales is the gross profit for the period. This element of the profit – gross profit – traditionally pays for the overhead/indirect costs of the organization. These costs are likely to include administration, marketing, personnel and other costs. In the main, these are costs that cannot be allocated to a specific good or service. In the pricing of goods or services these costs are generally apportioned on some reasonable basis so that the costs can be recovered through the pricing process.

Expenses

These are the overhead/indirect costs referred to in the previous paragraph. The nature of these expenses tend to be more fixed than those included in the cost of sales. Thus, many organizations try to minimize these types of expenses as they have to be paid for regardless of the success or otherwise of the organization.

Net profit

In the private sector, net profit is used to fund the payment of tax, dividends, the transfer of funds to reserves for future capital developments and so on. SEs could be in a position to use net profits for these reasons. If not, then they are likely to save any surplus for future developments or to fund an organization in a difficult financial period.

Expenses/expenditure

Expenses are included in both cost of sales and as charges against gross profit. As with income, it is important that general managers as well as finance managers have some appreciation of the nature of the expenditure being incurred by the organization and should be able to go a long way towards answering the majority of the following questions.

Is cash involved in incurring the expenditure?

A number of items of expenditure do not involve cash payments, but, rather, are non-cash items that need to be included in the accounts or financial statements to meet the requirements of accounting rules and regulations. Depreciation, for example, is a charge against profits, but no cash payments are involved. It is a charge for the use of an asset and is included in the accounts for the sake of completeness and to match all costs incurred with all income earned. Similarly, a provision for bad debts is a charge against profits yet no cash expenditure is incurred.

Are there alternatives?

Managers should always ensure that they are buying the most economical and effective goods or services available yet still match the ethos and mission of the organization. The sources of goods and services is an important consideration for many SEs and, increasingly, for other organisation, too.

Do we have to buy?

There are alternatives to buying, in the form of hiring and leasing arrangements, for example. While, in the main, such options might appear to be more expensive than buying, they have one great advantage – the full cost of purchase is not incurred in one lump sum payment. For example, a van might be hired on an 'as and when needed' basis rather than the organization buying a van outright and it being unused for significant periods of time.

Managers often say they do not understand financial statements and they do not play a significant part in a manager's life, but it is important for them to recognize that the financial statements of an organization reflect, in financial terms, the impact of the organization. If it is well run and managers are making good decisions *and* there is a demand for its goods/services, then the organization is likely to be financially sound, which will be reflected in the accounts. If there are problems within the organization and some of the above conditions do not apply, then it is likely that the organization will be facing some financial problems and those will be reflected in the financial statements.

In particular, managers should make themselves fully aware of the financial implications of their actions and use the financial statements as a checklist, as indicated in the previous paragraphs. Such constant questioning and reviewing of their actions by managers will go a long way towards ensuring that their organization has the best chance of achieving its aims and objectives and delivering its mission.

PERFORMANCE MEASUREMENT

The measurement or quantification of performance has been at the heart of managerial changes seen in many private- and public-sector organizations across Europe and North America in the last two decades. The limitations of financial measures, including profit or loss and break-even statements, as an indication of performance has led to management specialists searching for something more acceptable and appropriate. The shift of focus in the public services and, thus, inevitably, many not-for-profit organizations from bureaucratic procedures to a managerial emphasis has accentuated performance measurement in these services (Lapsley, 2008).

A significant performance measurement tool adopted by many profitmaking and not-for-profit organizations is the Balanced Scorecard (Kaplan and Norton, 1992) that was discussed in Chapter 3. Its guiding concept was the aim of moving managers away from looking at purely financial outcomes and towards considering a more balanced portfolio of multiple financial *and* non-financial measures closely linked to strategic objectives. The scorecard encourages managers to look to the future and less to the past. 'What can we achieve?' becomes more important than 'What have we achieved?'

The generic balanced scorecard (see Figure 5.2) consists of four interrelated quadrants, each containing objectives and measures from a distinct perspective:

- financial;
- customer;
- internal processes;
- learning and growth.

The scope of these perspectives is designed to cover the whole of the organization's activities – internally and externally, for the present and the future.

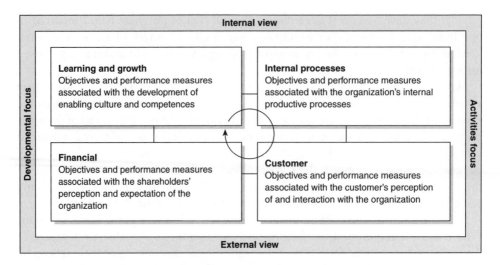

Figure 5.2   The balanced scorecard (Kaplan and Norton, 1992).
Copyright Harvard Business Publishing 1992. Reproduced with permission.

In comparison with profitmaking organizations, where the dominant requirement is likely to be return on capital employed, those of SEs and other not-for-profit organizations are likely to be more complex. The requirements of stakeholders in SEs are usually comprised of an extensive set of mostly non-financial objectives that address social, political and economic issues. 'Customers' of SEs are also likely to present demands that are more complex and open-ended than might be faced by a profitmaking organization. It is not difficult to connect the principles and values of the balanced scorecard with the concepts of corporate social responsibility mentioned earlier in this chapter.

Working out exactly how to articulate strategy for a not-for-profit organization is likely to be more complex than it is for a profitmaking one. There is no common 'default' goal that is shared by all non-profit organizations. Thus, determining a clear mission for an SE is essential to deciding whether the organization is successful or not.

Once it has been formulated, the organization's strategy is translated into specific objectives that can be classified within each of these four perspectives. Once those objectives have been identified, appropriate quantitative measures can be devised to monitor the success of the organization in achieving them. Figure 5.3 lists examples of the kinds of objectives and measures that are entered in each of the boxes for the four measurement perspectives. Figure 5.3 is drawn from the original article by Kaplan and Norton (1992). The entries in the boxes relate more obviously to a for-profit organization than an SE, but it is acknowledged by many, including Kaplan (2001) himself and Niven (2003), that the template can be relatively easily adapted and used by SEs and other not-for-profit organizations to equal effect.

The concept of performance measurement and management has a number of critics. It is difficult to compare one organization with another and one period with another, critics of performance management argue. However, despite these criticisms, it is evident that the wider public services and many for-profit organizations see performance management as core to their management processes.

Learning and growth		Internal processes	
Objectives	Measures	Objectives	Measures
'To value our staff'	Employee retention index	'To continually challenge competitors' products in the marketplace	Time to market for next generation of products
'To maximize productivity'	Output per head	'To compete on product reliablity'	Production defect rates
'To develop a skilled workforce	Number of training hours completed per head	'To compete on competitive logistics capabilities'	Stock replenishment cycle times
'To provide internal information'	Information availability survey index	'To compete on product delivery channel mix'	Volumes of transactions conducted through each of our delivery channels
'To create organizational alignment	Peer evaluation pleasures within/between teams	'To capture a unique supply chain'	Percentages of suppliers' revenues dependent on us
'To cultivate a core competence in …	Skill and technology measures related to desired competence	'To reinvent our value-creation system'	Benchmarking index for supplier of outsourced activities
Financial		Customer	
Objectives	Measures	Objectives	Measures
'To achieve a higher return on investment:'	ROI, ROCE	'To dominate our major markets'	Market share
'To see significant revenue from our new product launch'	Revenue growth on selected product lines	'To delight our targeted customers	Customers satisfaction survey results
'To maximize profitability per transaction	Unit costs	'To increase revenue through repeat purchases'	Customers retention over time
'To minimize the cost of obtaining funds	Credit rating	'To grow our business in a selected target group'	Customers acquisition from target group
'To delight our shareholders'	Value-added measures	'To add margin through image or fashion'	Marketing spend as a percentage of sales
'To improve our cash flow'	Creditor days	'To build customer recognition'	Corporate image or brand awareness polls

Figure 5.3   Possible measures (Kaplan and Norton, 1996).

CONCLUSIONS

This chapter has been written specifically with non-finance managers in mind. It has attempted to offer a signposts for such managers, guiding them through many of the constituent parts of the financial management framework. Further, it has amplified on those parts of the framework that are likely to be particularly useful to managers in their daily operational activities. It has also asked useful questions to this end. Who are our customers? What do we know about them? Should we buy or lease? How does the cash flow? How do we compare with the competition? Are we doing better than last year? These are questions for managers to consider and the financial processes, outputs and statements described can be very useful tools for doing so in the hands of those who know how to use them.

The continuing emergence of SEs and their increasing importance, both financially and socially, has led to an increasing requirement for managers to develop and use financial skills that previously they may not have needed. It is hoped that this book, and this chapter in particular, will support the modern manager in helping SEs achieve their aims and objectives.

REFERENCES

Bank of England (2003) 'The Financing of Social Enterprises', Bank of England Domestic Finance Division, London.

Borzaga, C. and Defourney, J. (eds) (2001) *The Emergence of Social Enterprise*. Abingdon: Routledge.

Coombs, H., Hobbs, D. and Jenkins, E. (2005) *Management Accounting: Principles and Applications*. London: Sage.

Drury, C. (2006) *Cost and Management Accounting* (6th edn). Stanford, CT: Thomson Learning.

DTI (2002) 'Social enterprise: a strategy for success', DTI London.

DTI (2006) 'Social enterprise action plan: scaling new heights', DTI, London.

Elkington, J. (1998) *Cannibals with Forks: The triple bottom line of 21st century business*. Gabriola Island, BC: New Society.

Kaplan, Robert S. (2001) 'Strategic performance measurement and management in nonprofit organisations', *Nonprofit Management and Leadership*, 11 (3): 353–70.

Kaplan, R.S. and Norton, D.P. (1992) 'The Balanced Scorecard: measures that drive performance', *Harvard Business Review,* January–February: 71–80.

Kaplan, R.S. and Norton, D.P. (1996) 'Using the Balanced Scorecard as a strategic management system', *Harvard Business Review*, January–February: 75–85.

Lapsley, I. (2008) 'The NPM agenda: back to the future', *Financial Accountability and Management*, 24 (1): 77–96.

Lewis, R., Hunt, P. and Carson, D. (2006) 'Social enterprise and community-based care', Kings Fund, London.

Niven, Paul R. (2003) *Balanced Scorecard: Step-by-step for government and nonprofit agencies*. Chichester: Wiley.

Pearce, J. (2003) *Social Enterprise in Anytown*. London: Calouste Gulbenkian Foundation.

Simon, H.A. (1953) *Studies in Econometric Methods*. New York: John Wiley & Sons.

6

MARKETING FOR SOCIAL ENTERPRISES

KEY THEMES

- The potential of marketing for SEs.
- The development of a market orientation.
- A critical analysis of the role of social marketing for SEs.
- Examining the potential role for a relationship marketing approach for SEs.
- Appraising the role of branding for SEs.

INTRODUCTION

Peattie and Morley (2008), in their monograph on SEs for the UK Economic Social Research Council (ESRC), argue that SEs have a poor understanding of marketing mix elements such as pricing and product dimensions (in particular, packaging). They also highlight the under-researched potential for SEs to differentiate themselves along social and ethical dimensions to achieve competitive advantage. This points towards the benefits of exploring in this chapter both the social and ethical dimensions of marketing.

Doherty and Tranchell (2007) propose the importance of combining mainstream distribution with 'the alternative High Street' when marketing fair trade products. Peattie and Morley (2008) also highlight the opportunity for SEs of developing partnerships with private-sector organizations wishing to align themselves with a social cause. Doherty (2008) points to the benefits of partnerships between SEs, giving as an example the partnership between the Co-operative Food group and Divine Chocolate Ltd (see under relationship marketing later in this chapter). Such a focus on partnerships shows the need to also explore in this chapter the potential of relationship marketing for SEs.

Despite the obvious potential for SEs in relation to ethical, social and relationship marketing, there has been little research carried out in the area of marketing management in SEs. Thus far, research focused on these aspects has looked mainly at certain organizational forms, such as fair trade SEs. As a result, we will draw heavily on this literature.

THE MARKETING CONTEXT FOR SEs

The social economy is notable for both its recent growth (see Chapter 1, the growth and positioning of social enterprises) and the diversity of social objectives the resulting organizational forms seek to address. Reasons for this rapid expansion are equally diverse, so no simple list will suffice to account for the range of organizations addressing issues such as fair trade, healthcare provision, employment enhancement, childcare, environmental protection, arts promotion and social housing. Managers of SEs are increasingly dealing with the impacts of such rapid expansion. These impacts include the following:

- resource shortages as more SEs compete for fewer grants;
- increased political pressure to replace grant funding with earned income;
- human resources bottlenecks due to a lack of appropriately skilled and experienced people seeking employment in the sector;
- more demanding requirements for transparency and accountability as SEs grow in number and size;
- increasing intra-sector competition due to overcrowding in some subsectors;
- increasing attention from, and collaboration with, for-profit organizations.

These impacts strengthen the case for SEs seeking a clear definition of their target audiences and programmes for service/product delivery internally and a clearly articulated corporate identity to support strategies for building relationships with key stakeholders externally. In short, adopting a strategic approach to marketing.

That is not to suggest marketing is entirely underdeveloped in the third sector. On the contrary, Andreasen et al. (2005) report that the rapid growth in the numbers of non-profitmaking organizations in the USA has impelled them to adopt for-profit marketing techniques to assist the transition from dependence on grants to financial independence. However, they conclude that certain areas of marketing are less understood and employed, but, with the common pressures operating in both contexts, SEs are able to adopt and apply mainstream for-profit marketing techniques.

Theories and concepts in the field of marketing can offer opportunities for managers of SEs to fashion unique marketing strategies to support the growth and development of their organizations. Specifically, strategic marketing has seen significant changes in our understanding of sources of competitive advantage and these changes support efforts by managers of SEs to cocreate sustainable product/service offers via stakeholder engagement and build social resources in the form of intangibles, such as reputation, trust, brand identity, relationships and social capital. These social resources support SEs' sustainability and, in turn, reinforce their competitive positions relative to for-profit providers.

This view is underpinned by a growing body of evidence on the link between corporate social performance (CSP) and corporate financial performance (CFP). In a bid to assist SE managers to devise appropriate strategic marketing plans, this chapter will begin by outlining the historical development towards a marketing orientation, further explore the dynamics of the SE sector and the potential for marketing applications before going on to review some key recent developments in the field of strategic marketing. This chapter also highlights how these methods, primarily aimed at for-profit organizations, can be relevant to the SE sector. In particular, it will look at social marketing, relationship marketing and ethical dimensions of branding.

MARKETING ORIENTATION

Business orientations evolved from a production orientation in the early twentieth century to the emergence of a formalized marketing discipline in the decades after World War II. This new thing called marketing was characterized by a transactional orientation (1950s–1960s), with emphasis being put on sales volumes rather than customer loyalty and repeat business. This was possible due to booming consumer demand, creating an excess of demand over supply (with limited competition in many sectors). However, as competition increased in the 1970s with the emergence of more competitors both at home and abroad, the need to differentiate product/service offers led to the emergence of brands, plus an emphasis on brand identity to attract customers and brand loyalty to retain them. As customers' experience and knowledge grew, they became more discriminating in their selection of products/services, leading companies in the 1980s–1990s to focus more than they had done before on customer retention via relationship marketing strategies. This was a response to the waning power of brands and the need for new tactics to ensure customer loyalty.

Latterly, from the 1990s until the present, there has been a further development in favour of 'value-based marketing'. This has been a response by companies to customers becoming very savvy about the products and services they consume as a result of access to ICT (especially the Internet). As Piercy (2002) puts it, 'sophisticated customers will define the relationship they want with us, not the other way round.' Thus, as all firms embrace relationship marketing, its value as a differentiator declines because it becomes the norm. Consequently, the marketing challenge is to develop capabilities for identifying and delivering customer value better than can competitors. Figure 6.1 summarizes this and the previous developments mentioned above.

The conventional marketing wisdom holds that embracing a market orientation provides a company with a better understanding of its customers, competitors and the environment in which it operates that, subsequently, leads to superior performance (Deshpande and Farley, 1998; Kohli and Jaworski, 1990; Slater and Narver, 1994). While these studies are primarily based on the for-profit sector, there is an emerging body of literature indicating its value to aspects of the performance of non-profitmaking organizations (Sargeant, 2005).

Operationalizing the marketing concept, according to Narver and Slater (1990), involves the organization actively understanding and responding to customers and competitors and coordinating its internal resources to create superior value for customers. Figure 6.2 highlights the components of market orientation.

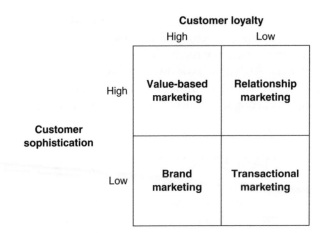

Figure 6.1 The evolution of value-based marketing (Piercy, 2002: 59)

This article was published in *Market-led Strategic Change: A guide to transforming the process of going to market*, N. Piercy, Copyright Elsevier (2002).

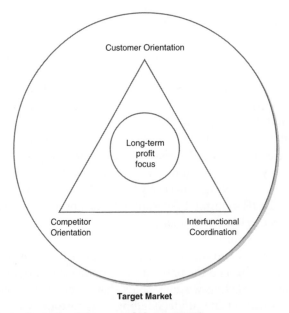

Figure 6.2 Market orientation (Narver and Slater, 1990)

In 1935, the American Marketing Association (AMA, 2008: 2) defined marketing as, 'the performance of business activities that direct the flow of goods and services from producers to consumers.' Levitt (1960) identified a shift in emphasis in the 1950s and posited that it was the principle function of business not to generate a profit but to create a satisfied customer, with profit being the final reward. However, this concept not wholly embraced by either academics or industries (Webster, 1988) and the focus again began to change. This time stress was put on the value of understanding marketing functions and viewing marketing from a broader economic and societal perspective (Webster, 1992). In 1969, Kotler and Levy suggested that marketing was a pervasive societal activity that went beyond the selling of goods to consumers.

Kotler (1979) explored this social dimension further and suggested that economic activity was viewed as a function of two main sectors: profit and governmental. However, in addition to this, he suggested that a third sector also existed, containing not-for-profit organizations such as charities and social agencies, and this sector was a 'middle way' for meeting social needs.

Vargo and Lusch (2004) challenged the dominant logic of the marketing mix – the 4Ps (McCarthy, 1960) – highlighting that new frames of reference, not based on a standard economics paradigm, had emerged, such as services marketing, relationship marketing, quality management, value and network analysis. There was a feeling that the old concept was inadequate in the service context and marketing had moved from a goods-dominant view to a service-dominant view, changing the focus from tangibles to intangibles, 'such as skills, information and knowledge, and toward interactivity and connectivity and ongoing relationships' (Vargo and Lusch, 2004: 15).

With the debates moving marketing towards being both a social and economic process, the AMA (2008: 2) saw fit to revise its official definition in 2004 in recognition of this changing landscape. Robert Lusch was instrumental in putting the revised definition together, which was:

> **Marketing is an organizational function and a set of processes for creating, communicating and delivering value to customers and for managing customer relationships in ways that benefit the organization and its stakeholders.**

Gronroos (2006) has further redefined marketing in response to the AMA, suggesting that it is limited in the following ways:

- value is not delivered solely by the firm but is cocreated by customer processes and interactions with customers;

- relationship management should not be advocated as a generic approach as there are times when customers do not want a relationship;

- marketing should not be confined to one organizational function – a customer focus should be pervasive in all functions of the organization.

A 'promising management' definition is offered as an alternative (Gronroos, 2006: 407):

> **Marketing is a customer focus that permeates organizational functions and processes and is geared towards making promises through value a proposition, enabling fulfilment of individual expectations created by such promises and fulfilling such expectations**

through support to customers' value-generating processes, thereby supporting value creation in the firm's as well as its customers' and other stakeholders' processes.

The AMA went on to further review the definition to reflect the ongoing debate and, importantly for SEs, include the role marketing plays within society and acknowledge the idea that it is equally relevant to market something to do good as it is to make profit. The latest definition, resulting from this review, was unveiled in January 2008 and reads:

Marketing is the activity, set of institutions, and processes for creating, communicating, delivering, and exchanging offerings that have value for customers, clients, partners, and society at large.

Similarly, the Chartered Institute of Marketing (CIM) in September 2007 embarked on a definition review and proposed the following:

The strategic business function that creates value by stimulating, facilitating and fulfilling customer demand. It does this by building brands, nurturing innovation, developing relationships, creating good customer service and communicating benefits. By operating customer-centrically, marketing brings positive return on investment, satisfies shareholders and stakeholders from business and the community, and contributes to positive behavioural change and a sustainable business future.

So, it can be seen that there is an acceptance of the social dimension in marketing, emerging acknowledgement of the third sector as a player in the business environment and marketing and 'customer' means more than just the buyer, with wider stakeholders from both business and the community needing to be acknowledged. The importance of stakeholders is key here, bearing in mind their significance in the definitions of SEs (see Chapter 2).

Andreasen et al. (2005: 47) suggest that there has been somewhat of a shift from the earlier scepticism on the part of not-for-profit organizations about marketing concepts, towards acceptance of a marketing orientation. Indeed, 'being a customer-centric organization' is one of the six strategic goals outlined by the restructured US organization The Futures Initiative.

A key element in both social and traditional marketing campaigns is putting the consumer at the heart of decisions and processes. However, this consumer orientation can be achieved in very different ways, as can be seen in the case of Quit & Save, a Scottish SE, who adopted a bottom-up approach, using a layperson to communicate and facilitate problemsolving directly with clients, as opposed to the top-down approach used by the NHS of a health professional doing so (Hastings, 2007: 290).

Let us now explore the potential of social marketing for SEs.

SOCIAL MARKETING

A large number of SEs will, very likely, have mission statements and business objectives that allude to improving personal and social welfare in addition to economic aspirations and many will look to achieve these via behavioural changes. Thus, social marketing is an area that can offer guidance to SEs when developing their strategies for success.

Social marketing is fast gaining credibility in both academic and commercial sectors, particularly the health sector. A government white paper in the UK talks of the 'power of social marketing' and how 'marketing tools applied to social good' can raise public awareness and change behaviour (Department of Health 2004: 21), which has led to the establishment of the National Social Marketing Centre (NSMC). This level of acknowledgment of the value of social marketing is replicated in other governments, too, such as Australia, Canada, New Zealand, the USA and Scotland.

The following definition by Lazer and Kelley (1973: 9), which refers to enhancing social as well as economic goals, best indicates the relevance of this area to SEs:

> Social marketing is concerned with the application of marketing knowledge, concepts and techniques to enhance social as well as economic ends. It is also concerned with analysis of the social consequence of marketing policies, decisions and activities.

This viewpoint has been adopted generally and can be seen in the majority of modern definitions of social marketing, as they include the use of traditional marketing methods/ knowledge. Andreasen (1994), for example, defined social marketing as 'the application of commercial marketing technologies to the analysis, planning, execution and evaluation of programs designed to influence the voluntary behaviour of target audiences in order to improve their personal welfare and that of society'.

Thus, social marketing goes beyond being just a communication campaign or advertising. These may be part of its marketing effort, but alongside other considerations, such as price determination, distribution and so on.

Social marketing, like traditional marketing, does not stand alone as a theory. It is a framework that encompasses economics, psychology, sociology, anthropology and communications theory to understand how to influence behaviour (Kotler and Zaltman, 1971).

Traditional marketing is often based on the 4Ps model posited by McCarthy (1960), but it was recognized that this did not take into account the issues of people, policy and physical evidence, which are so relevant to today's social marketer, so these were added to the 4Ps model to create the 7Ps (Booms and Bitner, 1981).

Andreasen (2002), in the USA, identified six criteria by which a campaign should be judged to determine whether or not it is a social marketing campaign – namely, behaviour change, consumer research, segmenting and targeting, marketing mix, exchange/ benefit and competition.

These have since been refined by French and Blair-Stevens (2006) for the UK National Social Marketing Centre. They outlined the following eight key attributes for social marketing in its list of social marketing benchmarks.

- customer orientation;
- behaviour;
- theory;

- insight;

- exchange;

- competition;

- segmentation;

- methods mix;

Let us look at each of these in turn.

Customer orientation

This means being focused on developing a robust understanding of the customer, based on drawing credible market and consumer research from a variety of sources.

When considering social marketing, the customer/consumer is considered to be an active participant in the change process. MacFayden et al. (2007) suggests that, at this stage, the customer-centred approach asks not 'What is wrong with these people, why don't they understand?', but 'What is wrong with us? What don't we understand about our target audience?' The role of the social marketer is to build and foster relationships with the customer over time and continue to consult and seek customer input to gain a greater understanding. Hastings (2007) suggests that stakeholders should also be included in this stage.

Behaviour

It is the focus on understanding and changing behaviour that is at the core of social marketing. It aims to achieve a measurable impact on what people actually do. It doesn't just focus on achieving changes in behaviour, though, but also broadens that out, aiming to promote, establish and sustain changes over time. As such, any strategy must have a clear focus on behaviour underpinned by strong behavioural analysis of the specific behaviour in question. This focus on social behaviour suggests the importance of a voluntary change in behaviour, the need to induce the change by making the benefits clear, the requirement for segmentation and targeted delivery and, ultimately, the delivery of personal and social improvement.

Theory

Any programme should be underpinned and informed by behavioural theory. One such is social cognitive theory.

The concept of social learning was first introduced by Miller and Dollard (1941) and extended by Bandura and Walters (1963) when they added the principles of observational learning and vicarious reinforcement.

Social cognitive theory (SCT) suggests that human behaviour is jointly determined by personal internal factors, such as the level of deprivation and external factors, such as the facilities available for a community to use and it explains how people acquire and maintain certain behavioural patterns while also providing the basis for intervention strategies (Bandura, 1986).

It is suggested that social marketers should consider the influence of the environment on individuals. The environment can be subdivided into the immediate environment, being that of family, friends and the local community, and the 'wider social context' of economic conditions, cultural norms and social mores. (Hastings, 2007). Considering and addressing both types of environments can limit the risks of failure.

SCT could be considered relevant by SEs that have as their primary objectives education and/or behaviour change programmes, and for example, it can provide the basis for intervention strategies.

Insight

A key social marketing objective is to understand the target audience, developing a deeper insight into the individual/group and issue. Any programme should be 'insight' driven.

The focus needs to be clearly on gaining a deep understanding and insight into what moves and motivates the customer by:

- drilling down from a wider understanding of the customer in order to focus on identifying key factors and issues relevant to positively influencing a particular behaviour – consideration of the wider social context (Hastings, 2007), mentioned above, is vital here;

- identifying and developing actionable insights using considered judgement rather than just relying on data and intelligence.

It is important when developing insights into behaviour to note that individuals do not make and action decisions in a simple, binary manner, especially when these relate to complex situations. Instead, they pass through a staged process – from ignorance or indifference, to change through trial, to, eventually, reaching a commitment to a behaviour change (Prochaska and DiClemente, 1982).

The five-stage process known as the transtheoretical model (TTM) suggests that a decision is made via:

- *precontemplation* when the person is aware of a new behaviour but has no interest in the changing of theirs;

- *contemplation* when there is a conscious evaluation of the relevance of making a behaviour change;

- *preparation* to put measures in place to make a change;

- *actions* taken to make the change happen;

- *confirmation and maintenance* the decision has been made, the effects have been realized and the desire to regress is limited.

It cannot be assumed that progression through stages is a given – inhibitors to progress can arise at any point. Bridle et al. (2005) suggest that the barriers to change for individuals will vary at different stages of the process and must be understood in order for the process to be effective. This is an insight that needs to be gleaned if the programme is to be effective.

While the TTM was developed for clinical use in psychotherapy, it can offer insights to those outside the health field, too. Lichenstein and Glasgow (1992) suggest that the attraction of the staged process is not just a result of its intuitive and theoretical plausibility but also due to its apparent ability to explain why campaigns aimed at large groups or the mass public might fail. They suggest that the 'one size fits all theory' is less effective than the targeted stage process.

Exchange

Social marketing incorporates an 'exchange' analysis – that is, understanding what the person has to give to get the benefits proposed. This highlights the fact that social marketing not only shares the traditional marketing philosophy of customer orientation but also that of exchange. Indeed, Bagozzi (1975) argues that marketing does not occur unless there are two or more parties, each with something to exchange and they have the ability to communicate and create a distribution network.

'Exchange' is defined as an exchange of resources or value between two or more parties, with the motivation being to satisfy need (Houston and Gassenheimer, 1987). MacFayden et al. (2007) suggest that social marketing puts an emphasis on voluntary behaviour and, to achieve an exchange, the individual must be offered something of perceived value in return for adopting a change in behaviour.

Therefore, we can see that, in order to effect change or influence behaviour, there is a need to provide the individual with a perceived benefit. Kotler (1979) suggests that there are five prerequisites to an exchange taking place:

- there are at least two parties;
- both have something that is of value to the other;
- each party is capable of communicating;
- they are all free to accept and reject any offer;
- each party has a desire to deal with the other.

The theory proposes that consumers will be likely to voluntarily adopt behaviour if its perceived benefits are shown to outweigh the perceived cost of purchase.

SEs and social marketing can involve the mutual transfer of psychological or other intangible entities – a symbolic or utilitarian exchange takes place. Such intangibility is not unique to SEs, though – it can be seen in the offerings of many commercial marketers who are 'selling' an experience or lifestyle benefit. Thus, this should not be seen as an obstacle to engaging in commercial marketing practices.

Competition

Social marketing should incorporate competition analysis so that it can be seen what things compete for the resources of the customer, such as time and money.

Competition is not influenced merely by what other companies do, but also by the fundamental forces operating in the marketplace (Hastings, 2007). Porter (1998) suggested that, when considering competition, five forces should be analysed:

- the power of the customer;
- the power of the supplier;
- the degree to which offerings can be substituted;
- new entrants into the marketplace;
- rivalry between existing organizations.

The fact that social marketers often deal with voluntary behaviour changes means that individuals have choice, indicating competition exists and needs to be overcome.

Wayman et al. (2007) suggests that social marketing faces a number of forms of competition, including that of individual behaviour and the social factors that may discourage a behaviour change and the initiatives of other organizations or companies, which may also see competition for funding and resources. They suggest that a competitor analysis should be a part of any social marketing campaign.

Segmentation

Any programme must avoid taking a blanket approach to marketing and communicating with the individual or group, developing an appropriate segmentation approach.

Social marketers recognize that different audiences have specific needs and, to achieve effective message delivery, it is necessary to analyse both audience demographic and psychographic data. These can include factors such as age, gender, marital status and personality dispositions. Segmentation is recognized as an essential tool for social marketers and assists in the determining of wants, needs, desires and tendencies of specific groups within a larger population. Hastings (2007) suggests that there are three commonly used segmentation criteria for social marketing – personal characteristics, past behaviour and perceived benefits.

Methods mix

The social marketing programme must draw on an appropriate mix of methods at both the strategic and operational levels. At the strategic level, the intervention mix draws on theories and concepts to inform policy and strategy, whereas at the operational level, the emphasis is on applying techniques to a specific planned process, such as a social marketing programme. It is here that the techniques of the

4Ps marketing mix (McCarthy, 1960) or the extended version, the 7Ps (Booms and Bitner, 1981), can be exploited:

- product;
- people;
- price;
- policy;
- promotion;
- physical evidence;
- place.

In conclusion, Hastings (2007) suggests that social marketing has the key elements of any marketing orientation – that is, a customer orientation, an exchange and a long-term planning outlook.

Thackeray et al. (2007) suggests that, when considering a social marketing programme, several key questions should be considered.

- What is the product?
- What is the purpose of the promotion?
- What message will be conveyed?
- What tools will be used?
- What promotional communication materials will be utilized?

They suggest that a promotional strategy is required and becomes part of the marketing plan, which is then effectively integrated into the strategic plan.

Social marketing is not solely about the benefits to an organization, but the benefits to an individual or community. This is one of the factors that distinguish it from all other forms of marketing – the level of customer involvement and interaction tends to be greater throughout the process.

Hastings et al. (2000) suggest that social marketing can be powerful in not only engaging citizens downstream but also educating and persuading stakeholders, such as doctors, upstream.

Golding and Peattie (2005) discuss the potential for promoting fair trade coffee using a social marketing-based approach. They propose an alternative to the view that fair trade organizations need to learn more from conventional commercial marketing.

Fair trade organizations aim to integrate social and environmental considerations into trade models and promote social justice and environmental welfare in developing countries (see the definition of fair trade in Exhibit 1.4, Chapter 1). They have clearly shown consumers the people, places and relationships behind commodities such as coffee, tea, cocoa, bananas, cotton and so on and created active engagement with consumers, as opposed to passive consumerism. Exhibit 6.1 looks at fair trade Coffee and Cafédirect. First the marketing challenge facing Cafédirect is discussed. Afterwards, there is some analysis of the application of social marketing to Cafédirect.

Exhibit 6.1   Fair trade, social marketing and Cafédirect

Fair trade coffee has been central to the growth of the fair trade market generally in the UK, with fair trade coffee sales in 2007 at £117 million, accounting for 24 per cent of the total fair trade market in the UK. Only the sale of bananas, at £150 million, are higher (Fairtrade Foundation, 2008).

Coffee is a product with social and symbolic significance and is the second most widely traded commodity in the world after oil – hence the term 'black gold', which is also the title of a film exploring the plight of coffee farmers in Ethiopia (Black Gold, 2007). Thus, market analysts regard the coffee market as a highly competitive one (Mintel, 2008).

Sales activities are particularly concentrated on the major manufacturers (Kraft, Nestlé, Proctor & Gamble and Sara Lee), who possess the long-established brands. The economies of scale afforded by the international resources of these leading firms make it increasingly difficult for smaller players to compete in terms of price, distribution, range of products and marketing spend (Blythman, 2004; Golding and Peattie, 2005; Tiffen, 2002).

Such a concentration of power is also exhibited at the retail level (Mintel, 2008). For example, in the UK coffee market, 83 per cent of all sales in 2007 were through multiple supermarkets. The growth of the coffee market suggests a thriving industry, but there is another side to the story.

The International Coffee Agreement, which controlled the price of coffee beans, collapsed in 1989. This caused the price of coffee to fall to a third of its pre-1989 level within a few years, which had a devastating effect on the incomes of small-scale coffee farmers globally (Barratt Brown, 2007). Three-quarters of the global supply of coffee is produced by small, family-owned farms. Their earnings are critical for countries such as Ethiopia, where 54 per cent of its foreign exchange earnings are derived from trading raw coffee beans. The declining and volatile prices reduce the producers' access to education, housing, food and medical services for their families.

The development of fair trade coffee is viewed as a reaction to this crisis. In 1991, a range of third-sector organizations, including Oxfam, Traidcraft, Equal Exchange and Twin Trading, got together and formed the branded fair trade coffee company Cafédirect. All four organizations were already involved in the distribution of fair trade coffee into the UK, but they realized that, collectively, they could achieve so much more. Cafédirect was born from this alliance of interested charities with one specific mission: to pioneer fair trade into the mainstream of consumer consciousness and purchasing in the UK.

By 2007, Cafédirect became the fourth largest hot beverage company in the UK, with a turnover of £23 million and a market share in the roast and ground coffee market of 9 per cent (Mintel, 2008).

King (2004) argues that Cafédirect's success is built on a focus on product quality and brandbuilding. However, Moore (2004) expresses

(Continued)

(Continued)

concern regarding the dilution of the fair trade ideology by the increase in commercialization of this segment and its subversion by profit-seeking companies, which aim to move the progressive fair trade movement into a profit-orientated niche marketing scheme.

The experience of Cafédirect at the hands of competitors and retailers perhaps gives some credence to Moore's arguments. In 2006, the company made its first after tax loss since 1995. During 2007, retail sales actually fell for the first time in the company's history (by 4 per cent to £17 million, Cafédirect, 2008). This is a concern as 70 per cent of the company's total turnover is via the supermarket retail channel.

Cafédirect is feeling the effects of increasing competition, from both like-for-like fair trade goods, which include supermarkets' own-label fair trade products, and new sustainable coffees. In fact, 39 per cent of fair trade coffee sales are now accounted for by supermarkets' own-label brands.

The application of social marketing to SEs

This section provides a critical examination of the application of SM to Cafédirect. Golding and Peattie (2005) propose the discipline of social marketing as a means of preserving the social mission of fair trade while also contributing to its commercial success. They argue that social marketing allows fair trade SEs such as Cafédirect to balance their social and commercial objectives and provide an alternative to relying solely on the principles of conventional marketing.

So, what is the case for applying social marketing to this context? Golding and Peattie (2005) argue that one of the defining characteristics of social marketing is that the beneficiary is the target audience and/or broader society, not the sponsoring organization (Andreasen, 1995). They argue that those working in fair trade are likely to be comfortable with this perspective.

Social marketing also works on understanding and overcoming barriers to behavioural change. Hence, a social marketing approach would first try to understand why people do not buy this coffee and how their objections can be overcome. This is in contrast to a conventional marketing approach, which might start by investigating why consumers might buy this coffee and how they can be stimulated to do so.

Social marketing could also be helpful to both fair trade and other SEs in that it demonstrates a track record in winning David versus Goliath scenarios – in this case, the competitive position of small SEs when pitted against larger, much more resource-rich rivals. For example, in the case of stop smoking compaigns, social marketing was up against the power of the tobacco industry. Such instances are not one brand competing against another, but, rather, there being a battle between competing ideas.

The fair trade coffee sector has faced counter-marketing from a number of sources. They have tried to discredit the fair trade model by proposing that the growth of fair trade coffee actually exacerbates the problem of declining coffee prices and the benefits to coffee farmers are minimal. Understanding that competition is a battle of ideas rather than the search for greater-tasting coffee could be vital, bearing in mind the increasing number of sustainable labelled coffees entering the market, such as Rainforest Alliance-certified coffee.

The suitability of social marketing to fair trade SEs is illustrated by asking the question, 'What is the fair trade consumer being asked to buy?' The consumer is being asked to buy into a fairer world where the central idea is to benefit others rather than the individual consumer via a lifestyle choice. Social marketing could therefore help to avoid the ethical dimensions of fair trade products being considered just another product augmentation. Social marketing could be seen as an opportunity to actually change the mass market in this area, as it has done in cases such as smoking and drink driving. Social marketing has effectively changed widespread attitudes towards certain behaviours, making them socially unacceptable. Potentially, this ambitious approach could allow the fair trade proposition to be the focus of the marketing strategy.

We should remember, however, the early lessons learned by the alternative/fair trade movement, when unbranded products were characterized by their poor quality (Nicholls and Opal, 2004). This reputation was overcome by the developments of quality products from fair trade brands such as Cafédirect and Divine Chocolate and led to the growth and mainstreaming of the fair trade ethos.

The successful marketing of fair trade and other SE brands, then, may require the careful crafting of both conventional and social marketing. The importance of dimensions such as product quality and packaging is evidenced by the experiences of both Divine and Cafédirect. A monitoring and evaluation report carried out to measure the impact of Divine Chocolate Ltd on the UK's confectionery market reported the following: 90 per cent of all key informants interviewed identified the quality of Divine Chocolate's products as being a key factor in the company's success in the mainstream market. Also, 80 per cent identified its pricing as appropriate. One leading supermarket retailer specifically mentioned the impressive quality of Divine Dark (70 per cent cocoa content): 'Divine Dark is one of our strongest-performing plain chocolate products, the recipe is excellent' (Twin Trading, 2008).

Combining social and conventional marketing

Doherty and Tranchell (2007), via Divine Chocolate Ltd as a case study (see Exhibit 6.2 for introduction), offer an approach to blending both conventional and social marketing by further developing the concepts of 'radical mainstreaming' and the 'alternative high street' that we met earlier. Originally, Lowe and Davenport (2005a, 2005b) proposed the development of both radical mainstreaming companies and the alternative high street in order to maintain the original transformative message of fair trade. Lowe and Davenport (2005a) argued that fair trade models such as Cafédirect, Divine and Agrofair show alternative approaches to the market where producer organizations from developing countries (farmers groups and so on) are shareholders in these fair trade companies (in the developed economies of Western Europe and North America). They describe the companies as examples of 'radical mainstreaming' projects that maintain the transformative message of fair trade while also competing in the mainstream. Exhibit 6.2 looks at how this blending of concepts can be achieved.

Exhibit 6.2   Divine Chocolate Ltd

Divine's mainstreaming objectives were clear from the outset and include (Tiffen, 1998):

- taking a quality and affordable range of fair trade chocolate bars to the mainstream chocolate market;
- raising awareness of fair trade issues among UK retailers and consumers of all age groups;
- being highly visible and vocal in the chocolate sector and thereby acting as a catalyst for change;
- purchasing all cocoa used according to fair trade criteria.

Balfour (2006: 2), chair of Divine, says:

> Our mission in addition to making delicious chocolate is to be highly visible in debates about fair trade, to act as a bridge between consumers and primary producers, and to act as passionate advocates for a trading system that brings dignity and respect to all its participants.

Driven by its mission to effect change in the international trading system, Divine has also concentrated its efforts on leading politicians. During Fairtrade Fortnight campaign tours organized by Divine in the UK, farmers from KK have met with both the then Prime Minister Tony Blair in 2002 and Chancellor of the Exchequer Gordon Brown in March 2004, to explain the benefits of Divine's business model. Tony Blair also visited a KK village society in 2002 on the Ghana leg of his African tour. In June 2006, a delegation led by two boys from KK cocoa farming families, along with three UK schoolchildren, handed the 'Chocolate Challenge' manifesto to the Minister for International Development (Department for International Development, 2006). The manifesto outlined the views of over 400 UK schoolchildren who had attended, fair trade cocoa summits in 2006. According to Jonathan Smith from Comic Relief (Head of Education Communications): 'Divine's mainstream clout combined with its unique business model ensures it is better positioned to effect real change in the international trading system, demonstrated by its ability to access leading politicians'.

Another example of Divine's campaigning style was illustrated in the lead up to the G8 Summit in Gleneagles, Scotland, in June 2005, when Divine ran a national advertising programme, printed in colour in *The Guardian* newspaper, reading 'Eat poverty history'. The campaign featured women from the KK community in Ghanaian settings, challenging consumers to try Divine. According to Charlotte Borger (Head of Communications at Divine), 'This national campaign successfully subverts the traditional chocolate advertisement and we believe some preconceptions about fair trade'.

Also during the G8 Summit in 2005, each delegate found a Divine Gift in their bedrooms and thousands of members of the world's media also received a Divine package with an information pack. Being able to provide a list of major supermarkets where Divine was stocked was important for journalists, campaigners and consumers. Bruce Crowther, Head of the Fairtrade Towns campaign at the Fairtrade Foundation commented: 'Being able to tell young people and adults that Divine and Dubble Fairtrade Chocolate are available in the local supermarkets was a huge advantage in ensuring our fairtrade campaign was practical and credible'.

This last point demonstrates how the mainstream and the alternative high street can be mutually supportive. Charlotte Borger (Head of Communications) from Divine is convinced that 'Without competing in the mainstream, gaining press coverage would have been a real challenge'. Thus, by competing in the mainstream, Divine has managed to secure mainstream media coverage on television, radio and in leading newspapers and magazines.

The media features focus on Divine's unique farmer ownership model, producers and the 'bean to bar' story. Strong (1996) identifies communicating the human element of sustainability as one of the key challenges for fair trade companies. From the evidence, it could be argued that Divine is an exemplar in how to do just that.

It is also worth noting that Divine does not just limit itself to the mainstream press, but also targets ethical titles (*Ethical Consumer* and *New Consumer*), political titles (*New Statesman, New Internationalist* and *Parliamentary Brief*), religious press (*Church Times*), SE magazines (*The Big Issue*), local and regional titles, youth (*Sugar Magazine*) and African titles (such as *The African Times*). This radical approach to the media tends to support the earlier work done by Strong (1997), who proposed that media interest is key in developing fair trade brands. Such broad media coverage allows Divine to speak to a wider audience in greater depth and so build the Divine and Dubble brands. According to Charlotte Borger (Head of Communications) at Divine, 'Journalists would often go out and shop in supermarkets to see if they could find Divine before covering the story'.

Divine's success in communicating the transformative message of fair trade is further evidence that it has not limited itself to the price and quality message, which, Lowe and Davenport (2005b) argue, is a danger that can come from being in the mainstream. It appears that radical mainstreaming companies such as Divine are able to maintain the transformative message of trade while competing in the mainstream. The Chair of Divine, Sandy Balfour summarizes by explaining that:

> Having fair trade brands in the mainstream allows you to talk to more people in greater depth about FT. Our brand puts farmer ownership at the centre of our values; being in the mainstream allows you to develop the message and protect from pretenders. The fact you are competing in the mainstream also attracts mainstream partners, such as the UK charity Comic Relief. Our partnership with Comic Relief has delivered a TV advertising campaign on Nickelodeon TV and a schools education pack on FT for 15,000 schools in the UK.

(Continued)

(Continued)

Despite Divine's success in the mainstream market, part of its strategy is also focused on the alternative high street. According to Lowe and Davenport (2005b), this is where social action and ethically based consumption are combined. The alternative high street can exist in virtual or physical space, providing a way to protect the integrity of fair trade while continuing to develop sales. They also propose examples of the alternative high street, including fair trade towns, universities and so on. Fair trade towns are localized, grass roots campaigns that work towards concrete targets to raise awareness and sales of fair trade items across the UK (Around, 2006).

Lowe and Davenport (2005b) also refer to the literature on the 'new dominant logic of marketing' (Vargo and Lusch, 2004) to explain that the alternative high street is another way to think about the cocreation of value by producers, retailers and consumers.

A few examples of Divine's own alternative high street include the following.

- A fair trade fan club called Dubble Agents, which was set up in 2001. It now has over 50,000 members, all of whom have signed up, via the Dubble website (www.dubble.co.uk), to change the world, 'chunk by chunk'. Being a Dubble Agent gives young people the opportunity to access information and downloadable tools to undertake fair trade.
- Divine's work in 15,000 schools with Comic Relief to develop consumer citizens by launching the Papapaa education pack.
- By 2002, distribution via over 400 Oxfam high street retail outlets and the Traidcraft fair trade catalogue.

Despite Divine's success in the mainstream, it is important to note that alternative trading organizations (ATOs) – that is, the alternative high street – account for a significant portion of Divine and Dubble's branded chocolate sales. For example, sales through ATOs such as Oxfam and Traidcraft showed a 60 per cent growth in 2006/2007. Also, Oxfam shops stock the entire Divine range. In the mainstream, only the UK multiple supermarkets Tesco, Waitrose, Sainsbury's and Co-operative Food stock more than one Divine flavour. Hence, Oxfam shops provide a very useful test market for Divine's products.

These findings show that Divine has a good range of customers on both the alternative high street and in the mainstream and that these can be complimentary. Success via the alternative high street also counterbalances some of the risks associated with competing in the mainstream. The case of Divine provides a good example of a blended approach to both social and conventional marketing.

The blend of social and conventional marketing practised by Divine provides valuable lessons for other SEs competing in the mainstream or trying to change people's behaviour and attitudes. Divine also provides an example of the blended approach to marketing proposed by Golding and Peattie (2005) that we looked at earlier.

Due to the emphasis on stakeholder partnerships in the definitions of SE, relationship marketing also has potential for SEs. This will be explored next.

RELATIONSHIP MARKETING

The more recent developments in marketing theory have sought to explain how tangible resources are being replaced by the intangible competences of knowledge, technology and relationships (Barney, 1991; Davenport and Prusak, 2000; Gronroos, 2000; Hamel and Prahalad, 1994; Nonaka and Takeuchi, 1995; Porter, 2001; Rayport and Jaworski, 2003; Srivastava et al., 2001). The focus in this section is thus on relationships and relationship marketing. Hastings (2007: 290) highlights how the SE Quit & Save approached the promotion aspect of its marketing campaign by favouring the benefits of relationship marketing over more conventional promotion tools to communicate the benefits of quitting smoking. As discussed earlier, changes in marketing orientation have also seen a paradigm shift from transactional to relationship marketing.

The Chartered Institute of Marketing has previously (CIM, 2007) defined marketing as the 'management process responsible for identifying, anticipating and satisfying customer requirements profitably'. This is closely aligned to transactional marketing and relies heavily on reference to the marketing mix – a combination of marketing inputs that affect customer motivation and behaviour, which traditionally include four controllable variables: product, price, promotion and place. However, as services marketing theory has evolved, this list has subsequently been extended to 7Ps, as we saw earlier, with additional attention being given to:

- *people*   the attitude, skills and behaviour of all staff need to be consistent with the organization's mission and marketing;

- *process*   an element of service that sees the customer experiencing an organization's offering, for example delivering a training seminar;

- *physical evidence*   the material part of a service – for example, the packaging, website, business cards and so on.

Gronroos's (2006) redefinition of marketing, given on p. 139, encapsulates the concepts of relationship marketing and clearly has implications for the way in which organizations operate in respect of the function of marketing, and changes in the business landscape have triggered the CIM (2007) to also rethink their definition so as to better reflect business and society today. Whilst not yet fully ratified the proposed new definition, given earlier on p. 140, does acknowledge the importance of relationships and the emergent role of SEs in this landscape.

Relationship management has much potential for SEs. Eagan (2004) argues that trust and commitment are the building blocks of successful relationship management partnerships. Golding and Peattie (2005) argue that perhaps the marketing of fair trade SEs is closest to the true spirit of relationship management as it is based on equity, openness and mutual benefit. The relationship management paradigm emphasizes the importance of other stakeholder relationships in addition to buyer/seller exchanges (Eagan, 2004; Gummesson, 1997; Hunt and Morgan, 1994).

Until recently, the use of ethics and social resources to build exchange relationships has not been the focus of attention. However, Murphy et al. (2007) propose that relationship marketing has a definable ethical basis. They argue that establishing, sustaining and reinforcing relationships is based on the virtues of trust, commitment and diligence. The establishment of trust and continued diligence leads to commitment in the relationship. Their model also proposes a number of supporting virtues, including fairness, integrity, empathy and respect. Murphy et al. also point out the need to use their model to test whether or not branding can be better connected with trust. This perhaps highlights the value of ethics in enabling SEs to compete via relationship marketing. Ed Miliband (2007), former Third Sector Government Minister, argues for SEs to compete on the basis of ethical values (see Chapter 2, section on definitions of social enterprise). Relationship marketing could provide a way to operationalize these ethical values.

Eagan (2004) suggests that older definitions of relationship marketing focused mainly on the traditional supplier–customer relationship. However, by the end of the 1990s, he argues, there was a growing consensus that, in addition to the customer focus, a company should be considering a range of partnerships with suppliers, internal customers, institutions and intermediaries (Clarkson et al., 1997: 173). In this respect, relationship marketing is similar to the much older stakeholder theory (Tzokas and Saren, 2000: 6). The common theme in the literature on relationship marketing is that firms should compete through the development of long-term relationships with all their stakeholders to develop partnerships. A number of authors identify four major groupings of partnerships, including customer partnerships (intermediates or final consumer), internal partnerships (business units, employees and so on), external partnerships (government, non-profitmaking organizations, competitors, alliances, knowledge relationships) and supplier partnerships (goods and service suppliers). This development in theory and practice offers a potential competitive approach for SEs. Stakeholder management is proposed by some as a defining feature of this business form (see the beginning of Chapter 2).

We have taken the Divine case study in both this chapter (Exhibit 6.2) and in Exhibit 2.2 and used an adapted form of Eagan's (2004: 127) diagrammatic representation to analyse the core firm and its relationships, shown in Figure 6.3. We will look at these relationships in more depth later in this chapter.

It can be argued that both transaction and relationship marketing have their place and, indeed, elements of both may be required in some circumstances. Bund Jackson (1985) positioned customers as existing on a spectrum ranging from lost-for-good (customers for whom changing supplier would be difficult and costly, but, once they changed, it would be difficult to get them back) to always-a-share (customers who may buy from you, but could just as easily buy from your competitors and be likely to buy from both of you on different occasions).

This spectrum could then be used to ensure that the appropriate strategy was used, such as relationship marketing for buyers near the lost-for-good end of the spectrum or transactional marketing for buyers near the always-a-share end of the spectrum. For customers in intermediate positions on the spectrum, intermediate approaches could be used.

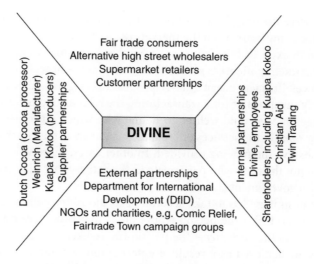

Figure 6.3   Divine Chocolate Ltd and its relationships

Corviello and Brodie (1998), through their research into marketing practices and attitudes to relationship marketing in 145 Canadian and New Zealand SMEs, support Bund Jackson's (1985) approach. They highlight three implications for managers:

- they need to understand the expansive nature of the concepts associated with both relational and transactional marketing;

- they should probe for the true relationship needs of their particular customer base;

- they must recognize the characteristics of their particular environmental context and understand how they may affect marketing practices and customer relationships.

It seems that relationship marketing theory, which at first evolved as a reaction to, and was seen as the antithesis of, transactional marketing theory is now being thought of as complementary to it or at least that there is a place for both disciplines to make a contribution to marketing strategy and practice.

Accepting the view that relationship and transactional marketing are complementary, to illustrate how SEs can combine them in practice, next we look at each of Divine Chocolate's stakeholders grouping (shown in Figure 6.3) in the light of the theory on partnerships and transactional marketing to illustrate the potential of such a complimentary approach for SEs.

Customer relationships

It may well have been that early followers of transactional marketing theory paid scant regard to 'customer relations' and an emphasis on the 4Ps assumed the product and its characteristics were the only factors to be considered in making a sale. This has not been the case for many years. Even the marketing mix theory was extended – not only by the addition of extra Ps but also so as to emphasize customers and their expectations. Now all marketing theorists place the customer at the heart of marketing strategies and practices. In fact, Eagan (2004) proposes that good-quality products and services are only the qualifier for a transaction – the relationship is the enabler.

The challenge for SEs could well be to define who/which customer to relate to. It may be that, for *some* of the services offered, the customers actually participate in or at least directly observe them being provided. In other cases, those who are purchasing the services are not the ones who participate in the activity that they are buying, such as contracts with government agencies.

The marketing strategy *has* to take account of relationships with both the *client* (or consumer of the service) – the person whose life is improved because of the service provided – and with the *customer* – the person (more likely the organization) whose own objectives are achieved as a result of entering into a contract with the SE. It is unlikely that the SE would be able successfully to complete its contractual commitments to the customer (outputs and outcomes) if good customer relationships with both clients and frontline colleagues in *partner* organizations were not developed and sustained. In the case of Divine, the initial customers include:

- multiple supermarkets;
- wholesalers;
- coffee shop chains;
- Oxfam Retail;
- catalogue companies, such as Traidcraft PLC;
- food service companies that distribute to workplace restaurants, student union shops and so on.

However, the person who actually consumes Divine Chocolate is the consumer, particularly ethical consumers.

The combining of both relational and transactional management approaches is illustrated by interview feedback from some of Divine's customers. For example, one leading supermarket retailer specifically mentioned the impressive quality of Divine Dark (which has a 70 per cent cocoa content): 'Divine Dark is one of our strongest-performing plain chocolate products, the recipe is excellent'. Combining both a RM and TM approach is illustrated by interview feedback with some of Divine's customers. A supermarket buyer explained, 'the quality of the Divine range as a whole is very good. Also, as far as the packaging is concerned, I think its eye catching' (this data is taken from Twin Trading's report, 2008).

In addition, the importance of Divine's relationships is shown by the comment of a senior executive from Co-op (Doherty, 2008): 214.

> the relationship is a real partnership with Divine Chocolate. We both have a shared vision and a shared ownership perspective on

key issues. Discussions are easier and there is a greater degree of flexibility in the relationship in comparison to the major players, which actually means the relationship between the Co-op and Divine is stronger. For example, the relationship with the major players is based on the need to make more money. With Divine it is a different level of relationship. Of course there is a need to make money, but what we are doing together is much broader than just making money.

This relationship between Divine Chocolate and the Co-operative Food Group is the subject of a research paper (Doherty, 2008), as mentioned earlier. The paper investigates the conversion of Co-op's own-label chocolate to 100 per cent fair trade. It was in 2002, that the Co-operative Food Retail Executive Committee decided to make this significant strategic move, switching its entire own-label block chocolate range to being made using 100 per cent fair trade-sourced cocoa. This is a large contract and shows the value of SEs partnering with the private sector.

Networking

Networks in marketing are central to relationship marketing theory. Gumesson (1997) believed that this was one of the ways in which the theory differed from earlier ideas about marketing, which dealt primarily with competition. Instead, the theory stresses collaboration, whereby all parties take responsibility for ensuring a functional relationship.

It could be argued that elements of networking are important for SEs because of the opportunities they offer as an output from the many hours they often invest in networking.

Active engagement with a wide range of networks – which may include existing and potential customers as well as competitors, at local, subregional, regional and national levels – can ensure good, up-to-date intelligence about the markets in which an SE functions. Also, it is an approach to building relationships with key external partners.

The key connections in Divine's value network are shown in Figure 6.4. Development of the company is guided by its board of directors, drawn from five organizations with strong commitments to Divine's social mission. While difficult to quantify, the value of the board's experience and guidance in shaping overall strategy and particular policies has been critical to the development of Divine's reputation as a good corporate citizen.

Divine's credibility is reinforced by Kuapa Kokoo's commitment to social and ethical business practices. For example, Kuapa invests its social premiums in sustainable development projects to enhance the long-term viability of farming communities. Similarly, it has a democratic governance structure and is committed to balanced gender participation in its management (that is, it actively promotes the development of female managers).

Beyond the immediate ownership structure, external organizations that Divine chooses to do business with are carefully considered in terms of their commitment to socially responsible business. For instance (as shown in Figure 6.4), only cocoa processors approved by the Fairtrade Labelling Organization (FLO) are used.

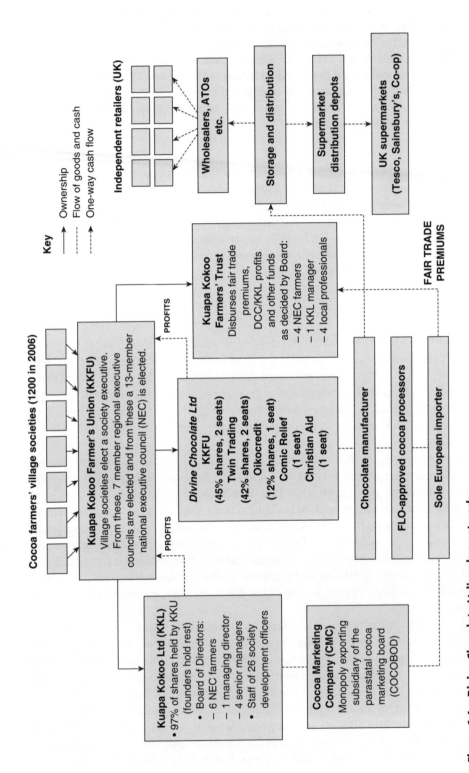

Figure 6.4   Divine Chocolate Ltd's value network

In Divine's marketing and distribution, associations between organizations with similar social commitments has resulted in synergistic benefits for both parties. For example, in November 1999, Divine launched a promotion with Sainsbury's supermarkets and Christian Aid supporters that involved a special feature in the Christian Aid Action mailing, accompanied by a 20p price reduction coupon, only redeemable in Sainsbury's stores. This resulted in an unusually high redemption rate of 6.2 per cent, persuading Sainsbury's to increase the distribution of Divine from 70 of its stores to 343. Similarly, development of the Dubble Fairtrade Chocolate brand (aimed at promoting fair trade among young people) involved awareness raising efforts with Comic Relief.

Of course, participating in networks has other advantages. Relationships are established with existing and potential customers and a level of familiarity, trust and recognition of professional competence may lead to commissioned or negotiated contracts and invitations to tender.

The value of building relationships with external partners such as government departments can also be of significant value for SEs. In 2000, the Department for International Development (DFID) guaranteed a bank loan to Divine Chocolate Ltd for £400,000 as part of it poverty alleviation programme in Ghana. It was the first time this financial instrument had been used. It was a good example of joined-up government, where the DFID worked with the DTI's small business analytical unit to assess the risk and then signed off the guarantee through the Ghana desk.

Internal partnerships

Marketing exists everywhere the customer has the opportunity to consider whether the company is doing a good job or not. Relationship marketing theory suggests that it is just as important to embrace the concept of internal marketing as the external kind – all staff are part-time marketers, Gummesson (1997). This approach works to build internal partnerships.

What must be done to ensure that all staff embrace the concept of relationship marketing and make a continuous and effective commitment to it?

Corviello and Brodie (1998) found that getting commitment to marketing from staff was difficult in larger organizations as there is a relatively high turnover of staff and the customer base is large and distant. Maybe by their very nature (to benefit multiple stakeholders) and their average size, SEs are in an advantageous position to elicit this kind of commitment from staff.

Some commentators have identified the possibility that use of the language of marketing may inhibit staff commitment to being part-time marketers (Gummeson, 1997; Laing and McKee, 2001). However, where there is ownership of the service delivery process and the activities are couched in terms of quality initiatives rather than being presented as marketing activities, then there is a general embracing of them (Laing and McKee, 2001).

SEs with flat structures – such that all core employees share in the responsibility for the future direction of the company and implementation of mutually agreed policies and initiatives – will surely be able to harness the benefits of such a commitment.

Some literature suggests that successful marketing will not necessarily require that companies dedicate a whole department to this and only this function and, indeed, doing so may not be a good way to deliver marketing – it may best be implemented where one person or a group of people within the organization act as marketing champions (Payne, 1991) or provide leadership. For SEs, it may be that they do not have the resources to establish a marketing department or even employ a dedicated staff member. In such instances, serious consideration needs to be given to how such leadership could be incorporated into the functioning of a company.

SEs' employees and volunteers are often passionate about the work they are doing, so internal marketing approaches would appear to have significant potential. Employee ownership (see Eaga Partnership in Exhibit 2.2, Chapter 2) and joint ownership with producer groups (Divine, Cafédirect and Agrofair) are examples of unique approaches to engaging employees in the same social mission. Employee ownership – a form of SE – is a significant force: the Employee Ownership Association reports this group of enterprises to be worth £20 billion annually (www.employeeownership.co.uk).

Supplier partnerships

The existence of trading partnerships is not new. Prior to the industrial revolution, an environment of limited legislation prevailed, which meant that trust when trading with others was key in developing relationships (Sheth and Parvatiyar, 1995: 403). However, the growth and formalization of mass market distribution resulted in traditional relationships between traders in the distribution chain becoming strained. As a result, marketers accepted a more transactional approach. Payne et al. (1995) argue that transactional marketing can be adversarial and shows a short-term focus on the single sale rather than an orientation towards customer retention, as in relationship marketing. Such a focus on the short term appears to be prevalent in commodity supply chains. According to Tiffen (2002), there is significant disconnect between smallholder farmers and consumers in commodity supply chains.

It is argued that the conventional trading model for cash crops is harmful to the interests of smallholder farmers and exploits their weaknesses, such as illiteracy and distance from urban centres. Tiffen (2002) suggests that farmers' needs and the right to a sustainable economic return for their labour are not respected. The value in such supply chains is concentrated downstream, with the manufacturer and the retailer.

The conventional trade of cash crops involves various middlemen, processors, manufacturers, retailers and consumers. Barratt Brown (2007) reports that these middlemen are sometimes known locally by farmers as coyotes, jackals or piranhas.

According to Barratt Brown (2007), there is a need to establish a more direct relationship with farmers in such supply chains. This is a challenge, however, as giant corporations are often both the traders and the processors, controlling, between them, 85–90 per cent of the market in each commodity, giving them the opportunity to control stocks.

Thus far in the relationship marketing literature, upstream supply chain partnerships are sought to achieve the desired quality and reduce costs. Downstream partnerships with customers to cocreate value are deemed desirable as a better route to improved product development and targeting (Prahalad and Ramaswamy, 2004; Leavy, 2004; Stabel and Fjeldstad, 1998).

The priority afforded to downstream actors (especially final consumers) reflects the disciplinary commitments to the market orientation ideology embraced by both marketing and, in the guise of the 'positioning school', strategy. It also reflects the governance structures prevailing in many Western countries (where the revised theory is under development). That is to say, revised models of value creation have so far implicitly accepted a particular distribution of the created value that is more consistent with profit-maximizing business models than anything else. SEs, however, can challenge the priority afforded to downstream actors.

SEs such as Divine, Cafédirect, Agrofair, Liberation and so on confront this reality by making farmers equity owners in fair trade-branded propositions downstream in the supply chain. These fair trade companies also make direct links with producer groups, usually cooperatives, and work with them as equity partners. The SEs operate a strong fair trade approach by:

- working proactively in partnership with smallholder cooperatives and other similar associations;

- making advance payments to farmers;

- paying the minimum fair trade price – above in some cases;

- paying a social premium to invest in community projects, such as boring water wells to supply clean water, medical care projects, income-generating projects and educational initiatives;

- on top of this, pay producer support and development monies based on a percentage of branded sales – this money is invested in producer groups to build organizational capacity, improve agronomy practices, product quality and environmental management, the ultimate goal being to strengthen the supply chain.

These fair trade SEs, such as Cafédirect and Divine, appear to provide a new form of supplier partnership based on strong ethical commitments. In the case of Divine, it is a unique farmer ownership model (Kuapa Kokoo have 47 per cent equity ownership), providing a contrast to conventional trade. The purchase of Kuapa Kokoo cocoa beans by Divine Chocolate, the social premium and the producer support and development monies are reported in Table 6.1.

In addition to the three income streams to Kuapa Kokoo, Divine also, in April 2007, announced its first dividend payment of £500 a share, equivalent to £47,379, paid to Kuapa Kokoo. This fourth income stream is due to the unique farmer ownership model that SEs such as Divine have pioneered. This approach to building partnerships to strengthen supply chains at the upstream part offers new thinking for relationship marketing. This could be of potential benefit to other SEs that have strong relationships in communities. Perhaps SEs such as Divine also provide Murphy et al. (2007) with the case studies they call for to illustrate an ethical basis to relationship marketing.

Another potential extension of relationship marketing theory that could have potential for SEs is the work of Alexander and Nicholls (2006) on consumer–producer relationships. Conventional marketing and relationship marketing do not look at the consumer–producer relationship – they look at customer loyalty from the retailer–consumer perspective and not really at all at multiple relationships or even the relationships that exist from the producer to the consumer via the retailer.

Table 6.1 The financial impact on Kuapa Kokoo of partnership with Divine

Year	Tonnes of cocoa	Fairtrade price ($)	Social premium ($)	Producer support and development (£)
2004/05	996	$1,593,600	$149,400	£107,426
2005/06	1165	$1,864,000	$174,750	£179,000
2006/07	1420	$2.272,000	$213,000	£214,000

Source: Divine annual report, 2008

Alexander and Nicholls (2006) argue that consumers search for connection and involvement as part of a developing consumer marketing network in which the consumption value of goods is partly defined by the links they generate with producers (Cova, 1997). They also say that this desire for connection is apparent in high-involvement purchases, such as fair trade products. Their work suggests that we need a deeper conceptualization of marketing networks to understand the consumer producer relationship. A central theme of Divine Chocolate Ltd's marketing communications is the 'bean to bar' story, which has connected both consumers and producers in addition to other stakeholders. According to Alexander and Nicholls (2006), this flow of information is strengthened by product quality and the assurances provided by the Fairtrade Mark certification. The flow of information in the networks is driven by concepts of social capital and solidarity (Putnam 2000). The value of social capital to SEs is discussed further in Chapter 7.

The potential for SEs to develop strong relationships built on trust and loyalty with stakeholders has significant potential in terms of developing a competitive position. Next, we will now look at the potential of branding for SEs.

BRANDING FOR SEs

Despite the anti-brand media lobby, brands are part of our everyday lives. The SE Bulky Bobs, based in Liverpool and part of the FRC Group (www.frcgroup.co.uk), is recognized by local residents and is part of the city' daily life, collecting domestic furniture for renovation in partnership with Liverpool City Council. For some organizations in the social economy, though, the term brand is associated with the private sector and can have negative meanings for them.

In this section, we propose that developing brands can, in fact, be a source of competitive advantage for SEs. For example, Cafédirect, in the Millward and Brown 2007 survey of 2000 global brands, was ranked number one as the most recommended brand (Cafédirect, 2007).

What is a brand?

A brand can be defined as 'a name, term, symbol, design or combination of all' (Aaker, 1997; Keller, 1993). It is agreed by many marketing academics that a brand serves two functions: identification and differentiation. It is also acknowledged that a brand can be differentiated on a tangible (product quality) or intangible level (relationships with stakeholders)'. Numerous brand experts offer a consumer-orientated definition of a brand, such as that given by Franzen and Bouwman (2001: 127):

> **Brands are not found in the factory or the studio, the sales channels or the supermarket shelves – not even on the television screen. You only find them in the minds of consumers.**

A brand is not a name, logo or advertising slogan; a brand is a person's dominant perception when the *stimulus* of a name, logo or slogan is presented. A brand, in short, is a reputation that develops most durably from customers' actual consumption experiences (Berry and Lampo, 2004).

Chiagouris (2005) describes two key brand elements that consumers need to see from SEs' brands. The first is the unique selling proposition (USP), which often reflects – in this case – what the brand will do for others. The second is the reason to believe (RTB), which builds the case for high credibility of such social brands.

These things are very important if you consider that Lafferty, Goldsmith and Newell (2002) show there is a growing body of evidence strongly supporting the view that positive corporate image is positively correlated to purchase intention. They propose that consumers discriminate between firms and their product/service offerings based on trustworthiness and expertise. Lafferty et al. (2002) also argue that corporate credibility plays a crucial role in creating partnerships and securing loan finance.

Why are brands important?

First of all, a brand offers ease of identification and allows the customer/consumer to lower their own search costs and perception of risk. However, more importantly for SE brands, they can take on personal meanings, giving the consumer the ability to express something about themselves. A brand, therefore, has the potential to enrich the life of a consumer (Keller, 1993). The value of a brand – known as brand equity – can be thought of in different ways:

- financial – impact on the balance sheet;
- strength of the consumer's attachment to the brand;
- a description of the associations and beliefs a consumer has about the brand (brand image) or even organizational associations.

Keller (1993: 3) defines brand image as being 'the perceptions about a brand as reflected by the associations held in the consumer memory'. He divides brand associations into three categories:

- attributes;
- benefits;
- attitudes.

Attributes are the descriptive features that characterize a brand. They can include price information, quality, packaging, user imagery and usage.

Benefits can be subdivided into three kinds. The first is the functional benefits, such as taste. The second is the symbolic benefits, with its more extrinsic advantages and often relate to non-product attributes, which could be important for SE brands. Third is the experiential benefits, which are what it feels like to use the brand.

Attitudes – the highest level of brand associations – are defined as the overall evaluations of a brand.

Keller (1993: 9) argues that attitudes 'form the basis of actions and behaviour which consumers take with the brand'. Brand experts further explain that brand attitudes can be related to beliefs about product-related attributes and symbolic benefits. This could have potential for SE brands, which have loyal customers and consumers.

Research into fair trade SE brands highlights the importance of loyalty. One supermarket buyer explains that Divine Chocolate has a loyal consumer base: 'Divine is actually about half way in terms of our performance ranking and that's completely driven by the fact that it has a very loyal consumer' (interview with supermarket trading manager). Perhaps the ethical dimensions to SEs can explain this loyalty to the Divine brand.

Ethical dimensions of brands

Hoffler and Keller (2002) assert that ethical marketing programmes can build brand equity by building brand awareness, establishing brand credibility, evoking brand feelings, enhancing brand image and creating a sense of brand community.

The importance of ethical dimensions to consumers is demonstrated by the growth in such markets. The Co-operative Bank's ethical purchasing index of 2005 reported that ethical consumerism in UK markets is worth £29.3 billion per year. Spending on ethical food (organic, fair trade and free-range) was up by 18 per cent to £5.4 billion. A further £11.6 billion was accounted for by ethical finance, up from £10.6 billion in the previous year.

The importance of ethical dimensions is also evidenced by recent research on the fair trade brands Cafédirect and Divine. Supermarket buyers were interviewed to find out to what extent these two brands competed in highly competitive markets. One supermarket buyer explained, 'I think the ethics behind Divine is what makes the quality different and, as I say, the consumers do feel that they are doing something for the world outside.' When asked to expand further to explain what was meant by ethics, the buyer replied, 'I think going back to the farmers and the countries where it's coming from, that they feel that they are giving a fair trade, you know a fair wage out to the people who are actually producing it.'

This suggests the potential of consumer – producer connections for developing the credibility of social brands. Some also posit that growth in consumer awareness and demand for fair trade products is driven by the interaction of a number of political, academic, cultural and informational influences, with informational and cultural influences being the strongest (Comfort and Jones, 2003; Nicholls, 2002). Shaw et al. (2006) also highlights the importance of political aspects and argues that buying fair trade items allows consumers to make statements about themselves.

A number of authors have proposed that the growth of ethical brands is due to the rise in ethical consumption. However, this chapter is not about ethical consumption and other authors have covered this topic extremely well (see Harrison et al., 2005). That said, we do need to highlight its potential here.

A range of authors (Harrison et al., 2005; Shaw et al., 2006; Tallontire et al., 2001) researched fair trade purchasing behaviour in the grocery shopping environment. Key findings include the importance of labelling on the products, together with appropriate information, product availability, religious beliefs and the belief of individuals that real change can be created as a result of individual consumption choices.

Shaws et al.'s (2006) work looks at the link between behaviour and belief and proposes a range of key themes emerging from their research:

- consumption of fair trade products displays to the rest of society an aspect of one's personality and identity;
- consumers are curious and interested in exploring new grocery products;
- buying fair trade products to change people's lives for the better is an ethical obligation;
- a way to correct social injustice.

Doherty and Meehan (2006: 307) also propose that 'social and ethical credibility are now viable bases for differentiation and competitive positioning in mainstream consumer markets.'

There is a growing realization that SE brands need to identify the triggers that are most effective in encouraging consumers to act on their ethical concerns. Central to the development of SE brands is the need to learn from the early success of fair trade brands as a result of increased consumer education and innovative marketing approaches as these approaches build brands and create a set of ethical values.

Soper (2004) proposes the existence of citizen consumers who choose, where possible, both fair trade and more environmentally friendly products due to not only the intrinsic pleasures the products bring but also their wider long-term social and environmental benefits. Varney (2002) supports this view and explains that consumer citizens act beyond their interests as consumers and take responsibility for long-term considerations beyond themselves.

The rise of ethical purchasing behaviour has brought with it notions of consumer responsibility. Seyfang (2004) proposes that consumption is an expression of citizenship. In this context, notions of consumer citizenship have become important, say Lang and Gabriel (2005). These authors propose that contemporary consumer citizenship possesses two distinct elements: an ethical consumer element and the concept of a consumer of public services. A number of authors (Parker, 1999; Urry, 1995) argue that the consumer acts not only as a purely economic agent or a purely political agent but as a hybrid of the two: as a consumer citizen whose identity, belief and practice is brought to bear via the market.

As a result of these developments, brands built on consistent ethical values could be attractive in terms of consumer citizenship. Brands need to be carefully managed to build this credibility, with people in different parts of the SE referring to the same statements about what makes their brand unique. Developing brand descriptors and agreeing the key brand values is thus an important part of this approach. It can be achieved by consulting internal and external stakeholders via market research. SEs developing brands must ensure that all literature and packaging is consistent with the brand. It is important to strictly adhere to the corporate house style of colours and logo. It is common for organizations to employ different printers for different products, merchandising materials and so on, so close attention needs to be paid to the consistency of the printing.

CONCLUSIONS

It is clear from the revisions to the definitions of marketing by both the CIM and the AMA that other stakeholders, such as the community, have become increasingly important. There is evidence that a stakeholder approach could be advantageous for SEs. This chapter supports Peattie and Morley's (2008) argument there is an under-researched potential for SEs to differentiate themselves along social and ethical dimensions to achieve competitive advantage.

Peattie and Morley (2008) also propose that SEs have a poor understanding of marketing mix elements, such as pricing and product dimensions (in particular, packaging). While this is perhaps true in general, there are some SEs – particularly fair trade SEs – that show a good understanding of these elements. Divine Chocolate, for example, has managed to blend social, relationship and conventional marketing, which has enabled them to compete in the highly competitive UK chocolate market.

This chapter has also illustrated the importance to SEs of developing a mission statement, that articulates the social/environmental objectives. First, it is the key to engaging with networks and partners that may share their social/environmental mission. Second, it is clearly an opportunity to communicate those values via a brand and the resulting marketing communications. This can lead to the creation of brand value via the ethical and trust dimensions associated with SEs.

The significant potential of social marketing for SEs has been clearly demonstrated. It has enabled a number of transformations in society – for example, quitting smoking. SEs often work to provide new solutions and transform markets and associated attitudes, so social marketing could be used to change attitudes to health and diet, recycling, energy use and so on. To develop such an approach, at a tactical level, it is important to be ambitious, consistent and clear in all marketing communications. Having such a clear social marketing strategy enables SEs to form networks with other organizations that are eager to see the same shift in behaviour and thinking.

We also looked at the value of developing a relationship marketing approach as a source of competitive advantage. Relationship marketing does not imply the adoption of a prescriptive approach in order to guarantee success. Rather, we have recommended developing a relationship marketing approach within the marketing planning process. The first step for any SE is to recognize the importance of stakeholders. During the situation analysis (audit) phase of the marketing planning process map, SEs should map their key stakeholders. An assessment of how effective the relationships with their key stakeholders are should be carried out. Also, as a key focus of relationship marketing is customer retention, an in-depth analysis of the nature of each kind of customer relationship should be implemented, which should be in addition to competitor profiling.

According to relationship marketing, the orientation should be towards cooperative rather than adversarial relationships. Therefore, SEs need to build structures to both manage and develop such long-term partnerships. Although much of relationship marketing theory has focused on the customer, SEs often work with socially excluded groups of people who are final service users or upstream suppliers, as in the case of fair trade producers. Utilizing this network of partnerships could be of significant value to SEs.

Finally, despite their often limited resources, we have shown how SEs can compete, calling on their ethical values (intangible elements) to develop a social marketing approach, a strong brand and an effective relationship marketing strategy.

REFERENCES

Interviews

Charlotte Borger, Head of Media Communications, Divine Chocolate Ltd, interviewed 2 April 2007, London.
Jonathan Smith, Head of Education Communications, Comic Relief, interviewed 6 March 2007, London.

Aaker, D. (1997) 'Should you take your brand to where the action is?', *Harvard Business Review*, September–October: 135–47.
Alexander, A. and Nicholls, A. (2006) 'Rediscovering consumer–producer involvement: a network perspective on fair trade marketing, *European Journal of Marketing*, 40 (11/12): 1236–53.
American Marketing Association (AMA) (2008) The American Marketing Association Releases New Definition of Marketing, 14 January 2008. [Accessed 9 April 2008: www.marketingpower.com/About AMA/Pages/PressRoom.aspx]
Andreasen, A. (1994) 'Social marketing: its definition and domain', *Journal of Public Policy and Marketing*, 13 (1): 108–14.
Andreason, A.R. (1995) *Marketing Social Change*. San Francisco, CA: Jossey-Bass.
Andreasen, A.R. (2002) 'Marketing social marketing in the social change marketplace', *Journal of Public Policy and Marketing*, 21 (1): 3–13.
Andreasen, A.R., Goodstein, R.C. and Wilson, J.W. (2005) 'Transferring "marketing knowledge" to the nonprofit sector', *California Management Review*, 47 (4): 46–67.
Around, E. (2006) *The Fairtrade Towns Initiative: Lessons from across the ocean*. Boston, MA: Oxfam America.
Bagozzi, R. (1975) 'Marketing as exchange', *Journal of Marketing*, 39 (October): 32–9.
Balfour, S. (2006) 'Chairman's report: The Day Chocolate Company annual report 2004–2005', Day Chocolate Company, London, p. 2.
Bandura, A. (1986) *Social Foundation of Thought and Action: A social cognitive approach*. Upper Saddle River, NJ: Prentice Hall.
Bandura, A. and Walters, R.H. (1963) *Social Learning and Personality Development*. New York: Holt.
Barney, J.B. (1991) 'Firm resources and sustained competitive advantage', *Journal of Management*, 17 (1): 99–120.
Barratt Brown, M. (2007) 'Fair trade with Africa', *Review of African Political Economy*, 112: 267–77.
Berry, L. and Lampo. S. (2004) 'Branding labour intensive services', *Business Strategy Review*, 15: 18–25.
Black Gold (2007) '*Black gold: Wake up and smell the coffee*', a film. More information at: www.myspace./blackgoldmovie
Blythman, J. (2004) '*Shopped: The shocking power of British supermarkets*'. London: HarperCollins.

Booms, B.H. and Bitner, M.J. (1981) 'Marketing strategies and organization structures for service firms', in J.H. Donnelly and W.R. George (eds), *Marketing of Services*. Chicago: American Marketing Association. pp. 47–52.

Bridle, C., Riemsma, R.P., Pattenden, J., Sowden, A.J., Matten, L., Watt, I.S. and Walker, A. (2005) 'Systematic review of the effectiveness of health behaviour interventions based on the transtheoretical model', *Psychology and Health*, 20 (3): 283–301.

Bund Jackson, B. (1985) 'Build customer relations that last', *Harvard Business Review*, 63 (9): 120–28.

Cafédirect (2007) 'Cafédirect PLC report and financial statements 2006/2007', Baker Tilly International. London.

Cafédirect (2008) 'Cafédirect PLC report and financial statements 2007', Baker Tilly International. London.

Chiagouris, L. (2005) 'Non profit brands come of age', *Marketing Management*, 14 (5): 30–3.

Chartered Institute of Marketing (CIM) (2007) Leading body calls for a new definition of marketing, 21 September 2007. [Accessed 10 December 2007: www.cim.co.uk/NewsAndEvents/MediaCentre/PressReleaseIndex.aspx]

Clarkson, R.M., Clarke-Hill, C. and Robinson, T. (1997) 'Towards a general framework for relationship marketing', a literature review paper presented at the Academy of Marketing's conference. Manchester.

Cova, B. (1997) 'Community and consumption: towards a definition of the linking value of product or services', *European Journal of Marketing*, 31 (3/4): 297–316.

Comfort, D. and Jones, P. (2003) 'Retailing fair trade food products in the UK', *British Food Journal*, 105 (11): 800–10.

Corviello, N.E. and Brodie, R.J. (1998) 'From transaction to relationship marketing: an investigation of managerial perceptions and practices', *Journal of Strategic Marketing*, 6: 171–86.

Davenport, Thomas H. and Prusak, Laurence (2000) *Working Knowledge: How Organizations manage what they know*. Boston, MA: Harvard Business School Press.

Department of Health (2004) '*Choosing health: making healthy choices easier*', Government White Paper, Department of Health. London. Available at: www.dh.gov.uk/en/Publicationsandstatistics/Publications/PublicationsPolicyAndGuidance/DH_4094550

Department for International Development (2006) 'Young Fairtraders from UK and Ghana present "Chocolate Challenge" manifesto to International Development Secretary', DfID News. London. Available online, accessed on 30 July 2006.

Deshpande, R. and Farley, J.U. (1998) 'Measuring market orientation: generalization and synthesis', *Journal of Market-focused Management*, 2: 213–332.

Divine (2008) 'Divine Chocolate Ltd: annual report, 2007–2008', Divine Chocolate Ltd. London.

Doherty, B. (2008) 'A truly co-operative venture: the case study of Co-operative Food – a retailer response to fair trade', *Journal of Strategic Marketing*, 16 (3): 331.

Doherty, B. and Meehan, J. (2006) 'Market entry based on social resources: the case of the Day Chocolate Company in the UK confectionery sector', *Journal of Strategic Marketing*, 14 (4).

Doherty, B. and Tranchell, S. (2007) 'Radical mainstreaming of fairtrade', special edition *Equal Opportunities International Journal in Culture and Diversity in Marketing*, 26 (7).

Eagan, J. (2004) *Relationship Marketing: Exploring relational strategies in marketing* (2nd edn). London: FT Prentice Hall.

Fairtrade Foundation (2008) 'Fairtrade Foundation annual review, Fairtrade Foundation. London.

Franzen, G. and Bouwman, M. (2001) *The Mental World of Brands, Mind, Memory and Brand Success*. Henley-on-Thames, Oxfordshire: WARC, UK, Admap Publications.

French, J. and Blair-Stevens, C. (2006) 'Social marketing national benchmark criteria', NSMC. London. Available at: www.nsms.org.uk (click on 'Resources, documents and presentations', then 'Leaflets and documents' and it is listed.)

Golding, K. and Peattie, K. (2005) 'In search of a golden blend: perspectives on the marketing of fair trade coffee', *Sustainable Development*, 13: 154–65.

Gronroos, C. (2000) *Service Management and Marketing: A customer relationship management approach*. Chichester: John Wiley and Sons.

Gronroos, C. (2006) 'On defining marketing: finding a new roadmap for marketing', *Marketing Theory*, 6 (4): 395–417.

Gummesson, E. (1997) 'Relationship marketing as a paradigm shift: some conclusions from the 30R approach', *Management Decision*, 3 (5/4): 267–72.

Hamel, G. and Prahalad, C.K. (1994) *Competing for the Future*. Boston, MA: Harvard Business School Press.

Harrison, R., Newholm, T. and Shaw, D. (2005) The *Ethical Consumer*. London: Sage.

Hastings, G. (2007) *Social Marketing: Why should the devil have all the best tunes*. Oxford: Butterworth-Heinemann.

Hastings, G., MacFayden, L. and Anderson, S. (2000) 'Whose behaviour is it anyway: the broader potential of social marketing', *Social Marketing Quarterly*, 1 (2): 46–58.

Hoffler, S. and Keller, K. (2002) 'Building brand equity through corporate societal marketing, *Journal of Public Policy and Marketing*', (1, spring) 21: 78–9.

Houston, F.S. and Gassenheimer, J. (1987) 'Marketing and exchange, *Journal of Marketing*, 51: 3–18.

Hunt, S.D. and Morgan, R.E. (1995) 'The comparative advantage theory of competition', *Journal of Marketing*, 59: 1–15.

Keller, L.K. (1993) 'Conceptualizing, measuring and managing customer-based brand equity', *Journal of Marketing*, 57 (1): 1–22.

Kholi, A.J. and Jaworski, B.J. (1990) 'Market orientation: the construct, research propositions and managerial implications', *Journal of Marketing*, April: 1–18.

King, P. (2004) 'Presentation given at the ICO Roundtable on Equitable Trading and the World Coffee Economy'. London.

Kotler, P. (1979) 'Strategies for introducing marketing into non-profit organizations', *Journal of Marketing*, 43: 37–44.

Kotler, P. and Levy, S. (1969) 'Broadening the concept of marketing', *Journal of Marketing*, 38 (January): 10–15.

Kotler, P. and Zaltman, G. (1971) 'Social marketing: an approach to planned social change', *Journal of Marketing*, 35 (3): 3–12.

Lafferty, B.A., Goldsmith, R.E. and Newell, S.J. (2002) 'The dual credibility model: the influence of corporate and endorser credibility on attitudes and purchase intentions', *Journal of Marketing Theory and Practice*, 10 (3): 1–12.

Laing, A. and McKee, L. (2001) 'Willing volunteers or unwilling conscripts?: professionals and marketing in service organizations', *Journal of Marketing Management*. 17: 559–75.

Lang, T. and Gabriel, Y. (2005) 'A brief history of consumer activism', in R. Harrison, T. Newholm and D. Shaw (eds), *The Ethical Consumer*. London: Sage. 39–53.

Lazer, W. and Kelley, E. (1973) *Social Marketing: Perspectives and viewpoints*. Homewood, IL: Irwin.

Leavy, B. (2004) 'Partnering with the customer', *Strategy and Leadership*, 32 (3): 10–13.

Levitt, T. (1960) 'Marketing myopia', *Harvard Business Review*, 38 (July/August): 24–47.

Lichtenstein, E. and Glasgow, R.E. (1992) 'Smoking cessation: what have we learned over the past decade?', *Journal of Consulting and Clinical Psychology*, 60: 518–27.

Lowe, W. and Davenport, E. (2005a) 'Postcards from the edge: maintaining the "alternative" character of fair trade', *Sustainable Development*, 13: 143–53.

Lowe, W. and Davenport, E. (2005b), 'Has the medium (roast) become the message?: The ethics of marketing fair trade in the mainstream', *International Marketing Review*, 22 (5): 494–511.

MacFayden, L., Stead, M. and Hastings, G. (2007) 'Social marketing' in M.J. Baker and S.J. Hart (eds), *The Marketing Book*, (6th edn.) Oxford: Butterworth-Heinemann.

McCarthy, E.J. (1960) *Basic Marketing: A managerial approach*. Homewood, IL: Irwin.

Miller, N.E. and Dollard, J. (1941) *Social Learning and Imitation*. New Haven, CT: Yale University Press.

Miliband, E. (2007) 'Foreword by the Minister of the Third Sector', *Social Enterprise Journal*, 3 (1).

Mintel (2008) 'UK coffee report', Mintel. London.

Moore, G. (2004) 'The fair trade movement: parameters, issues and future research', *Journal of Business Ethics*, 53 (1–2): 73–86.

Murphy, E.P., Laczniak, R.G. and Wood, G. (2007) 'An ethical basis for relationship marketing: a virtue ethics perspective', *European Journal of Marketing*, 41 (1/2): 37–57.

Narver, J.C. and Slater, S.F. (1990) 'The effect of a market orientation on business profitability', *Journal of Marketing*, Oct: 20–35.

Nicholls, A.J. (2002) 'Strategic options for fair trade retailing', *International Journal of Retail and Distribution Management*, 30 (1): 6–17.

Nicholls, A. and Opal, C. (2004) *Fair Trade: Market-driven ethical consumption*. London: Sage.

Nonaka, I. and Takeuchi, H. (1995) *The Knowledge-creating Company: How Japanese companies create the dynamics of innovation*. Oxford: Oxford University Press.

NSMC (2007) www.nsms.org.uk/

Parker, G. (1999) 'The role of the consumer-citizen in environmental protest in the 1990s', *Space and Polity*, 3 (1): 67–83.

Payne, A. (1991) *Relationship Marketing*. Oxford: Butterworth-Heinemann.

Payne, A., Christopherm, M. and Peck, H. (eds) (1995) *Relationship Marketing for Competitive Advantage; Winning and keeping customers*. Oxford: Butterworth-Heinemann.

Peattie, K. and Morley, A. (2008) 'Social enterprises: diversity and dynamics, contexts and contributions a research monograph', ESRC Centre for BRASS. Cardiff.

Piercy, N. (2002) *Market-led Strategic Change: A guide to transforming the process of going to market*. Oxford: Butterworth-Heinemann.

Porter, M. (1998) 'Clusters and the new economics of competition', *Harvard Business Review*, 76 (6): 77–90.

Porter, M.E. (2001) 'Strategy and the Internet', *Harvard Business Review*, 73 (March): 63–79.

Prahalad, C.K. and Ramaswamy, V. (2004) 'Co-creating unique value with customers', *Strategy and Leadership*, 32 (3): 4–9.

Prochaska, J.O. and DiClemente, C.C. (1982) 'Transtheoretical therapy toward a more integrative model of change', *Psychotherapy: Theory, Research and Practice*, 19 (3): 276–87.

Putnam, R. (2000) *Bowling Alone: The collapse and revival of American community*. New York: Simon & Schuster.

Rayport, J. and Jaworski, B.J. (2003) *e-commerce*. Maidenhead: McGraw-Hill.

Sargeant, A. (2005) *Marketing Management for Nonprofit Organizations* (2nd edn). New York: Oxford University Press.

Seyfang, G. (2004), 'Eco-warriors in the supermarket?: Evaluating the UK sustainable consumption strategy as a tool for ecological citizenship', CSERGE Working paper, EDM 04–07.

Shaw, D., Newholm, T. and Dickinson, R. (2006) 'Consumption as voting: an exploration of consumer empowerment', *European Journal of Marketing*, 40 (9/10): 1049–67.

Sheth, J.N. and Parvatiyar, A. (1995) 'The evolution of relationship marketing', *International Business Review*, 4 (4): 397–418.

Slater, S.F. and Narver, J.C. (1994) 'Market orientation, customer value and superior performance', *Business Horizons*, Mar/Apr: 22–8.

Soper, K. (2004) 'Rethinking the "good life": the consumer as citizen', *Capitalism Nature Socialism*, 15 (3): 115–16.

Srivastava, R.K., Fahey, L. and Christensen, H.K. (2001) 'The resource-based view and marketing: the role of market-based assets in gaining competitive advantage', *Journal of Management*, 27: 777–802.

Stabel, B. and Fjeldstad, Ø.D. (1998) 'Configuring value for competitive advantage: on chains, shops, and networks', *Strategic Management Journal*, 19 (5) 413–37.

Strong, C. (1996) 'Features contributing to the growth of ethical consumerism – a preliminary investigation', *Marketing Intelligence and Planning*, 14: 5–9.

Strong, C. (1997) 'The problems of translating fair trade principles into consumer purchase behaviour', *Marketing Intelligence and Planning*, 15 (1): 32–7.

Tallontire, A., Rentsendorj, E. and Blowfield, M. (2001) 'Ethical consumers and ethical trade: a review of current literature', Natural Resources Institute. Chatham.

Thackeray, R., Young, B., Neiger, L.B. and Hanson, L.C. (2007) 'Developing a promotional strategy: important questions for social marketing', *Health Promotion and Practice*, 8 (4): 332–6.

Tiffen, P. (1998) *The Day Chocolate Company: a commercial opportunity*. London.

Tiffen, P. (2002) 'A chocolate-coated case for alternative international business models', *Development in Practice*, 12 (3 & 4): 383–97.

Twin Trading (2008) 'Monitoring and evaluation report on Divine Chocolate in the UK confectionery market and on farmer livelihoods in Ghana', for the Department for International Development. London.

Tzokas, N. and Saren, M. (2000) 'Knowledge and relationship marketing: where, what and how?' 2nd WWW Conference on Relationship Marketing, 15–16 November 1999 15/11/99-15/2/00 Paper

Urry, J. (1995) *Consuming Places*. London: Routledge.

Vargo, S.L. and Lusch, R.F. (2004) 'Evolving to a new dominant logic for Marketing', *Journal of Marketing*, 68: 1–17.

Varney, R.V. (2002) *Marketing Communication: Principles and practice*. London: Routledge.

Wayman, J., Jennifer, J., Beall, T. and Thackeray, M.C. (2007) 'Competition: a social marketers' friend or foe?', *Health Promotion Practice*, 8 (2): 134–9.

Webster, F. (1988) 'The rediscovery of the marketing concept', *Business Horizons*, May/Jun: 29–39.

Webster, F. (1992) 'The changing role of marketing in the corporation', *Journal of Marketing*, 56: 1–17.

7

BUSINESS ETHICS AND SOCIAL ENTERPRISES

SCOPE

The purpose of this section is to provide a quick lead into how SEs connect with the business ethics agenda. It should be realized that business ethics – that is, ethics related to business situations – like any other branch of ethics, draws on a history of ethically related philosophical discourse spanning millennia. In the focus of discussion here, we are concerned with what is right and wrong in the context of business activities and decisions. Pedagogic experience indicates that the way to understand the meaning, nuances and usefulness of ethical theory is to apply it to real-life cases or instances from your own work life. To this end, cases of SEs are discussed in this chapter.

There are many situations in business in which ethical issues are encountered. These include a wide variety of considerations, which are quite often complex. The issues are concerned with the needs, rights and expectations of a range of internal and external stakeholders.

Brief reflection on business ethics reveals a range of issues and, on deeper analysis, a number of these can be seen to be interrelated. The issues include, for example, fair pay, the remuneration of business leaders compared to that of workers, gender, race, age and disability discrimination, treatment of trading partners, including the exploitation of suppliers, with fair trade as a specific aspect of the latter, equal operating standards in the global context of corporate entities and dealings with customers and clients, to name but a few. Also of particular importance to the considerations here are the inter- and intra-generational equity notions of sustainable development, expressed in social, economic and environmental dimensions. These strands point towards an analysis that addresses the maintenance and development of social, financial, human, manufactured and natural capital (Defourney and Nyssens, 2006; Elkington, 1997; Evers et al., 2004; Pearce, 2003; Porrit, 2005). The discussion below aims to show us the links between sustainable development and business ethics.

Considering sustainable development issues on a global scale, many would argue that, at this juncture in human development, we have arrived at a previously unexperienced crisis point. This crisis has several varied aspects, such a global issues, including, for example, global warming; the clash between Western and Eastern philosophies; the rapid resource take arising from the emergence of Chinese and Indian economies; globalization and the linked growing inequalities between the rich and poor and between the developed and developing worlds; current re-emphasis on food shortages for the rapidly expanding world population; and the current crisis in global financial markets.

It is axiomatic that these global forces have marked effects at the local level and for sustainable development in the local context. Our purpose here is to consider the activities of SEs and so our focus of attention is brought to sustainable development at this local level. Issues concerning the failures of the market system and the role of SEs in alleviating this were introduced in Chapter 1.

Regarding what sustainable development means at the local level, it is argued that it is created as a process deriving from stakeholders' interactions. In this it is apparent that, at the local level, it is a social construction (Rotheroe and Richards, 2007). It is a 'local reality' created by the stakeholders concerned. This stakeholder context at the level of the individual SE has particular resonance from the business ethics perspective and is discussed further below. Relevant ethical theories for consideration here might include, by way of example, ethics of duties, feminist ethics, ethics of rights and justice and virtue ethics.

Returning to the above brief reflection on the range of business issues that business ethics applies to, it is apparent that many of these business ethics issues apply to SEs in a similar way to how they apply to 'mainstream' business entities. However, a number of specific aspects surface when the operating context of SEs is considered. Some of these are emergent in character.

Interestingly, in this vein and as discussed further below, some issues arise concerning the often tense public sector–SE interface. In a number of cases, this is connected with the provision and distribution of welfare and the traditional view of top-down public services provision versus the emerging enabling view. It includes a consideration of what some would consider as dysfunctions at the public sector–SE interface in the client and commissioning relationship.

Concerning the application of business ethics, the theories of utilitarianism, duties and rights and justice, discussed further below, can be brought to bear here. The consideration of the public sector–SE interface is relevant to the matter of the public sector's failure in relation to service delivery. Here, resources that are innovative, residing in the social economy sector, are sought after.

In a related context, perceived public-sector failures to take account of feedback arising from practice in strategic policy development are relevant. One aspect of this is a slowness to understand what user participation in service delivery really means. A discussion of the Kantian ethics of duties is undertaken below as a result.

SUSTAINABLE DEVELOPMENT AS A FRAMEWORK FOR THE CONSIDERATION OF BUSINESS ETHICS IN SEs

Reflection on the inter- and intra-generational equity aspects of sustainable development usefully provides us with an explicit link to the discussion of ethical theory below.

This is perhaps particularly true of the ethics of rights and justice and of duties. It is also true of the stakeholder dialogue aspects, which are grounded in feminist ethical theory.

On how SEs are connected with sustainable development, as indicated, they are characterized strongly by the interrelationship of their activities with the social, environmental and economic notions of sustainable development. Shaw and Carter (2007) point to the positive impacts of SEs in this context and refer to the perception of commitment in the sector to community, place and capacity building. As discussed above, the meaning of this is expressed through the interaction of SEs with their internal and external stakeholders. Success in progressing towards sustainable development is indicated by the creation of a dialogue with stakeholders at different levels. Attention is on the primacy of the social aim and, within this, addressing the needs of a range of stakeholders. Via such stakeholder interaction, the reality of sustainable development can be locally derived and is a social construction – it is a local creation of reality (Rotheroe and Richards, 2007).

One key success factor in moving towards sustainable development is the adoption of innovation and new ways of working. A second important factor is the development of community, at various levels.

Innovation and new ways of working, are very relevant to all three elements of sustainable development – they embrace social, environmental and economic aspects (Hart and Milstein, 2003; Rotheroe et al., 2003). They apply in the business, social economy, and public sectors. Importantly for SEs, they also apply at the public sector–SE and business sector–SE interfaces. Arising from practice, it becomes clear that good-quality cross-sectoral stakeholder relationships at these interfaces can be an indicator of positive progress towards sustainable development and it is notable that the reverse position also applies. This aspect is taken up further below.

Clearly, for many SEs, it is their focus on a locality that produces the emphasis on community, the generation of social capital and capacitybuilding. Innovation and community are linked through SEs, activities in various ways. For example, as a result of:

- the creation of community interaction, social infrastructure and social inclusion;
- building on the local sense of place and space;
- linking recycling and other environmental initiatives to the achievement of wider social objectives;
- initiatives in community-based arts;
- initiatives to stimulate employment for disabled groups;
- transport initiatives;
- innovation in social housing and mixed development;
- initiatives for the unemployed;
- user participation in the delivery of range of health-related activities.

The exhortations of policymakers in relation to their views on the purposes of SEs provide clear indications that their stance is sought-after. In addressing social inequalities and environmental problems and improving public services, reference, by policymakers, is made to SEs providing innovative solutions (particularly by comparison to traditional public-sector approaches) to meeting the needs of their user groups. They are seen as vehicles for fair trade and improving on existing private-sector approaches to corporate responsibility. In the UK context, this is evidenced by the content of the DTI's (2002) 'Social enterprise; a strategy for success' and the OTS' (2006) 'Social enterprise action plan: scaling new heights'. In a wider policy context, these documents are intended to be linked explicitly to the drive for well-being through the social and environmental imperatives indicated in the UK's sustainable development strategy (DEFRA, 2005).

Considering sustainable development in a broader international context, it is perhaps interesting to reflect on fair trade in relation to 'The millennium development goals report' (UNDESA, 2007). The case study of fair trade and the Divine Chocolate Company given in Exhibit 7.2 later in the chapter is relevant here. It provides an illustration of the links between sustainable development and the ethics associated with intragenerational equity. It brings our attention to the ethics of duties and of rights and justice, discussed below.

CORPORATE SOCIAL RESPONSIBILITY AND BUSINESS ETHICS

It is useful to examine where some of the debates concerning 'mainstream business' stand in relation to business ethics. Current discussion of business ethics is substantially taking place in the global context and talks the language of globalization. This is discussed further below when we consider egoism. Part of the debate brings attention to the absence of regulation regarding the social responsibility of transnational corporations (TNCs) in the global system. Dicken (2007: 538) pinpoints this as follows:

> The major dilemma of any attempt to establish a global regulatory framework for ... TNCs is the sharp conflict of interest inherent in the process involving TNCs, states, labour groups and CSOs. Should the focus be on regulating the conduct of TNCs (the viewpoint of most developing countries, some developed countries, labour and environmental groups) or should it be concerned with protecting TNCs' interests (the latter referring to intellectual property rights and so on).

The considerable body of globalized protest against the 'evils' of TNCs is articulated in the context of poor perceived performance in the social, economic and environmental terms pertinent to sustainable development. Most large companies have seen that they need to move on this and the business response to stakeholder concerns in this respect has been the widespread growth of voluntary corporate social responsibility (CSR) programmes and reporting.

However, there has been much criticism of the voluntary CSR concept, to the effect that it lacks clear definition and has been hijacked, in a number of instances, by corporate organizations as some form of public relations exercise. There is a view that CSR is being utilized as a strategic marketing stance in relation to the protection of brands. Critics suggest that, in the application of the concept, there has been an

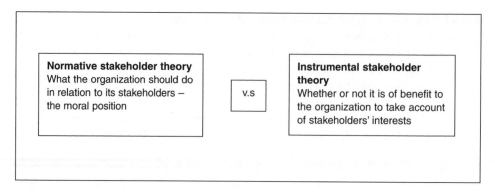

Figure 7.1   Stakeholder approaches: contrasting positions

insufficient grounding in ethics, with little consideration given to the application of ethical theory in the development and implementation of many approaches currently adopted by companies.

Some developments in CSR thinking can be tracked in the work of the Global Reporting Initiative (GRI). The GRI is a formative movement comprised of cooperating global interests with the aim of promoting a progressive approach in relation to CSR. It has produced the 'Sustainability reporting guidelines' (GRI, 2006), which are refined on an ongoing basis. In the light of the understanding developed, the later refinements made to the published GRI documentation have increased the emphasis on the need for companies to achieve stakeholder engagement. The associated discussions have recognized this area as a weakness in companies' approaches. Parallel social accounting movements also echo this point, emphasizing the need for engagement with stakeholders in the accounting process (see, for example, the social accounting standard AA1000 (ISEA, 1999) and linked documentation that has been developed to complement the GRI).

This issue of listening to stakeholders is advocated explicitly in the SEs, social reporting context by the Social Audit Network (SAN) (Pearce and Kay, 2005). SAN looks to promote best practice in SEs in what is an emerging activity in the sector. However, in the general business context – from the ethical standpoint of what is actually happening on the ground in many businesses – there are criticisms of and a degree of cynicism arising in relation to the nature of many companies' CSR approaches. As indicated, this is in relation to stakeholder engagement and to businesses taking responsibility for addressing stakeholders' concerns. Examples of this viewpoint are abundant and easily evidenced by a quick review of the campaigning material on the websites of the socially and environmentally concerned civil society organizations (CSOs) (see, for example, the websites of Christian Aid, Action Aid, Greenpeace and Friends of the Earth).

The essence of the concerns can be expressed as relating to the tension between normative and instrumental approaches to stakeholders, as illustrated in Figure 7.1. Normative stakeholder theory tells us why businesses should take account of stakeholders' interests from a moral standpoint – what firms should do. This is in relation to not only shareholders but also a wider group of stakeholders and, hence, runs contrary to Friedman's (1970) well-aired arguments against businesses' social responsibility in this context discussed further later in this chapter under the heading Egoism.

There is a well-established body of work on normative stakeholder theory in relation to business. The key proponent of this theory is Freeman (1984). Freeman's (1984: 46) definition of stakeholders is: 'any group or individual who can affect, or is affected by, the achievement of the organisations' objectives.'

Stakeholder theory is informed by Kantian ethics, which is discussed further below, and draws on Kant's categorical imperative. The latter points to the duty to treat human beings as ends in their own right. Here, the moral approach is to treat people as having their own needs and expectations, rather than as a resource to be exploited or their interests ignored in the relentless pursuit of profit maximization. Evan and Freeman (1993) developed this through a further consideration of the rights of stakeholder groups pertaining to the actions and activities of businesses. (Stakeholder theory is discussed in more detail later in this chapter under the heading Egoism.)

The essence of the criticism of current CSR approaches in business and other organizations is that the normative model, indicated by Freeman and others, has enjoyed a fairly limited application. Rather, most current approaches, in practice, lean more towards the instrumental. In instrumental stakeholder theory, the focus is on whether or not it is beneficial to the business to take into account stakeholders' interests. In terms of ethical theory, this approach is classified as egoism.

Given the continuing popularity and growth of CSR in the business, consultancy and practitioner communities, what, then, can a perusal of CSR theory tell us about the approach to CSR that it indicates? What does this mean in the context of the relationship of the latter to business ethics?

In this, the work of Carroll (1979) has been important in defining the obligations of businesses to society and moving the debate beyond the view of Friedman (1970). As discussed further below, the latter is that the responsibility of business should be limited to a fiduciary responsibility to shareholders only, while complying with the law. In contrast, Carroll advocates a progressive view and defines the responsibilities of businesses in society more widely.

In this he developed a theoretical construct to depict CSR that is known as the pyramid of corporate responsibility (Carroll, 1991). This contains four elements – economic, legal, ethical and philanthropic responsibilities. The model has subsequently been utilized by a number of scholars. Carroll's model is shown in Figure 7.2, with some examples to illustrate its meaning.

At this juncture, it is perhaps interesting to consider also the earlier work of Sethi (1975), which attempted to provide some way of enabling society to carry out a comparative analysis of how well businesses perform in terms of CSR. It aimed to provide a way of classifying performance in different dimensions, using categories that would retain the same meanings over time. In part resonant with the Caroll's depiction, these dimensions of behaviour are:

- search for legitimacy;
- ethical norms;
- social accountability;
- operating strategy;

- response to social pressures;
- activities pertaining to government actions;
- legislative and political activities;
- philanthropy.

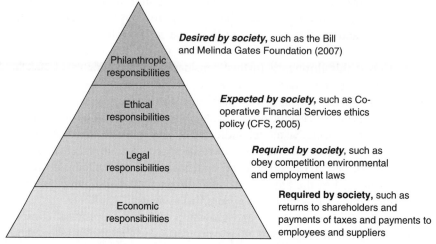

Figure 7.2 Carroll's four-part model of CSR (adapted from Carroll, 1991)

Reprinted from *Business Horizons* 34(4), Archie B. Carroll, 'The Pyramid of Corporate Social Responsibility: Toward the Moral Management of Organizational Stakeholders', p. 10, Copyright 1991, with permission from Elsevier.

Briefly, the model classifies organizations into one of three schema for each of the dimensions of behaviour listed above – namely, proscriptive, prescriptive and anticipatory and preventative.

These represent progressive levels of development. The lowest level, proscriptive, equates to complying with the law and providing returns to shareholders. Social and environmental costs are externalized and, thus, born by the environment (such as exploitation of resources, environmental pollution, depletion of habitat and species) or other stakeholders in society (in terms of labour rights, property rights and so on) where the law does not prevent this. Hence, this level of performance does not meet with the aims of sustainable development.

The next level, prescriptive, corresponds to taking a wider view of responsibility to stakeholders other than shareholders, though the latter are still the prime beneficiaries. At this level, organizations act according to salient social norms, moving beyond just complying with the law.

The highest level of social responsibility development is characterized by reaching the third state – anticipatory and preventative. Such organizations view cultural and social acceptance of their behaviour on a par with their legal and economic responsibilities. A long-term strategy is developed to communicate with and be responsible to stakeholders. The latter are often key to the decisionmaking process and, thus, take part in dialogue with these organizations – it is not just a consultation. There is special emphasis on accountability and the role of such organizations within a dynamic social system. These ideas can be seen to intersect with those in the discussion above on what has come to be seen as best practice in social accounting. The current state of affairs is that some international ratings of corporate performance may reveal a degree of progression towards this state. The case study in Exhibit 7.3 later in this chapter gives the example of Co-operative Financial Services, which is notable for making a significant contribution in this area, recieving a United Nations Environment Programme environmental award for its work (CFS, 2005).

As noted Sethi's model is intended to remain stable against the backdrop of changing public expectations over time. In line with ethical relativism, encountered in globalized operations, the model recognizes that any assessment of performance regarding CSR is culture-bound (relativism is discussed in relation to ethical theory below). The model is useful in that it illustrates the direction of the progressive stance, which is indicated in terms of closing the legitimacy gap between performance regarding CSR and societies' (stakeholders') changing and developing expectations.

In brief, while there are limitations, it is certainly true that the application of the Sethi model and Carroll's pyramid model surface issues pertinent to CSR if applied to companies or sectors. Further, in this vein, a useful treatment is provided by Meehan et al. (2006) concerning progressing the implementation of CSR approaches in organizations. This is achieved by building strategies based on competing through social resources, the authors describing the interrelated components of these in the form of a model.

In relation to our consideration of ethics here, however, these models do not give explicit guidance on how to examine ethical performance per se or carry out a detailed analysis with recourse to ethical theory. Some progress was made in this respect when the Carroll model was revisited with a view to refining and progressing it. A new theoretical construct, the three domain approach, was proposed (Schwartz and Carroll, 2003).

Some of the limitations and misconceptions associated with the pyramid model were considered, including the implicit hierarchy of the pyramid form. One of the refinements was to change philanthropic activity from being a separate 'domain'/responsibility. Instead, it became subsumed into the ethical domain. Also the overlaps between areas were incoporated so an activity could now be classified as ethical *and* economic if desired. This change was made because philanthropic activities can be in organizations' economic interests, perhaps enhancing brand image and so on. It also possible for an ethical interpretation to be applied in that a philanthropic activity could protect the property rights of shareholders as it would enhance a brand's image.

In the case of the first ethical argument, the authors make recourse to the ethical theory and consider different aspects. One of these is a justification of this in terms of Kant's categorical imperative, which is considered further below. As we will see, this is concerned with treating people not as a means to some organizational objective, but, rather, as an end in their own right, philanthropic activity ensuring that they are supported in the achievement of their own objectives for their lives. In these circumstances, the purpose of philanthropic activity could be to support this, which would mean that it would also be justified as an ethical activity. Schwartz and Carroll give other arguments, too, regarding the ethical context.

As indicated, treatment of the ethical domain in the earlier model was somewhat limited. Another limitation was the lack of any substantial indication of how to address overlaps or conflicts, which were revealed when if came to applying the model.

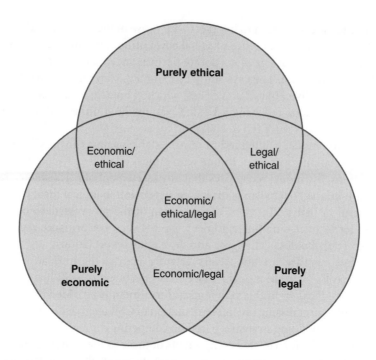

Figure 7.3   The three domain model of corporate social responsibility (Schwartz and Carroll, 2003: 509)

The new theoretical construct is depicted in the form of a Venn diagram, reproduced in Figure 7.3. In this new model, Schwartz and Carroll, in referring to the central segment of the model – Economic/ethical/legal – point to this as the area where firms should seek to locate their operations wherever possible. However, they describe and analyse a range of situations where this is not the case, using the analytical facility provided by the model. They also analyse in depth the overlaps in the ethical, legal and economic domains – the seven categories depicted in Figure 7.3.

As noted, the ethical domain is treated in a more sophisticated way in the new construct. The authors address relativism, like Sethi, recognizing that some ethical issues are viewed differently in different societies. However, they emphasize that, in their view, this relativism is limited by the imperative to comply with 'a set of minimum ethical standards.' For them, universal ethical standards are defined by consequentialist and deontological ethics. These aspects of ethical theory are described and discussed further in the next section.

In the three domain model, a utilitarian justification places an action in the ethical category. The thrust here is for it to do the maximum good for a range of stakeholders. The latter are defined in broad terms that correspond with the discussion in this chapter on stakeholder theory. It is interesting to note that, according to Schwartz and Carroll, actions that can only be justified on the grounds of egoism – those of benefit to the organization only – are excluded from being classified in the ethical domain of the three domain model.

The three domain model exhorts users to comply with minimum ethical standards. It also utilizes a duties-based – or deontological – standard, but this is more fully defined than it was in the earlier pyramid model. The earlier model referred to moral rights and justice when defining ethical responsibility. The three domain approach extends this to emphasize further other duty-based theoretical perspectives, including, as indicated above, Kantianism. These aspects of ethical theory are discussed further below.

What we can take from this brief consideration of CSR theory so as to assist our discussions here, is that approaches need to be underpinned by ethical analysis in the circumstances of the particular business realities. Key to the considerations is analysis of the issues that are pertinent to a range of stakeholders.

ETHICS: ADOPTING DIFFERING PHILOSOPHICAL POSITIONS

SEs have been described as being values-led and market-driven. The formation and declaration of values derives from the organization determining that it will take a moral approach – do what is right and wrong in the reality in which the business finds itself. How can a moral approach be determined and defended in a robust way? That is the purpose of ethical theories – they aim to determine what is right and wrong in that reality. Figure 7.4 illustrates this.

It is important to realize, however, that the application of different ethical theories can give us different and, at times, contrasting answers and, indeed, the purpose of utilizing the different theories is to deal with complexity. It is important to identify as many of the aspects around an issue-or set of circumstances as we can. An example of

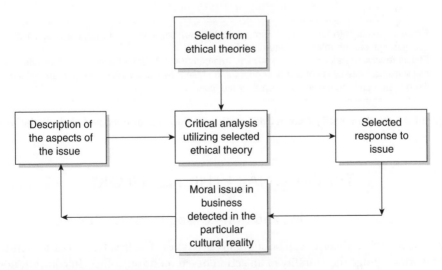

Figure 7.4   Using ethical theory to analyse business situations
(adapted from Chryssides and Kaler, *An Introduction to Business Ethics*, 1993: 16)

this might be in the provision of welfare in the sense of state provision models. (Note that Utilitarian ethics are discussed below concerning this and the potential conflict with ethics of duties is highlighted. Also, issues relating to the dignity of those receiving services are surfaced in this respect.)

The thrust is that, in order for better, more informed business decisions to be made, a range of theories should be understood and applied. This is so that 'all' the facets are considered. Advantage can be gained from considering situations in which right and wrong are addressed from a variety of perspectives. In the process of this analysis, taking contrasting philosophical positions from different schools of ethical theory can prove productive.

It is appropriate now to consider what these different perspectives are, their meaning and areas of application, with illustrations from the rich world of SEs.

Drawing on Greek philosophy, there are two fundamentally contrasting positions that can be taken: ethical absolutism and ethical relativism. These are discussed, for instance, by De George (1999) and Crane and Matten (2007). Figure 7.5 provides a summary. Within this framework of contrasting philosophical views, we will go on to consider what traditional and contemporary ethical theories can offer to the ethical analysis of business issues. Before moving on to consider particular theories, it is valid to note that, as usefully highlighted by Crane and Matten (2007: 87), 'most traditional ethical theories tend to be absolutist in nature [however] … contemporary ethical theories tend towards a more relativist position.' According to Crane and Matten, with respect to finding solutions to ethical problems in the real world of business, an approach somewhere in the middle ground – pluralism – is most appropriate. Reinforcing the discussion above, this indicates the application of a range of ethical theories.

Thus, a useful entry point to the next stage of the discussion is reached and we can move on to consider some of the ethical theories in more detail.

- Ethical absolutism (refer to cognitivism, Plato 427–347 BC) – right and wrong are objective qualities that can be rationally determined
- Ethical relativism (refer to non-cognitivism, Aristotle 384–322 BC) – there are no absolute moral truths. Morality is context dependant and subjective – depends on the person making the decision and the culture in which they are located.

Figure 7.5   Fundamentally contrasting positions: ethical absolutism and ethical relativism

TRADITIONAL ETHICAL THEORY

Consequentialist and non-consequentialist theories

Traditional ethical theories can be split into two types. The first type – consequentialist theories – judge the morality of an action based on its outcomes. In contrast, non-consequentialist theories purport that the morality of an action should be judged from the perspective of predefined principles.

Consequentialist theories

Egoism

The origins of egoism are attributed to ancient Greek philosophical thinkers. Egoism proposes that, to pursue a moral course of action, actors – expressed in this context as people or business entities – should follow their own short-term desires or long-term interests.

This does not equate necessarily with hedonism or selfishness. In fact, the sense of what beneficial outcomes are for egoistic people or business entities is not defined. In this vein, what is, in the long term, self-interest may coincide with acting in a beneficial way for other stakeholders in the eyes of wider society. Doing good for others in one's own interest is expressed as the enlightened self-interest argument. Egoism, however, is often attributed to the activities carried out by multinational corporations under the banner of CSR, in that they are, in fact, undertaken to protect the brand and to enhance market share or, in some cases, avoid legal intervention by governments.

The activities of individual philanthropists have been associated with egoism, in that these activities are self-actualizing. Doing good for others makes individuals feel better about themselves. Philanthropic activity is at the forefront of attention in the contemporary context as a result of the large sums donated by the corporate world – for example, by Bill Gates of Microsoft and by the tycoon Warren Buffet.

The connectivity of egoism to the free market thinking of Adam Smith (1723–1790) is widely discussed in literature concerned with CSR and normative stakeholder theory. Smith's notion of the 'invisible hand' of the marketplace – by which he meant individuals, in the frame of the economic system, pursuing their own self-interest generate net welfare through the outcomes in the economic system – is well known.

More recently, this was reinforced by the free market school of thought – notably Milton Friedman (1970). It gained particular expression in the neoconservative approaches promoted in the Thatcher and Regan era. In brief, and built on egoism, the thrust of Friedman's arguments are that the only business of business is business and, in this, businesses owe a duty to maximize returns for their shareholders only. Also, companies should comply with the law, but responsibilities wider than this are the remit of governments and civil society.

Stakeholder theory was introduced above, but let us look at it in a bit more detail. Normative stakeholder theory provides substantial counterarguments to Friedman's views – see, for instance, Freeman (1984) and Evan and Freeman (1993). In essence, and drawn substantially from Kantian ethics (see later in this chapter under the heading Deontology and Kant), normative stakeholder theory asserts that businesses owe duties to wider groups of stakeholders than just the shareholders and the former have corresponding rights in connection with the firm and its activities.

It should be noted that there is a body of academic writing on stakeholder theory and efforts are made by theorists to provide a wider theoretical grounding for it. As indicated, Kantian ethics are discussed in the literature in relation to this. Feminist ethics are also addressed below. For a consideration of feminist ethics as a grounding for stakeholder theory, see, for instance, Burton and Dunn (1996).

Also in this vein, human rights as a basis for stakeholder legitimacy are considered by Van de Ven (2005) in the context of international business. Further, in the contemporary context of globalization, Lepineaux (2005) considers civil society in stakeholder theory, taking a social cohesion perspective. The interests of civil society and social cohesion are identified as being centrally important in the justification of stakeholder theory. In the context of social cohesion, Lepineaux addresses the growing social exclusion in developed economies, inequalities between the developed and developing world and other such matters. Social cohesion provides a powerful linking point with the moral purposes of SEs in the context of business ethics. (This is discussed further later in this chapter under the heading Deontology and Kant.)

In a related societal context, it is notable that businesses rely on a stable society to provide the social, economic and legal infrastructure that will enable them to operate. Businesses are thus dependant on a wide range of stakeholders to operate, and society at large provides it with a licence to operate.

In consideration of egoism, Smith's notions of the invisible hand of the marketplace clearly had utility in the circumstances of the economy that he described at the time. However, it is apparent that the current version of capitalism, in the circumstances of rapidly developing globalization, presents a very different economic and social reality to that of Smith's period. In the contemporary context, the results of egoism in the unfettered globalized capitalist model are under fire. Much criticism resides around perceived market failure, where businesses are seen as culpable. This arises in relation to crises in global warming, global financial meltdown, perceived abuse of stable enterprises by a rampant private equity sector and other issues. As indicated above, all this connects powerfully with our considerations in relation to sustainable development; it links to the debate on overconsumption and that on the ethics of justice in terms of the fair distribution of economic outcomes between the developed and developing world. Issues of equity are central here and return us to the discussion in this book on the reasons for the growth of SEs and of the perceptions of their values-led, mission-based imperative.

It is acknowledged that the global capitalist economy is now almost totally dominant (interesting analysis of globalization is provided, for instance, by Dicken (2007) and Scholte (2005)). Scholte (2005: 8) points to positive and negative human consequences:

> Contemporary globalization could yield much better results in terms of human security, social equality and democracy with a change of policy course from neoliberalism to a blend of ambitious reformism and cautious transformism, although the political challenges of achieving this reorientation must not be underestimated. (Scholte, 2005: 8)

> He captures the phenomenon of increasing globalisation thus (Scholte, 2005: 327): 'the general welfare gap between the South and the North has grown during the contemporary periods of accelerated gloablisation ... the advances have generally been greater in the already privileged North.These misfortunes can be partly attributed to local and national circumstances of the countries concerned, but globalisation has also played a part in deepening North-South inequality.'

Figure 7.6 illustrates the contrasting worldviews of the neoliberalists and those who take a reformist approach, wanting to tame what they see as the excesses of the current version of global capitalism.

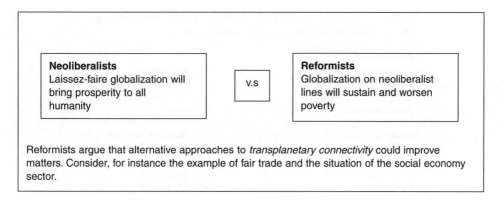

Figure 7.6   Justice in the globalized economy – conflicting worldviews

As indicated in Figure 7.6, the growing fair trade movement can be seen as one aspect of the reformist agenda. The case of the Divine Chocolate Company, given in Exhibit 7.2, later in this chapter, captures the contribution of this one SE to the promotion of fair trade. (This is discussed further later in this chapter under the heading Rights.)

Further, relating to equity and the role of the social economy sector in the global system, it is apparent that many of the activities of SEs are geared to addressing issues of social exclusion within countries in the developed world. These issues relate to justice and rights and, increasingly, derive from the reality of localized, often regionalized, structural decline within national economies resulting from the forces of globalization. Arising in a framework dominated by egoism in the capitalist society, attention is on inequality of income and access to employment and opportunity.

Consideration of these inequalities in the context of globalization is the subject of, for example, Dicken's (2007: Chapter 17) book. As indicated, the contributions and effectiveness of SEs in acting as part of the solution to these problems is currently the focus of much policy attention.

In this, it is perhaps interesting to view the position of SEs against the characteristics of mainstream companies given in Table 7.1, which is adapted from Dicken (2007). It emphasizes the points of difference between the mainstream economy and the place occupied by SEs – some of these differences being a matter of degree. Pedagogic experience indicates that it is useful to ask people who are leaders or managers in SEs to analyse their own organizations against these points. The results emphasize the greater and lesser extent of distinction, in terms of the characteristics listed, for individual SEs. It is a useful way to promote thinking about the ethical aspects associated with SEs, including the values base. It can also be used to embed an understanding of the differentiation of different types of SEs from each other and of the social economy sector from mainstream businesses in the current context of globalization. Applying this process to develop consideration and development of an ethical approach for SEs is suggested. Doing so in the context of strategic management can provide traction in the particular operational setting.

Utilitarianism

In so far as SEs are felt by some to be part of the reforming agenda discussed above, it is perhaps interesting to reflect that, in the historical context, utilitarianism is seen as

Table 7.1   Contrasting the characteristics of SEs with those of mainstream globalized capitalist companies

Predominant characteristics of mainstream capitalist companies (globalization)	Contrasting predominant characteristics of SEs sector
Aspatial/global	Attached to place
Specialized	Diversified
Singular	Multiple
Large-scale	Small-scale
Competitive	Cooperative
Centralized	Decentralized
Acultural	Culturally distinctive
Socially disembedded	Socially embedded
Non-local ownership	Local ownership
Agglomerate	Dispersed
Integrated	Autonomous
Export-orientated	Orientated towards local market
Privilege short-term returns	Value long-term investment

Source: Adapted from Dicken, 2007: 551

being linked with social and political reform. Leading thinkers, including the British philosophers Jeremy Bentham (1748–1832) and John Stuart Mill (1806–1873), articulated the concept in this way. At the time, it was set against the despotic power and control of the Establishment.

Utilitarianism falls into the consequentialist category of traditional ethical theories and judges morality in relation to the outcomes arising from actions. According to De George (1999: 57):

> Utilitarianism is an ethical theory that holds that an action is right if it produces, or if it tends to produce, the greatest amount of good for the greatest number of people affected by the action. Otherwise the action is wrong.

Contrasting with some of the deontological approaches discussed in the next section, utilitarian decisionmaking is fundamentally situated in the reality of the case, in the particular circumstances. It is concerned with empirical evidence and weighing up data in terms of a particular set of circumstances in order to make a decision.

In the context of the emergence of SEs, some may see that utilitarianism lends itself to considerations of the role of the state in providing welfare and the case for the involvement of SEs in the provision of welfare. Utilitarianism is concerned with improving total welfare, of maximizing the ratio of good outcomes to bad. It contrasts with egoism in that it requires these considerations to be applied to *all* affected stakeholders when considering the outcomes of a particular course of action.

Maximizing the provision of welfare by giving consideration to service delivery mechanisms is a very resonant current issue. In the UK setting, the developing dynamics in the relationship between the public sector and the private sector as well as the public sector and the third sector, including SEs, has a bearing here. In this respect, it is useful to consider the case study of the Liverpool ADHD Foundation given in Exhibit 7.1, a little later in the chapter, as it illustrates some aspects of this developing dynamic.

As indicated, the utilitarian approach is focused on consequences, on the outcomes of particular activities or interventions. It defines the moral course of action as one that provides the greatest amount of good for the greatest number of stakeholders affected by the action.

At one level, utilitarianism is hedonistic – the maximization of pleasure and avoidance of pain. An alternative interpretation of utilitarianism may promote it being viewed in wider terms, taking into account human concerns such as relationships and trust. This latter interpretation can assist us in linking ethical theory in a more explicit way to the notions of social capital. For a discussion of this, see, for instance, Field (2003), Hooghe and Stolle (2003), MacGillivray (2004), Putnam (1993), Kay (2003: 74–5). writing in the context of the social economy sector, summarizes the concept as follows:

> Social capital consists of resources within communities which are created through the presence of …
>
> 1. trust:
> 2. reciprocity and mutuality;
> 3. shared norms of behaviour;
> 4. shared commitment and belonging;
> 5. both formal and informal social networks; and
> 6. effective information channels.
>
> … which may be used productively by individuals and groups, to facilitate actions to benefit individuals, groups and the community more generally.

The progressive concerns of policymakers in promoting welfare by building positive aspects of social capital are articulated, for instance, in the UK context, by the 'Social capital discussion paper' produced for the Cabinet Office (2002). The particular implications for government strategy link strongly, for example, to the well-being strand of the British Government sustainable development strategy (DEFRA, 2005).

In the context of business, utilitarianism is seen to align with economic and business theory and analysis – the idea of applying utility to cost – benefit analysis being a derivation. Further, from the study of businesses, descriptive theory shows us that managers tend to take the utilitarian approach in practice.

The fair trade case study of the Divine Chocolate Company provided in Exhibit 7.2 is discussed later in this chapter in the sections on rights and justice and is considered also in relation to virtue ethics. In this vein, it is interesting to note that Nicholls and Opal (2004) apply utilitarianism to the analysis of ethics in supply chain relationships in the context of fair trade. In this, they weigh up the harms and benefits to stakeholders. As we might anticipate, Nicholls and Opal (2004: 67) find the following in relation to exploitation in the supply chain: 'In the case of trading arrangements where one party makes a profit by buying commodities at below subsistence price (resulting in starvation of the producer), it is clear that a utilitarian analysis would define this as unjust and unethical.' However, we can see that a consideration of these circumstances lends itself to the application of the ethics of duty, discussed further below, and the issue can be considered in the light of Kant's categorical imperative. The latter may be perceived as providing a more definitive framing of this particular issue.

Non-consequentialist theories

Deontology and Kant

Deontology, or the science of duty, has it that all our moral decisions should be based on ideals that are largely universally accepted. According to Trevino and Nelson (2004), deontological theory focuses on 'what's right on broad abstract universal principles or values such as honesty, promise keeping, fairness, loyalty, rights … justice, compassion and respect for persons and property.'

The essential difference of this from the utilitarian view is that what is right is not based on outcomes such as the optimization of social welfare, but, rather, the course of action based on ideals should be followed *irrespective* of the outcomes.

One of the dilemmas of state-provided welfare is that it may overlook the rights of minorities or minority groups in the drive to 'maximize' efficiency. A problem with state provision can be that a bureaucratic approach is too much in the ascendancy and this acts to counter the advantages provided by the underlying public service ethic.

Some would argue that the skill and innovation residing in the social economy sector equips it to challenge the negative aspects of the bureaucratic approach. In this, it can provide a valuable resource, delivering parts of the welfare agenda with a focus on the rights of particular groups or minorities and fulfilling corresponding duties to them.

To the forefront of deontological philosophy is the work of Immanuel Kant (1724–1804). Kantian thinking has been very influential in setting the frame of moral debate and his influence is felt strongly in normative stakeholder theory. As indicated above, the latter argues against the views of the free market thinkers and requires a consideration of duties to stakeholders generally, not shareholders alone (Freeman, 1984; Evan and Freeman, 1993).

Thus, the essential point about Kant's thinking, which is absolutist and based on describing duties, is that it is not circumstantial. In this, it does not rely on knowledge of or the weighing up of a particular set of circumstances or a particular reality in order to make a decision. Unlike utilitarianism, it is not based on considerations such as those provided by empirical data or factual knowledge of a set of conditions or relationships. This is in contrast to, for instance, the position of feminist ethics, which is discussed later in this chapter. Rather, the approach is categorical – that is, it works on the premise that a prescribed set of rules must be followed without regard, in this sense, to any consideration of desired outcomes or the needs of stakeholders or the relationships between them. For Kant, then, moral decisions derive from good will, driven by reasons of principle, drawn from a sense of duty. Kant describes this as the categorical imperative. This comprises rules that must be applied in all cases to determine whether or not an action is moral. De George (1999: 89) captures it thus:

> The Categorical Imperative, the ultimate principle of morality, according to the dominant deontological position, requires that any second-order moral rule or maxim must be capable of being consistently universalized, must respect the dignity of persons, and must be acceptable to rational beings.

The categorical imperative thus gives us principles or maxims that we should, in this view, apply to each decision to determine whether or not it follows a moral course. Chryssides and Khaler (1993) consider the ways in which Kant expresses the categorical imperative and conclude that they are not in fact equivalent – rather, they are separate but mutually supporting. The same authors cite definitions of the categorical imperative derived from a translation by Patton (1964), which are provided in Figure 7.7.

Two of the major elements of the categorical imperative.

1. 'I ought never to act except in such a way that I can also will that my action shall become a universal law.'
2. 'Act in such a way that you always treat humanity ... never simply as a means, but always at the same time as an end.'

Figure 7.7   Elements of Kant's categorical imperative (Chryssides and Kaler, 1993: 98–99)

Element 1 is referred to as consistency or universality. This means that we look at the principles on which we act from this perspective. What would be the result if 'it' were universally carried out? Using an extreme example, the test of universality would clearly preclude killing because, if every one acted in this way, then a functioning society would not be possible.

Returning to the business idiom, cynics assert that 'business ethics' is an oxymoron, that there is no such thing as ethics in business, implying that dishonesty is implicit. However, it is clear that business could not proceed if lying in transactions was accepted as a principle. The principle of honesty in transactions between players is essential to allow business to operate. Hence, lying is excluded by applying the universality test.

Element 2 addresses human dignity. In the business context, this refers to the treatment of a range of stakeholders. Applying it means not treating employees as means of production (no more than a cog in a machine), not treating customers and trading partners as 'facilities' to be exploited and so on. It asserts the fundamental view that people have their own needs, aspirations and life objectives that should be considered in the process of the carrying out of a business. As noted earlier, this view is a driver for normative stakeholder theory. It is also concerned with the duties owed to groups of stakeholders wider than just the shareholders. From the business ethics perspective, then, stakeholders, as a result of the duties of the business operation, have rights in connection with the activities and operations of the business entity.

On the latter point, the following is a brief consideration of the range of issues and stakeholders this relates to. Typical examples, often to the forefront of attention, include the need for businesses to provide career and personal development for employees, safe and healthy working conditions, protect the ecological environment, provide adequate information to customers regarding products and good levels of service to clients and so on.

Clearly these aspects apply to all businesses, including SEs. Considering SEs explicitly, though, it is appropriate here to apply a Kantian analysis to aspects associated with the specific roles and functions of SEs. As indicated in the scope section at the beginning of this chapter, some issues reside around the public sector–SE interface and, by way of illustration, it is useful to consider this further. Proponents of SEs would see one of their strengths as being the development of innovation in service delivery. This is in contrast to the traditional public-sector top-down delivery paradigm that is seen as not being successful in this respect and is articulated as being part of the public-sector's failure. Here, the framework is tackling problems associated with, for example, poverty, special needs, social exclusion and so on. We are referring to places where SEs are seen by the government and others as having a key role.

As indicated above, one aspect of this public sector–SE interface relates to strategic policy development where there is a perceived failure to take account of feedback arising from the experiences of SEs delivering on the ground. This is concerned with what works and what does not work in improving the life chances of stakeholders. Here, in Exhibit 7.1, we will look at an example of what slowness to perceive what user participation in service delivery really means and the loss caused by squandering the opportunity presented – that is, the learning provided by experience from SEs operating on the ground not being utilized to develop policy and funding regimes.

Exhibit 7.1   The Liverpool ADHD Foundation

Attention Deficit Hyperactivity Disorder (ADHD) is a major issue. According to the National Institute of Clinical Excellence (Department of Health, 2006):

> ADHD is among the most commonly diagnosed behavioural disorders ... A sizeable proportion of children referred continue to have problems into adulthood, including emotional and social problems, substance misuse, unemployment and involvement in crime. It is estimated to affect 3–9% of school-age children.

Centred on a leading innovative approach, the mission of the Liverpool ADHD Foundation, an SE established in Liverpool UK, is as follows:

> We aim to transform the services for children with ADHD. We have demonstrated that ADHD need not be a pathological condition which isolates and stigmatizes those affected by it. When parents and children learn to understand and manage it they are empowered to join with agencies to make positive improvements. This changes their role from being passive recipients of services for which there are long waiting lists to being stakeholders in the design and delivery of services. To work in partnership with all stakeholders to provide a focused and consistent approach to ADHD using its values of Understanding, Communicating,

---

Encouraging, Involving and Empowering to deliver outcomes for Children's Services, locally and nationally.

Central to the philosophy of the Foundation is an explicit focus on the duties it has to the recipients of the service it provides. It makes specific recognition of the fact that, while the condition has a medical diagnosis, for the stakeholders, it is fundamentally a public health issue. The effect of the condition is that it encompasses the full range of interactions that make up a child's life – in the home, in the school and in the community. The parents and children express anguish in terms of the social isolation and exclusion the condition brings in the context of their social interactions in everyday terms.

The response and innovation of the Foundation is in its recognition, in the circumstances of the children and their families, that its duty is to defend the right to social inclusion. It achieves this through the careful design of the way in which it exercises its intervention, in a multistakeholder context. The drive is to meaningfully engage the users of the service – the parents and children – in its design and execution. The model recognizes the key need to facilitate real engagement with the stakeholders that define the reality of the child's life. In this, the building of bridging social capital with those perceived to be 'in authority' is important. This is as well as building bonding social capital with others in the same circumstances.

Thus, the service model developed by the Foundation provides a multistakeholder approach. It engages with children identified with ADHD and their families. It provides services to parents, young people, schools and agencies. This is to provide a framework in which all the stakeholders can understand and manage ADHD.

As indicated, the recipients of the service are involved in the design and delivery of services. Parental involvement ranges through a spectrum, from volunteering, engaging with the child's school, completing the organization's accreditation programme to some recipients becoming paid workers at the Foundation.

According to Liz Miller, the manager of the Foundation:

> We have worked hard to understand how the service model can be improved by looking at the whole life situation of the children and their families, of understanding what the condition means in relation to their life chances, to their opportunities and fulfilment. In this we have attempted fundamentally to measure ourselves, as an organization, by the outcomes we have achieved for our service recipients. This in terms of their own measure and not in terms of some conveniently measurable form of statistic or output. This approach clearly demands resources and the qualitative appraisal needed does not easily satisfy the tick boxes of funders' requirements. We read from the purported agenda of policymakers that the approach we take is what accords with best practice. However, we are not confident that what this means in terms of practical approach on the ground and what the actual resource implications are is properly assimilated in

(Continued)

(Continued)

> policymaking/funders' circles. Further, it is clear that lessons from our user participation service model are transferable to other areas of provision or for wider dissemination, but we do not see a readily apparent/accessible mechanism to give this traction.

This case of the Liverpool ADHD Foundation brings home the application of element 2 of Kant's categorical imperative. It illustrates what is meant by moving away from the top-down, telling approach to one that is sensitive to the views, needs and involvement of those receiving services. It emphasizes the categorical imperative to treat users of services as ends in themselves, with their own perceptions, their own life opportunity needs and so on. It is based in the reality of what they need to be achieved in order to be able to progress. We can measure the success of the Liverpool ADHD Foundation's approach from the perceived quality outcomes for the users of the service.

This is in contrast to the often criticized public sector-led approach where the measurement of success is by means of 'forced' outputs rather than outcomes. These outputs would typically be the number of cases 'treated' rather than the outcomes achieved for those individuals. This arrangement is enforced to satisfy the reporting needs of the bureaucracy, not the needs of those that it sets out to serve.

Rights

So far, we have focused on deontological theory from the perspective of duties, obligations and principles. Another part of deontological theory that is very influential in determining the approach taken in business ethics is that of rights. Duties and rights are connected in that they are both concerned with human dignity and that the duties of one person or group of stakeholders correspond with the rights of another. In the context of our discussions, the duties are owed by the business entity.

Trevino and Nelson (2004) point to the origins of the notions of 'natural rights' in Greek philosophy that derive from 'natural law'. According to Chryssides and Kaler (1993), by the seventeenth century, the original notions of rights – framed as a form of protection for the citizen against the unjust use of power by governments – were reframed as a social contract – the focus being on the facility of control possessed by the people to 'set up and empower the government', which would then act according to the imperatives set by the people. In this way, the principle of democratic government was established.

The 'natural law' is centred on the dignity of human beings and so human rights are concerned with the value of individuals and the development of their potential. More recent notions of the role of governments in protecting human rights are widely attributed to the philosophy of John Locke (1632–1714). In a more modern context, the conflict of World War II gave rise to the United Nations' Declaration of Human Rights in 1948. The list of 'identified' human rights is continually expanding. Adding to early interpretations, a contemporary list would include the rights to life, liberty, shelter, nutrition, justice, property, freedom of expression, belief, association, education, welfare, fair trial, employment, fair pay and good working conditions.

The role of parts of the social economy sector can be seen as very much associated with the ethics of rights and the protection and provision of the rights of individuals and the protection of their human dignity. On a general level, this is illustrated, for example, by the UK Government's stance of the role of SEs in the provision of welfare and reduction of social exclusion. A review of the activities of the social economy sector soon reveals areas where SEs are concerned with the defence and provision of social rights. The latter are discussed in relation to ethics and the corporate sector by Matten and Crane (2005: 170), who usefully define social rights as serving to 'provide the individual with freedom to participate in society, such as right to education, healthcare, or various aspects of welfare.'

Examples of SEs proriding services with respect to the protection of the social rights of a number of groups are evident. A list of examples, which is not exhaustive, would include SEs' services in the following categories:

- mental disability;

- physical disability;

- homelessness;

- special educational needs;

- employability and training;

- fair trade;

- community arts;

- aged;

- intermediate labour market;

- drug dependency and rehabilitation

As mentioned earlier, our discussion of business ethics in the social economy sector takes place against the backdrop of globalization and the struggle to move towards sustainable development. An overview of the websites of pressure groups such as Christian Aid, Action Aid, Greenpeace, Friends of the Earth and so on rapidly brings into focus the range of accusations of failure made against corporate businesses concerning their respect for the rights of a range of stakeholders. Set in the context of globalized business, these concerns and dynamics are discussed, for instance, by Crane and Matten (2007), Dicken (2007) and Scholte (2005). The human rights records of some companies have, in a number of instances, been very damaging to them and their brands. Obvious examples include the treatment of workers in the supply chains of sports and garment industries and brands such as Gap and Nike. Recently, by way of example, the pressure group Action Aid has criticized Tesco over issues relating to fair trade (Wijeratna, 2005).

Businesses have responded by developing policies concerned with human rights and publicly reporting on these in the form of their ethics, CSR and sustainability reports. The trend now is to move further towards transparency and accountability. In this respect, third-party auditing, verifications of reports and the data that underpin the claims in them are at the forefront of best practice. The approach is now beginning to gain a foothold in small- to medium-sized enterprises and is nascent in SEs, too, through social auditing (Pearce and Kay, 2005) and measurement of social return on investment (Rotheroe and Richards, 2007).

Illustrative of business and civil society responses to concerns about the exploitation of workers in supply chains and producers in commodity markets have been the efforts to improve the moral management of supply chains reported by large players, in some cases with verifiable, audited reports. One response to issues in the commodity and other markets has been the rapid growth in fair trade retailing (fair trade and ethical consumption are also discussed in the section on virtue ethics after the next section).

In relation to our discussion of rights, it is useful to consider the place of SEs regarding fair trade. SEs have an established and growing presence in the fair trade market (Doherty and Tranchell, 2007). This is illustrated by the case study of Divine Chocolate in Exhibit 7.2. In the context of this section, it illustrates the defence and provision of human rights that have resulted from the intervention of a SE. It also connects us to other aspects of ethical theory discussed in this chapter.

Exhibit 7.2   Divine Chocolate Ltd and business ethics

The case of the SE Divine Chocolate Ltd. was discussed in Chapter 6 in Exhibit 6.2, from a marketing perspective. Here, it is considered again, but from the perspective of our discussion of business ethics and, as part of this, sustainable development. Concerning the discussion of virtue ethics later in the chapter, it is evident that the mission of Divine Chocolate Ltd. corresponds with a virtuous approach. The mission is to: (Tranchell, 2008: 5)

> Improve the lives and opportunities of small-scale cocoa farmers in West Africa by establishing a dynamic, branded fair trade chocolate marketing company in the large UK chocolate market, thus putting the farmers higher up the value chain.

As stated at Exhibit 6.2, the mission drives the following objectives, which are to (Tiffen, 2002: 384):

- take a quality and affordable range of fair trade chocolate bars on to the mainstream chocolate market;
- raise awareness of fair trade issues among UK retailers and consumers of all age groups;
- be highly visible and vocal in the chocolate sector and thereby act as a catalyst for change;
- purchase all cocoa used under Fairtrade Mark criteria.

The company sets itself the task of confronting the global problem of developing world commodity producers becoming poorer while multinational corporations increase their profits and market share from the sale of manufactured products derived from the commodities provided by these producers. To do this, Divine engages in the chocolate market according to a fair trade model that seeks to protect and provide human rights and justice to smallholding cocoa farmers in Ghana. Richly interwoven in the approach is a stance that is indicative of progress towards sustainable development (the connectivity between such innovation and sustainable development was discussed earlier in this chapter under the heading Sustainable development as a framework for the consideration of business ethics in SEs). At Divine Chocolate this is associated with its intrinsic innovation of the business model and principles of democracy in terms of its structure and governance, transparency, accountability and trust.

To accomplish its mission, a unique business model is followed by Divine Chocolate. Kuapa Kokoo, a Ghanian farmers' union, owns 45 per cent of the organization and is the recipient of the fair trade benefits. The remainder of the equity is owned by the founder organizations, including Christian Aid, Body Shop, Comic Relief and Twin Trading. The Kuapa Kokoo shares cannot be diluted, apart from by the inclusion of other farmers. This secures the enterprise from takeover, while the Northern hemisphere equity allows for an innovative and a very business like trading approach in the Northern markets. Divine Chocolate Ltd is based in London and directed and managed from there.

Divine's purpose is explicitly to pursue market transformation, utilizing a sustainable business model. This is to address the problems raised in the discussion in the section on egoism and, within this, the criticism of the predominant neoliberal market system in the globalized economy. Divine Chocolate's agenda follows that of the reformists. Thus, the business model aims to achieve progressive outcomes. Here, the virtuous approach is marshalled by virtue of by using the resource of a brand in the Northern market. The business model makes this facility available to the producers in the Southern hemisphere so that they can earn their way out of poverty by providing them with fair access to Northern markets. The model allows for the payment of a transparently set guaranteed fair trade price to the farmers for their cocoa beans. It moves them away from income dictated by world commodity markets, set by the forces of speculation, often at prices at or below subsistence level. In addition to this, a social premium is also paid, on a per tonne basis. This is used by the farmers to assist in their social and environmental community infrastructure, including education, health, access to safe drinking water and so on. These projects are designed and implemented through the resources of the farmers cooperative, which operated according to democratic principles. As well as the direct benefits arising from the dividend paid to farmers as a result of their ownership of shares, the producers also benefit from the significant investment in their producer support and development programme.

In the context of this section on the ethics of rights, it is apparent that issues concerning rights are addressed by the efforts of the company. Property rights – making it possible to receive a fair return on investment of effort in the production of a commodity – are central. In the extreme, such rights may include the right to life through the avoidance of a precarious existence carried out below subsistence levels. The investment available for social infrastructure upholds rights to healthcare, access to clean water and access to education and opportunity.

(Continued)

(Continued)

The relevance of the application of Kantian ethics, discussed above, also becomes apparent in the fact that there is the provision of opportunities for individuals in the farming community to achieve their life chances. Further, justice is also seen to be upheld by this approach, in the context of the discussion next.

Thus, Divine Chocolate takes an ethical approach to trading through its resources of innovation, management intensity, knowledge intensity and marketing intensity (see Chapter 6). With respect to the creation of a sustainable business model, it has achieved very successful penetration of the chocolate market in the UK and elsewhere. This is illustrated in Table 7.2. Table 7.3 shows the associated purchases of cocoa beans from Kuapa Kokoo, illustrating the value of this system to the growers in Ghana.

The discussion in Chapter 6 gave some indication of the extent to which the reformist mission is deployed by the key figures at Divine Chocolate. In terms of virtue ethics, its evident virtuous approach could be framed in terms of wisdom, bravery in confronting the predominant economic system and integrity. It can be seen that the efforts of the company are very wideranging and astutely targeted to influence society through high-level social and political interactions (Doherty and Tranchell, 2007).

Table 7.2   Success of the Divine Chocolate brand

Year	Turnover	Profit	Sales growth
2004/05	£ 7,673,298	£497,481	36%
2005/06	£ 8,988,071	£453,091	18%
2006/07	£10,702,500	£434,554	19%

Source: Tranchell, 2008

Table 7.3   Associated purchases of Kuapa Kokoo's fair trade cocoa beans

Year	Tonnes	Fair trade price	Social premium	PS&D
2004/05	996	$1,593,600	$149,400	£107,426
2005/06	1165	$1,864,000	$174,750	£179,000
2006/07	1420	$2,272,000	$213,000	£214,000

Note: April 2007, Divine announced its first dividend of £500 a share
Source: Tranchell, 2008

Justice

The determination of justice between groups and individuals covers a wide range of aspects encountered in the human condition and is the subject of age-old philosophical consideration.

Two extreme positions can be taken in the consideration of justice. One is the egalitarian position – that justice is the same as equality. This view would have it that all should receive equal rewards. This does not seem helpful when one considers the different abilities, skills and qualities that individuals bring to bear in their contributions to society. The other is non-egalitarian, which essentially looks to the 'free' market to provide just outcomes. As discussed, it seems clear that unreformed capitalism, in the contemporary context of the globalized economy, fails to deliver just outcomes in many situations.

The literature offers us these two polar positions in order to provide a framework for critique and analysis. Consensus indicates solutions that are situated in between the extremes. In the context, and seeking to address the 'problem' of justice, Rawls (1971) identified two principles of justice:

- each person is to have an equal right to the most extensive system of basic liberties compatible with a similar system of liberty for all;
- social and economic inequalities are arranged so that they are both:
  - to the greatest benefit of the least advantaged; and
  - attached to offices and positions open to all under conditions of the fair equality of opportunity.

For a detailed treatment of this, see, for instance, Boatright (2003) or Beauchamp and Bowie (2004).

The first of Rawl's principles is designed to protect basic rights. The requirement is that this should be satisfied before moving on to the second principle. The second principle accepts inequalities, provided that the opportunities of the most disadvantaged are maximized in the context of their circumstances.

This might take us on to consider the arguments made by some for the justification of multinational corporations in situating their production operations in developing countries to reduce their labour costs in the home market. This is while still giving a fair return by way of pay and employment conditions to those people employed in developing countries, for whom the alternative may be starvation or a standard of living limited to some form of subsistence existence. However, in the circumstances of globalization, this does not address the subject of justice from the perspective of those suffering job losses in the home economies, career termination/disruption, curtailment of pensions and, in some cases, social devastation of their communities. It is interesting to note that a number of SEs have been formed at various locations to provide support to communities in just these circumstances.

Returning to consider the facets of justice at a broad level, Boatright (2003) refers to Aristotle's analysis of justice in specific situations – *particular* justice. This considers three aspects:

- *distributive justice*   the distribution of benefits and burdens;
- *compensatory justice*   compensating people for wrong done to them;
- *retributive justice*   the punishment of wrongdoers.

For the purpose of our discussion, we are primarily focused on justice in relation to business activities. Reflecting on SEs in this is context, as actors in the market system, many would aspire for them to have a role in reforming capitalism. This revolves around the provision of amelioration with respect to the social, economic and environmental harms arising in the now globally dominant form of capitalist economy operating today, as discussed above.

As indicated, considerations of justice – commonly viewed as fairness to one actor in relation to another – come into play when there is something to distribute. The social economy sector is situated, in the view of policymakers, in relation to its importance in the provision of welfare. As introduced above, in the section on consequentialist ethics, arguments for the market as an efficient distributor of welfare are utilitarian in nature and draw from the philosophy of Adam Smith. However, in the globalized economy, current injustice in the dominant neoliberal system of globalized capitalism resides in its relation to the distribution of welfare and, thus, to justice in this respect. As discussed above, this is within societies in the developed world and here is articulated in relation to the formation of a socially excluded underclass. Also as discussed above, it is between the growing disparity of benefits in the developed and developing worlds and also between the developed world and emerging economies (for more on this debate, see, for instance, Dicken (2007), and Scholte (2005). The perceived failures of the market system have been discussed above, together with the emergence of SEs as part of a reformist agenda.

Concerning this reformist agenda in the international setting, the ethics of justice can be pinpointed in the consideration of fair trade. The fair trade movement stems from a view that the distribution of the balance of benefits and burdens in the relationship between business organizations in the Northern hemisphere and, for example, commodity producers in the Southern hemisphere are not reconcilable in terms of justice. Fair trade aims to provide redress in this respect. Nicholls and Opal (2004) refer to fair trade at the institutional level: 'the role of fair trade organizations has been both to develop a commercial model for social justice and to act as advocates for the rights of farmers of the South.' The approach illustrated by Divine Chocolate in Exhibit 7.2 captures this imperative perfectly in its implementation of an innovative business model geared to this reformist agenda.

CONTEMPORARY ETHICAL THEORY

Virtue ethics

The ethical theories we have looked at so far have taken the philosophical position that the moral course can be followed if the rules-based approach of these traditional normative theories are followed. Virtue ethics has its origins in ancient philosophy – from Plato and Aristotle, for instance. It takes a completely different standpoint from the traditional ethical theory discussed so far. Here, the focus is on the moral character of the decisionmaker. Virtue ethics, then, derives from the position that moral decisions come from moral persons. According to Trevino and Nelson (2004: 93), 'A virtue ethics perspective considers primarily the actor's character, motivations and intentions.'

Aristotle defined the virtues as including intellectual ones with wisdom to the fore, and also the moral virtues. The latter included for example, courage, honesty and friendship. Virtue ethics is concerned with building a habitual pattern of behaviour that is learned and, with reference to a community of practice, being concerned with the particular community and tradition within which it is embedded. The imperative is to express these virtues as a habitual pattern of behaviour, which accords with Aristotle's notion of the 'good life.' Thus, the formation of character and character constancy is central. The 'good life' is explicitly linked with a flourishing society.

In framing the matter of a flourishing society in a contemporary context, it is interesting to note that there is a considerable and growing moral debate around the growth of affluence and the associated growth in consumption in the West in the post-World War II years. (For a treatment of ethics and consumerism, see Barnet, Cafaro and Newhol, 2005). In relation to virtue ethics, they (2005: 18) cite the following from Aristotle's *Nicomachean Ethics*: 'The many, the most vulgar, would seem to conceive of the good and happiness as pleasure, and hence they also like the life of gratification. Here they appear completely slavish, since the life they decide on is a life for grazing animals.'

Centuries after his time, this reflection of Aristotle seems to resonate with some of the current concerns regarding overconsumption and the consumer society. As indicated, Barnet et al. provide an analysis of what ethical consumption might mean and indicate the complexities of this debate. Specifically in relation to the associated considerations of a flourishing society, Offer (2006) discusses the considerable growth in affluence and consumption in the USA and UK since 1950. He points to research findings that reveal this has not corresponded to an increase in social well-being, which perhaps provides a perspective for us in terms of virtue ethics and modern society.

Also in the contemporary context, but focusing on SEs, it is interesting to note the view expressed by Chryssides and Kaler (1993: 139) that, in terms of the discussion here on what is meant by the 'good life', 'the good person would certainly not be a bureaucrat.' This is resonant with the above discussion on the public sector–SE interface in relation to funding and commissioning. This nuance is brought into focus by the Liverpool ADHD Foundation case study in Exhibit 7.1, which showed the importance of a focus on outcomes for the recipients of service innovations, rather than on bureaucratically determined outputs demanded as surrogates of quality by commissioners in the public sector. It is also resonant with the closely related expectations concerning the capacity for innovation in the social economy sector and the entrepreneurial resources available in the form of some of its leaders/promoters. Here, aspects of entrepreneurship, courage, foresight and a values-driven outlook link us to the notions of the 'good life.' In this vein, Nicholls and Opal (2004) refer to the actions of pioneers and leaders in the context of their discussion of fair trade. The meaning of this is brought out in the fair trade case study of Divine Chocolate provided in Exhibit 7.2. The intellectual and moral virtues of the instigators of its business model and the value of the business model in its own right can be seen in that case.

Further, regarding the realm of fair trade and ethical consumption, Barnett et al. (2005) review the application of ethical theory. They consider how traditional ethical theory can be applied to the analysis of ethical consumption. They argue that deontological approaches, which derive from obligation and consequentialist approaches and assess good outcomes, have their place in explaining behaviour. However, they conclude that these traditional approaches in ethical theory tend to be too abstract in terms of analysis. As an alternative, they explore the rationale for ethical consumption utilizing virtue ethics and find this more convincing. In these discussions they report that this approach links usefully to the related debate on sustainable development in that the habits and practices advocated by virtue ethics in the 'good life' may lead us to act in ways that are more environmentally and socially sustainable, by modifying our consumption patterns. They (Barnet et al., 2005: 24) point to research on ethical consumption that reveals:

- the reasons given for ethical behaviour are that it is driven by a sense of self, personal integrity;
- 'a sense of moral integrity is more fundamental to the ethical consumer than either a concern for consequences or rules (though both are evident).'

Turning to business ethics more generally and, again, providing a contemporary setting for virtue ethics in business, Crane and Matten (2007), for instance, point to the good life in the business sense as being concerned with the following factors:

- being more than just a profitable company;
- economic success being just one part of the good business life, other aspects including:
  - satisfaction of employees;
  - harmonious relations with all stakeholders.

To further deepen the meaning of contemporary virtue ethics in the business setting, it is useful to consider the work of Moore (2005). He considers modern business ethics in relation to the current predominant capitalist form of corporate business. Ethical criticism of the latter is implicit, but the work provides a positive dynamic in that it enables the articulation of a reformist agenda in the context of the critique of globalization discussed above. As also indicated above, it is productive to consider the situation of SEs in relation to the location of this agenda.

Moore defines what virtuous corporate character is and differentiates it from the related and mutually influencing concept of corporate culture. On his road to a definition of virtuous corporate character, he cites and develops MacIntyre's (1985) modern virtue ethics–virtues–practice–institution schema. Within this discussion he considers 'business-as-practice' in relation to moral development. Briefly summarized, this relates to the development and maintenance of a virtuous approach, depicted as 'internal goods' that are 'goods of excellence'. These are characterized by Aristotle's notion of the good life. However, a tension between the building of habitual virtuous traits, characterized as 'internal goods', and the necessary achievement to some degree, for business survival, of 'external goods' is highlighted. These 'external goods', which are 'goods of effectiveness', are characterized in Moore's discussion as factors such as prestige, status or money. The organization has to be concerned with the latter to maintain its existence and, thus, be able to continue to act also as bearer of the internal goods, which are the determinants of good practice. Both kinds of goods are recognized as being intrinsic and interdependent in business and the elimination of one versus the other is not argued for. However, in light of the pressures and predilection towards avarice in the business world, some way to maintain the place of internal goods is sought after. The prevention of attrition of the virtues necessary for the achievement of internal goods is the objective. Moore considers this, in depth, utilizing the notion of corporate character.

In this respect, the virtues–practice–institution schema indicates that the business-as-practice resides in the institution of the corporation. Within this relationship, Moore's (2005: 661) analysis shows us that the preponderance of businesses to fail to act in a virtuous manner is because they 'fail to provide the kind of conducive environment within which the virtues may flourish and internal goods (goods of excellence) may be achieved.' This takes Moore (2005: 661) on to consider a solution to this by way of defining virtuous corporate character in the context of virtue ethics thus:

> Virtuous corporate character is the seat of the virtues necessary for a corporation to engage in practices with excellence, focusing on those internal goods thereby obtainable, while warding off threats from its own inordinate pursuit of external goods and from the corrupting power of other institutions with which it engages.

What does this mean in practice? Regarding the corporate sector, as that is where the analysis here was conceptualized, Exhibit 7.3 reproduces an article from *The Guardian* (Treanor, 2008) concerning a company trying to put virtue ethics into practice. Many would see the organization discussed in the article as being at least on a trajectory towards forming virtuous corporate character. The behaviour concerned is displayed in the trading stance taken by the Co-operative Insurance Society, based in Manchester. Details of the strategy and operational arrangements that underpin this stance can be found in the CFS's sustainability report (CFS, 2005).

Exhibit 7.3 'Co-op refuses to invest in six companies' (Jill Treanor, 2008)

Co-operative Insurance Society refused to invest in six major companies last year because of their stance towards corporate governance and has taken a tough line on at least three others over boardroom issues.

The Manchester-based group has £19bn under investment, including £2.5bn in unit trusts. It is the fund management arm of Co-operative Financial Services, a key part of the cooperative movement.

Its exclusion list contains retailer French Connection, publisher Euromoney Institutional Investors, home shopping group N Brown, cruise line Carnival, technology company Amstrad and – until recently – Asian miner Kazakhmys.

(Continued)

(Continued)

The fund manager also provides three examples where issues such as boardroom pay have led to serious discussions about investment decisions and prevented the group from taking a more positive stance. These are banking groups HSBC and Royal Bank of Scotland, and fund manager Aberdeen.

Ian Jones, head of responsible investment at CIS, said there were some companies with governance issues so bad that the group could not consider investing in them. Much of his concern stems from 'dominant shareholders', which he regards as a 'potential threat'.

The group held a stake in French Connection until deciding to sell after failing to extract changes from chairman and founder Stephen Marks. Euromoney Institutional Investors is also on the list because of the stake held by Daily Mail and General Trust, and N Brown is there because of the 33 per cent stake held by Lord Alliance, its chairman.

Carnival is excluded because CIS found the group 'very difficult in terms of willingness to engage' with shareholders. This is despite CIS's assessment that it is an attractive investment as it operates in a duopoly with Royal Caribbean and has good prospects for long-term growth. CIS sold off its holding in Carnival because of its broader concerns about corporate governance.

CIS objected to Amstrad, bought by BSkyB in September, because of its relationship with Sir Alan Sugar.

Kazakhmys was recently removed from the exclusion list because it has moderated its stance towards corporate governance by appointing new non-executive directors. It is the only one of the six companies on last year's list to have outperformed the FTSE All-Share index in 2007. French Connection's performance is almost a negative 50 per cent, Euromoney Institutional Investors' close to 40 per cent, N Brown's almost 30 per cent with Carnival's not far behind. Amstrad's underperformance is close to 10 per cent.

The CIS claims to be the only fund management group in the UK to 'fully embed' environmental, social and governance issues into its decisions about which stocks to buy and sell.

There are instances where corporate governance assessments reinforce the investment case. For instance, the improvement in management of telecoms group Vodafone and its strong cash generation were backed up by 'profitable sustainability opportunities'. Similarly, Scottish & Southern Energy's good management of power generation assets was supported by high scores on governance and environmental issues.

Copyright Guardian News & Media Ltd 2008

Within the concept of virtuous corporate character, Moore goes on to consider features of the corporation, as the institution in virtue ethics' virtues–practice–institution schema, which will better enable it to not distort the practice in which moral management may flourish through the achievement of internal goods. In brief, Moore:

addresses corporate culture, which he sees as being separate from corporate character and situated in order to obtain external goods. Thus, Moore identifies the tension between corporate character and corporate culture. They are seen to be interdependent, but, in this relationship, corporate character needs to be protected. This is in the context of the protection of internal goods, which are the seat of the virtues. In relation to this, he identifies a number of factors associated with the defence of virtuous corporate character in the framework of the schema, some of which are summarized in Figure 7.8.

- Within business-as-practice in relation to moral development – the development and maintenance of a virtuous approach and the organization's recognition of the need for active steps to be taken to sustain it are central.
- Strategic and managerial oversight to ensure encouragement of the pursuit of excellence in business-as-practice.
- While there must be a focus on external goods, such as profit and reputation, this should only be to the extent necessary to sustain and develop the business-as-practice.
- 'The character of the virtuous organization should be such as to resist the corrupting powers of organizations with which it in turn relates.'
- The just purpose of the particular practice–institution combination is represented by the corporate entity.
- A power balance structure allows the various constituencies to be fairly represented.
- Systems and processes allow challenge of the status quo. This prevents the organization from becoming out of synch with other parts of society.
- A supportive culture in terms of the definition of culture that is provided as part of the framework of this analysis.

Figure 7.8   Virtuous corporate character in the virtues–practice–institution schema: business-as-practice in moral development (adapted from Moore, 2005: 676–7)

Moore also underlines the point that character grows through time to become relatively fixed. It is by this means that the pursuit of external goods can be prevented from becoming too dominant and the attrition of corporate character in a changing business environment also avoided. The importance of maintaining character over time – virtue constancy – is explicit.

As indicated, this work has been developed in a corporate sector context, but it is resonant for SEs also. Indeed, it is suggested that the use of this virtue framework can be useful in developing ethical approaches in the strategic and operational management of SEs. Two aspects are readily apparent here, the first being the perceived problem of mission drift. In the current circumstances, this is where a number of SEs are in the process of moving or have moved away from grant dependency to a business operating model. In these cases, the 'original' values of the organization may be challenged by the adoption of a more commercial paradigm.

The second aspect concerns the emphasis on the sometimes pivotal role of influential individuals in the instigation and maintenance of a virtuous approach. Moore raises this in the context of the corporate sector, but in SEs it can be particularly crucial because of their generally small size. Checks and balances available to a greater or lesser extent in the corporate sector through non-executive board members, the chair, range of management staff and so on are unlikely to be available to most SEs because of their small scale and the contingencies of their operating context.

Exhibit 7.4, detailing the SE Happen 4 U, an organization in the North West of England, addresses the notions of virtue ethics in the social economy sector through the focus of a 'new business' formation. It provides context by drawing on the experiences and views of a leading practitioner.

Exhibit 7.4   Happen 4 U

David Atkinson is the Chief Executive of HITS, a charity making social service provision for young people. He holds an MA in Social Enterprise and, from his studies, he has an interest in business ethics in the sector. Deriving from this interest, he has provided the following reflection on some of the ethical aspects arising from the strategic stance taken in the formation of the SE Happen 4 U, in which he was involved:

Happen 4 U is the name of a community interest company (CIC) which was instigated in November 2005 by four voluntary organizations based in Halton, Greater Merseyside, UK. It was formed when four charities, Halton Voluntary Action, Kings Cross Project, Age Concern and HITS began to explore the possibility of acting to secure the future of these charities by setting up a jointly owned trading arm. This was to provide an additional source of finance to support the core charitable activities, but also to address the following objectives:

- using social enterprise itself as a new vehicle for achieving existing charitable objectives (rather than just raising money for the charities);
- trading in the market to create economic opportunity and generate income for the benefit of local people (typically a goal of social enterprise but not explicitly an objective of any of the charities).

In embarking on the project, the four charities placed Happen 4 U at the heart of a web of obligations to, and potentially competing interests of, stakeholders from the public, private and voluntary sectors. There was a notably high level of motivation and synergy on the part of key individuals in the four charities. The implicit and explicit ethical basis of the behaviour and motivation of the key individuals is therefore of interest. The principle players in the collaboration were the chief executives of the charities. They were well known to each other with crossover relationships on management boards and a history of joint understanding. Indeed relationships were key, with the collaboration itself as much a matter for celebration and preservation as the explicit goal of bringing about Happen 4 U. Feminist ethics, emphasizing relationships in the process of making choices and achieving goals, rather than the choices and goals themselves, offers a useful perspective in this analysis.

The decision to embark on the Happen 4 U project was not a conscious choice between alternatives, and the assumption that the considerable expenditure of human resource time required was worthwhile because of the perceived potential benefits went unchallenged. To a significant degree, this arose because of the character and structure of the charities and the positions of the key players within them.

From the perspective of virtue ethics, neither the principle players, nor those around them, would have perceived themselves as 'virtuous' in the Aristotlean sense. There are, however, two reasons why virtue ethics, and its limitations, are significant in the decisionmaking in the Happen 4 U project.

The first reason stems from the character of charities as 'good' organizations by virtue of their serving 'good' causes. This has legal expression in their constitutions (or memorandum and articles of association), where the 'objects' require an explicit statement as to the benefit brought about by that charity. In the sense that charitable objects are a statement of the good consequences for beneficiaries (or for society as a whole), they echo the socially beneficial dimension of Aristotlean virtue (and Pearce's 'good work' value for social enterprises). The unquestioned assumption that the activities of the charities had 'good' consequences for their beneficiaries – and, by implication, the charities themselves were 'good' and their future security a desirable end – implicitly gave to the quest a virtuous character.

The traditional Aristotlean notion of virtue, however, applies to people, not organizations or activities, and the quest ultimately owes any virtuous character it had to the activities of individual people working in the charities. Individuals may engage with the 'good' character of a charity in various ways. Many people are attracted to work for a charity (often for less pay than in equivalent jobs in the public or private sectors) by the 'good' work it is doing. Aspirant staff may be asked to confirm their agreement with the organization's value base.

Organizational culture and priorities promote behaviour that reflects the values, ultimately enforceable through disciplinary codes. While none of this necessarily gave the principle protagonists a virtuous character, in their commitment to the virtuous quest, they may be said to be, implicitly, 'virtuous'.

The second reason relates to the relative power enjoyed by the charity chief executives arising from the structural and sapiential basis of their authority. All four reported to management boards largely comprising volunteers serving as charity trustees (and company directors) that included a chairperson who was formally responsible for line supervision of the chief executive. In three of four cases, the chairperson combined these responsibilities with full-time paid employment and a different three had spent significantly less time in their roles than the chief executives had in theirs. Overall, the chief executives' knowledge and position advantage over their unpaid superiors meant that there was relatively little scrutiny of their actions and a high reliance on their virtuous character guaranteeing that the 'right' judgments were made.

(Continued)

(Continued)

Attention was paid by all four charities to checking the new organization's legal documents, but at a stage when they had already made significant tangible commitments (staff appointed, funding in place), making the absence of scrutiny earlier on more evident.

These valuable reflections from a senior sector practitioner provide us with some interesting perspectives. As we have seen from the discussion in this section, contemporary conceptions of virtue ethics, in the business setting, focus on the organization as an entity. Considering virtue ethics in the SE sector; it seems clear, in the light of the operating scale, available resources and particular contingencies of the sector that the power of key individuals can be particularly crucial. Here it can be more pivotal than in corporate entities, the latter possessing more resources for checks and balances. It is axiomatic that this is also true of other small- to medium-sized enterprises, but it is argued that there is a particular importance here in the SE sector. This is because of the particular explicit and implicit social aspects in the stakeholder relationships and the related ethical considerations. Thus, the importance of virtuous character as part of virtue ethics, is arguably accentuated in the sector, particularly with regard to its exhorted role.

Feminist ethics

Feminist ethics is another type of contemporary ethical theory. Feminist theorists argue that the male view of the world regards the individual in a threatened or threatening position.

Traditional ethical theories are predicated on the male view of self. This drives a philosophical approach to ethics that is born out of conflict and strives to protect the individual. Hence, we have deontology, built on notions of justice, rights and corresponding duties. Traditional ethical theory is meant to be 'applied through reasoned calculation' (Burton and Dunn, 1996: 135). Thus, Kant's view of reason is the basis for the categorical imperative. In similar vein, utilitarianism concerns itself with the calculation and distribution of harms and benefits. These theories are designed for universalization and to express impartiality. As indicated, they are based on the protection of the individual and are situated in the male paradigm of conflict and competition.

The feminist view of ethics, however, is that the moral course is situated around the maintenance and protection of relationships. The feminist articulation of self is that it can only obtain meaning through relationships with others. Moral worth and self-actualization is achieved by carrying out the responsibilities inherent in relationships. Whereas deontology points us towards abstract definitions of duties and rights and so on, feminist ethics engages with morality through the notion of caring. In this, 'humans only know through relationships' (Burton and Dunn, 1996: 135). The focus is on emotions and responsibilities to others rather than the abstract notions of what is right and wrong. In the context of business, this feminist conceptualization takes us to a consideration of relations with stakeholders.

In their consideration of feminist ethics as an ethical underpinning for stakeholder theory in business, Burton and Dunn make reference to the feminist theory of Noddings (1984). Noddings points to the route to the resolution of moral dilemmas as being through the carrying out of dialogue. This is within the context of the reality of the relationships that exist between those involved. This assertion of stakeholder dialogue, drawn from feminist ethics, can provide us with particular meaning in the debate around the formation of local sustainable development. Building on the discussion of sustainable development earlier in the chapter, we could argue that achieving progress towards it is the key moral challenge of our time. If we reflect on how to achieve this, a range of ethical dilemmas in social, economic and environmental contexts are thrown up and conflicts revealed. These are set within the context of duties, rights and justice, the distribution of harms and benefits and so on.

Turning to consider the scale and operating environment of SEs, it is evident that local sustainable development, certainly in terms of the social context, is built on a feminist paradigm through a process of stakeholder dialogue. As Burton and Dunn point out, this occurs by engaging those affected by SEs' 'business' decisions in the process of making those decisions. As discussed earlier regarding sustainable development, it is through a local construction of reality, utilizing stakeholder dialogue, that progress towards sustainable development is achieved. Thus, this dialogue between stakeholders has particular meaning in this context of failures in traditional local government approaches to engage with communities (addressed, for instance, by Rotheroe et al., (2003). In so far as we might hope that local government would provide a framework for the local expression of sustainable development, this remains of some concern. Anecdotal evidence drawn from SEs reveals that there is a strong view, in the social economy sector, that local government and the public sector more generally is slow to comprehend the meaning of this (a matter that is the subject of current research). In this respect, the importance of SEs is that they are particularly capable of harnessing the feminist ethics-based approach. This is due to the sorts of relationshipbuilding, based on stakeholder dialogue, that they achieve when operating at their innovative best.

It is interesting to observe that innovation of this nature is exhorted by the policymaking and commissioning community when they consider the social economy sector. However, as indicated above, the evidence of real understanding of what this means, on the part of that community is far from being universally apparent. This is at national, regional and local levels, as is discussed above in the deontology section and the ADHD Foundation case study in Exhibit 7.1.

Central to feminist theory, the case study of the Women's Business Network given in Exhibit 7.5 provides an illustration of the perspectives that can be gained from the application of feminist ethics. The case also indicates some of the relationships between feminist ethics and social capital theory, as well as the values-led philosophy of SEs and progression towards sustainable development.

Exhibit 7.5 The Womens' BusinessNetwork – illustrating the ethics of care

The material for this case study is taken from an article by Livesey and Rotheroe (2007). The intention is to draw on some of the key points they make that bear on our discussion of feminist ethics. This paper addresses case study research carried out at the SE Women's Business Network (North West) Ltd (WBN), established in the North West of England.

With economic and social objectives, the WBN has as its aim supporting the creation of new women's business networks in the North West of England and linking them together across the region. At a strategic level, the WBN's mission is to encourage the entrepreneurial aspirations of women and create opportunities for expanding social capital and, thus, links to notions of sustainable development. This is in line with the assertion of Rubin and Bartle (2005: 1) that, 'The international community of nations has publicly committed itself to promoting gender equity, reflecting the realization that the equality of men and women is essential for sustainable economic growth and full social development.' This, though, is set in the context of the problem of there being a relative lack of participation of women in business ownership and business building.

The study addresses the propensity of gender-specific networks to contribute to the rectification of this deficit. The releasing of latent female entrepreneurial talent is explicit and, as indicated, framed in terms of economic and social sustainability. In the consideration of sustainability, the release of innovation and provision of the facility to assist new and existing businesswomen to fulfil their potential and life chances is central.

The research emphasizes the important point that, drawing on the ethics of care, these considerations should not be hijacked by the dominant power discourse emanating from the male literature. In this, indications from feminist theory are brought out and space is created to perceive differences that may exist with respect to the feminist view of business success. Briefly, to illustrate this and consider entrepreneurship, the paper refers to the 'alternative' approach of Greer and Green (2003: 18) who assert that:

> A traditional approach to entrepreneurship would focus on how to assist women business owners with growth and income generation, two areas where they typically lag behind. A more feminist and sociological approach recognizes the additional validity of a low-growth, less aggressive approach to earnings, along with the importance of business survival as a criterion of business success.

It seems apparent that some resonance can be found here with the values-led approach of SEs and their wider social purposes. Also, in the vein of the feminist approach, this research contrasts the male, conflict-driven, rule-based view with the view of Calás and Smircich (1992: 230) that 'women on the other hand, conceive of themselves as embedded contextually in an interpersonal network where the primary imperative is to be responsible to others and caring to maintain the web of connections. Actions are justified with reference to their impact on others.'

Thus, regarding feminist theory and the ethics of care, the different male and female views of self are acknowledged in the context. The research is also framed by network theory and social capital theory. It highlights the importance of networks in bringing about business success. Network theory is linked to social capital theory in that 'it is the brokerage across "structural holes" between groups that provides the mechanism by which social capital is accumulated.' This accumulation of social capital is sought after in the business context and its importance in relation to success in business terms is explored. Livesey and Rotheroe (2007: 15).

This work by Livesey and Rotheroe articulates the overarching framework offered by the ethics of care and supports the premise that women-only business networks provide the kinds of facilitating conditions to create network ties that have been successfully facilitated by WBN. It finds that feminine contributions, which may be defined as collaboration, cooperation, participation and empowerment, do shape and influence the network process. It is demonstrated that this lays the foundations for creating enabling environments in which women business people encounter an enabling utility and, it is suggested, this builds bridging and bonding social capital, which is very valuable in the context of sustainable business.

CONCLUDING COMMENTS ON ETHICAL THEORY

It is apparent that the stakeholder theory of Freeman (1984) conflicts with the free market view. The latter is predominant in the globalized economic system and is based on egoism. It is valuable to underpin stakeholder theory by using ethical theory. Arguments from traditional ethical theory, particularly Kant, can be useful in this respect. Perspectives from contemporary ethical theory, including feminist ethics, are also applicable. Feminist ethical theory can be seen to provide grounding for stakeholder approaches to business management. Contemporary versions of virtue ethics, discussed here, indicate the approach needed to set out and maintain ethical mission and values in the light of operating pressures.

It is productive to utilize these and other perspectives drawn from ethical theory when considering the place and justification for SEs. Operating at their best, and based on a values-led approach, SEs offer a potential vehicle for moral management. This is situated in the positive interactions it creates via dialogue with the range of stakeholders involved in its operations.

REFERENCES

Barnett, C., Cafaro, P. and Newholm, T. (2005) 'Philosophy and ethical consumption', in R. Harrison, T. Newholm and D. Shaw (eds), *The Ethical Consumer*. London: Sage.
Beauchamp, T.L. and Bowie, N.E. (2004) *Ethical Theory and Business*. Upper Saddle River, NJ: Pearson.

Boatright, J.R. (2003) *Ethics and the Conduct of Business*. Upper Saddle River, NJ: Pearson.

Burton, K.B. and Dunn, C.P. (1996) 'Feminist ethics as moral grounding for stakeholder theory', *Business Ethics Quarterly*, 6 (3): 133–48.

Cabinet Office (2002) 'Social capital discussion paper', produced for the Cabinet Office. London.

Calas, M.B. and Smircich, L. (1992) 'Using the "F" word: feminist theories and the social consequences of organisational theory', in, A.J. Mills and P. Tancred *Gendering Organisational Analysis*. London: Sage. pp. 222–34.

Carroll, A. (1979) 'A three-dimensional model of corporate social performance', *Academy of Management Review*, 4: 497–505.

Carroll, A. (1991) 'The pyramid of corporate social responsibility: toward the moral management of organisational stakeholders', *Business Horizons*, 34 (4): 39–49.

CFS (2005) 'CFS sustainability report', CFS, Manchester.

Chryssides, G.D. and Kaler, J.H. (1993) *An Introduction to Business Ethics*. London: Thompson.

Crane, A. and Matten, D. (2007) *Business Ethics*. Oxford: Oxford University Press.

Defourney, J. and Nyssens, M. (2006) 'Defining social enterprise', in M. Nyssens (ed.), *Social Enterprise: At the crossroads of market, public policies and civil society*. London: Routledge.

DEFRA (2005) 'Securing the future: UK Government sustainable development strategy', The Stationery Office. London.

Department of Health (2006) National Institute for Clinical Excellence Report on Services for Children with Attention Deficit Hyperactivity Disorder. HMSO National Institute of Clinical Excellence. Available at www.nice.org.uk.

De George, R.T. (1999) *Business Ethics*. Upper Saddle River, NJ: Prentice Hall.

Dicken, P. (2007) *Global Shift: Mapping the Changing Contours of the World Economy* (5th edn.). London: Sage.

Doherty, R. and Tranchell, S. (2007) '"Radical mainstreaming" of fair trade: the case of the Day Chocolate Company', *Equal Opportunities International*, 20 (7): 693–711.

DTI (2002) 'Social enterprise: a strategy for success', DTI, London.

Elkington, J. (1997) *Cannibals with Forks: The triple bottom line in the 21st century*. Oxford: Capstone.

Evan, W. and Freeman, R.E. (1993) 'A stakeholder theory of the modern corporation: Kantian capitalism', in W.M. Hoffman and R.E. Frederick (eds), *Business Ethics Readings and Cases in Corporate Morality* (3rd edn). New York: McGraw-Hill.

Evers, A., Laville, J.L., Borgaza, C., Defourny, J., Lewis, J., Nyssens, M. and Pestoff, V. (2004) 'Defining the third sector in Europe', in A. Evers and J.L. Laveille (eds), *The Third Sector in Europe*. London: Edward Elgar.

Field, J. (2003) *Social Capital*. New York: Routledge.

Freeman, R.E. (1984) *Strategic Management: A stakeholder approach*. Boston, MA: Pitman.

Friedman, M. (1970) 'The social responsibility of business is to increase profits', *New York Times Magazine*, 13 September.

GRI (2006) 'Sustainability reporting guidelines', GRI, Amsterdam.

Bill and Melinda Gates Foundation (2007) Available online at: www.gatesfoundation.org/default.htm

Greer, M.J. and Greene, P.G. (2003) 'Feminist theory and the study of entrepreneurship', in J.E. Butler (ed.), *New Perspectives on Women Entrepreneurs*. Chanotte, NC: Information Age Publishing. pp. 1–24.

Hart, S.L. and Milstein, M.B. (2003) 'Creating sustainable value', *Academy of Management Executive*, 17 (2): 56–69.

Hooghe, M. and Stolle, D. (2003) *Generating Social Capital: Civil society and institutions in perspective*. New York: Palgrave Macmillan.

ISEA (1999) 'Accountability 1000 (AA1000) framework', ISEA. London.

Kay, A. (2003) 'Social capital in building the social economy', in J. Pearce, *Social Enterprise in Anytown*. London: Calouste Gulbenkian Foundation.

Lepineux, F. (2005) 'Stakeholder theory, society and social cohesion', *Corporate Governance*, 5 (2): 99–110.

Livesey, R. and Rotheroe, N. (2007) 'Women's business networks: do they contribute to sustainability by facilitating bonding and bridging social capital ties, increasing confidence and encouraging creativity and sharing of good ideas?', *Journal of Finance and Management*, Special Edition: Social Enterprise.

MacGillivray, A. (2004) 'Social capital at work: a manager's guide', in A. Henriques and J. Richardson, *The Triple Bottom Line: Does it all add up?* London: Earthscan.

MacIntyre, A. (1985) *After Virtue*. London: Duckworth.

Matten, D. and Crane, A. (2005) 'Corporate citizenship: toward an extended theoretical conceptualization', *Academy of Management Review*, 30 (1): 166–79.

Meehan, J., Meehan, K. and Richards, A. (2006) 'Corporate social responsibility: the 3C-SR model', *International Journal of Social Economics*, 33 (56): 386–98.

Moore, G. (2005) 'Corporate character: modern virtue ethics and the corporation', *Business Ethics Quarterly*, 15 (4): 659–85.

Nicholls, A. and Dpal, C. (2004) *Fair Trade: Market-driven ethical consumption*. London: Sage.

Noddings, N. (1984) *Caring: A feminine approach to ethics and moral education*. Berkeley, CA: University of California Press.

Offer, A. (2006) *The Challenge of Affluence: Self-control and well-being in the United States and Britain since 1950*. Oxford: Oxford University Press.

Patton, H. (1964) *Immanuel Kant, Groundwork of The Metaphysics of Morals*. Trans. H. Patton. London: Harper Row.

Pearce, D. (1991) *Blueprint 2: Greening the world economy*. London: Earthscan. Ltd.

Pearce, J. (2003) *Social Capital in Any Town*. London: Calouste Gulbenkian Foundation.

OTS (2006) 'Social enterprise action plan: scaling new heights', OTS, London.

Pearce, J. and Kay, A. (2005) *Social Accounting and Audit: The manual*. Exeter: Social Audit Network.

Porrit, J. (2005) *Capitalism: As if the world matters*. London: Earthscan.

Putnam, R.D. (1993) *Making Democracy Work: Civic traditions in modern Italy*. Princeton, NJ: Princeton University Press.

Rawls, J. (1971) *A Theory of Justice*. Cambridge, MA: Harvard University Press.

Rotheroe, N., Hunter, S. and Milne, L. (2003) 'Delivering sustainable development in the local government context: linking strategic and operational aspects', Corporate Social Responsibility and Environmental Management Conference Proceedings, University of Leeds, 30 June–1 July.

Rotheroe, N. and Richards, A. (2007) 'Social return on investment and social enterprise: transparent accountability for sustainable development', *Social Enterprise Journal*, 3 (1): 31–48.

Rubin, M.M. and Bartle, J.R. (2005) 'Integrating gender into government budgets: a new perspective', *Public Administration Review*, 65 (3), Special report.

Scholte, J.A. (2005) *Globalisation: A critical introduction*. London: Palgrave Macmillan.

Schwartz, M.S. and Carroll, A.B. (2003) 'Corporate social responsibility: a three domain approach', *Business Ethics Quarterly*, 13 (40): 503–30.

Sethi, S.P. (1975) 'Dimensions of corporate social performance: an analytical framework', *California Management Review*, 17 (3): 63–75.

Shaw, E. and Carter, S. (2007) 'Social entrepreneurship: theoretical antecedents and empirical analysis of entrepreneurial processes and outcomes', *Journal of Small Business and Enterprise Development*, 14 (3): 418–34.

Tiffen, P. (2002) 'A chocolate-coated case for alternative international business models', *Development in Practice*, 12 (3 & 4): 383–97.

Tranchell, S. (2008) Presentation on Divine Chocolate Ltd, made at Liverpool Business School, July, unpublished.

Treanor, J. (2008) 'Co-op refuses to invest in six companies', *The Guardian*, 24 March, p. 29.

Trevino, L.K. and Nelson, K.A. (2004) *Managing Business Ethics: Straight talk about how to do it right*. Chichester: John Wiley.

UNDESA (2007) 'The millennium development goals report', UNDESA. New York.

Van de Ven, B. (2005) 'Human rights as a normative basis for stakeholder legitimacy', *Corporate Governance*, 5 (2): 58–9.

Wijeratna, A. (2005) *Rotten Fruit: Tesco profits and women workers pay a high price*. London: Action Aid.

8

GOVERNANCE AND SEs

INTRODUCTION

The social and economic value of SEs is being increasingly recognized on an international scale. As this book has already made clear, these organizations have a key role in local, national and international regeneration and development. On a national level, it is estimated that 'there are more than 55,000 SEs ... with a combined turnover of £27 billion. Social Enterprises account for 5 per cent of all businesses with employees, and contribute £8.4 billion per year to the UK economy' (SEC, 2008).

Communities concerned with defined social, environmental and/or economic issues can use SEs to mobilize support for their chosen causes. Therefore, it becomes apparent that the 'value' they contribute is more than merely the economic impact they have. Moreover, the focus is on laudable outcomes, such as employability for excluded or minority groups, gender empowerment and social regeneration. It is on these economic and non-economic terms that the value of SEs is best understood.

On an international scale, the EU stresses its support for SEs as a valuable part of the social economy sector across its economic region. Furthermore, there is a long-established and thriving non-profit sector in the USA and Canada that encompasses SEs, while international support organizations, such as the Non-profit Enterprise and Self-sustainability Team (NESsT), work to promote international SEs and related projects. The latter organizations play an increasingly influential role in the development of SEs in emerging and developing economies, such as South America, India and South East Asia (UNIDO, 2002).

This snapshot of the global presence of the social economy highlights its relevance to contemporary society as we work to alleviate social, environmental and economic suffering. In tandem with this growth are a number of emergent issues and challenges that policymakers, trade and umbrella organizations, as well as social entrepreneurs and academics will have to face. One of the principal challenges requires an understanding of the bases for their governance, which is the focus of this chapter. By the term 'governance', I refer to the ability of SEs' boards to meet the needs of their stakeholders in both strategic and operational terms. These critical elements of the board's remit are discussed throughout this chapter. However, rather than provide a blueprint for 'good governance' by offering solutions to the key governance issues raised throughout, this chapter focuses on a discussion of these contemporary challenges as they are relevant to the sector.

The central tenets of governance are based on finding and maintaining the most appropriate arrangements for the protection of specified, stakeholder interests. Given that this chapter is concerned with the role of the board, it should be noted that the field of governance research transcends industries and sectors. Of course, one of the key variables that differentiates corporate from public and non-profitmaking sectors is *whose* interests are being protected in the process of governance. So, this chapter intends to look more closely at governance of SEs and some of its key concepts and practical realities. In so doing, we are really interested in addressing some questions about governance from a practical, as well as academic, viewpoint.

Principally, this concerns non-profitmaking organizations in terms of what governance is and how it has developed. The first section of this chapter deals with this subject in a succinct fashion, as well as explaining why governance in SEs is different from other types of governance. Having set the context for exploring governance of SEs, the chapter then develops a discursive account of the outcomes of governance, as well as the groups involved in the act of governing. In so doing, the chapter explores some of the most pertinent issues that tend to influence the effective governing of the SE. These include board member selection and recruitment, training for board members and embedding effective performance measurement systems.

As will become apparent, there are many differing perspectives on what constitutes 'effective' governance, which is perhaps infused with the high degree of enthusiasm and realism found among social entrepreneurs, boards and managers. This drive typically enhances the critical debate between these groups and leads political and academic institutions to provide an overview of the prescient governance challenges facing SEs. These include:

- mitigating 'failure' of SEs;
- enabling self-sufficiency through regular, sustainable trade;
- reconciling different types of accountability, including democratic and financial efficacy;
- developing a culture of transparent practice at board level, including board member effectiveness;
- managing the delivery and measurement of social benefits.

Each of the above points is covered in this chapter and an attempt made to signify the severity of their influence on governance, given the environmental pressures boards and staff are required to accommodate. The chapter also presents a conceptual 'committee' model for governance of SEs. This model is proposed in an attempt to pave the way for solutions to some of the critical issues raised in the course of the chapter, leading to a reflective comment on the future challenges for governance of SEs.

GOVERNANCE AND SEs

A brief overview of governance

The governance of organizations, as a concept and a practice, has a deep history. Much has been made in recent times of the problems associated with 'white-collar crime' and the myriad examples of high-profile governance misdemeanours bear testament to this. The most notorious examples are often recounted in newspaper or journal articles as symptomatic of governance failure, including Enron, WorldCom, Parmalat and BAE. (Zandstra, 2002) As a result, the term 'governance' (often, but not always 'corporate governance') has become synonymous with the wrongdoings of executives, directors, chief executives and other key individuals and groups involved in organizations. Current issues surrounding Japanese corporate governance continue to cause problems, as well as individual global corporations crying foul in big emerging markets (for example, BP in Russia).

There is also an international perspective, with the UK, USA and the EU demonstrating a keen awareness of the challenges facing organizational governance. More recently, Japan, the Middle East nations as well as the USA and Europe are providing legislative support to the political rhetoric, calling for greater protection for those stakeholders affected by governance issues at both national and supranational levels (Black et al., 1999; Vinten, 1998).

Governance of SEs

The practice and study of governance has revealed techniques and mechanisms for managing organizations to realize the interests of their primary beneficiaries. With origins in economic and legal fields, corporate governance as a set of practices arose in tandem with the growth of the 'corporate' form itself (Grant, 2003). This, however, was not corporation as we understand it today and actually refers to the chartering of 'public corporations' in the UK. Over time, a particular legal framework has evolved around socially orientated organizations. This framework broadly encompasses:

- the legal form used to incorporate the organization:
  - trusts/unincorporated associations:
    - clubs/village halls;
    - partnerships;
  - industrial and provident society companies;
  - limited by guarantee;
  - limited by shares, PLC:
    - community interest company;
    - limited liability partnership;
    - charitable incorporated organization;

- the rights and responsibilities of board members, as defined by the Charities Act 2006, as well as official guidance, such as Trustee Remuneration Guidance;

- the supervision of some types of SEs by defined institutions (the Charity Commission – see Locke et al., 2003).

While consideration of the merits of the various legal forms is not within the remit of this chapter, it is worth noting that the types of board members are often prescribed by the legal structure of the organization. Legal structures have facilitated the development of board 'roles' (for example, company secretary, non-executive directors), each of which will have a particular governance role and associated responsibility.

Governance can be defined broadly as a 'set of relationships between [an organiza-tion's] management, its board ... and other stakeholders' (OECD, 2004, p. 11), In this definition, the word 'company' has been deliberately replaced by 'organization', because the principle commonality in governance of organizations is the role played by the management, the board (however it may be comprised) and stakeholder groups. This catch all definition, however, stems from the corporate view of governance and neglects some of the different objectives of SEs that should be included. Nonetheless, it does provide an overview of the key elements of governance in general, such as the management of relationships between key groups and working towards an overarching objective.

So, the next, logical step is to try and conceptualize an appropriate definition of governance for SEs. First, we must consider what constitutes a SE before we can feasibly define what governance of SEs might be. According to various authors, SEs exist for a variety of reasons, including (Paton, 2003; Pearce, 2003):

- democracy;

- social justice;

- empowerment of minority or excluded groups;

- entrepreneurship;

- sustainable development;

- working in partnership.

These elements generally fit with the aims of SEs – that is, they work in partnership with staff, service users and support groups to achieve social (or environmental and economic) outcomes. They do so through entrepreneurship and aim to alleviate or redress issues concerning defined groups. This leads us on towards broader aims, such as can be classified under the umbrella of 'sustainable development', which includes regeneration and social inclusion.

If these elements represent some of the aims of SEs, then we must consider how they link with governance. Some of the expectations stakeholders might have of the governance of SEs might be those listed in Table 8.1.

The points made above illustrate how governance might fit with the expected characteristics of SEs as well as the potential groups that might affect or be affected by the governance of such organizations.

Table 8.1 **Stakeholders' expectations of the governance of SEs**

Stakeholder groups relevant to governance	Expected features of governance of SEs
Service users	Ethical governance
Internal staff (managers, directors, trustees)	Board-level strategic leadership
Local communities	A requirement to manage stakeholders' interests
Local government	Enabling and supporting an internal culture of maximizing social benefits
Funding bodies	Promoting inclusion of stakeholders
Support groups	Managing the establishment of a culture of accountability and transparency

'Governance' involves leadership of the board (including, but not limited to, a group of trustees) and management of different interests (Alexander and Weiner, 1998). 'Interests' here covers the financial and non-financial claims that various groups have on the organization – particularly defined communities and external sources of funding and political support (Huse, 1998). The SE needs to represent these interests and integrate them into the strategic decisions made by the organization.

This leads us towards the development of a more relevant definition of governance for SEs:

> **strategic and operational board-level leadership, enabling service users, managers, trustees and other defined stakeholders to create and maximize social benefit.**

This definition encapsulates a number of linked elements:

- the general tasks of the board in the SE, recognizing that it has strategic and operational responsibilities;
- the groups they influence and are influenced by;
- the raison d'être of the SE – creating and maximizing social benefit.

In this chapter, we are interested in the relationships between three disparate groups: the board, internal staff or other influencers in terms of the creation of social benefit and the group(s) in receipt of this benefit. We are particularly concerned with how the needs of each are satisfied or limited by behavioural dynamics and formal measures of 'performance'.

The former issue, 'behavioural dynamics', is the informal, unique and highly contextual interpersonal activities that occur within and between each group in the governance triumvirate (Huse, 2005). These influences often dictate how the organization operates and such aspects as the degree of freedom given to managers by the board and the power held by key stakeholders at board level, including the chair and chief executive.

The latter consideration, formal systems of performance measurement, include measures such as testing how well the organization has performed against its objectives and the processes used to check performance. Such systems typically examine financial performance – for example, through the periodic compilation of financial statements and audits – yet there is a growing tendency to check other bases of performance that analyse the social and environmental impact made by an organization (Elkington, 1997).

In light of this shifting and challenging emphasis on performance measurement and the role of governance in SEs, it is notable that the process can be viewed as an opportunity, too. A brief summary of some of these opportunities and challenges is given in Table 8.2. Suffice to say that the challenges and opportunities are often symptomatic of the antagonistic relationship between two issues. For example, there is a contrast between the need for effective leadership at board level and board-level individuals who wield too much power in the decisionmaking process. The implications posed by this dichotomy are explored throughout this chapter.

Table 8.2 Opportunities and challenges in the governance of SEs

Opportunities	Challenges
Establish strong strategic leadership	Board management difficulties
Provide staff empowerment and upskilling	Identifying and resolving leadership issues
Enhance democratic accountability	Prohibitive cultural barriers to change
Establish a level of competitiveness in new and existing markets	Enabling the inclusion of stakeholders
Foster and maintain board-level transparency	Managing function-specific expertise (such as marketing)
Manage and deliver benefits to a range of identified stakeholder groups	Problems with identifying and managing diverse stakeholder interests

SEs share traits with other non-profitmaking organizations (although the term 'non-profitmaking' here is used with a deal of caution). For example, an SE's board commonly comprises trustees or directors, a chief executive and chair. The unique element of an SE's board, and its governance activity, is the management of the defined social/business objectives. This is a trait it has in common with other non-profitmaking organizations that engage in enterprise activities. The boards of these organizations have the difficult task of ensuring that the organizations can meet their (often conflicting) objectives (Mason et al., 2007). Objectives are considered to conflict when their simultaneous pursuit entails trade-offs, resulting in lowered performance in the attainment of one or more of the objectives. Furthermore, they face a further pressure in that governance, as an organizational process, ensures that board members can be and are held to account for their actions and performance. To this end, the board must also consider *how* they are made accountable to various groups of stakeholders.

As the prior discussion has made clear, there are several 'groups' involved in the process of governing. In the traditional corporate view of governance, the board is charged with ensuring that managers are working towards the agreed goals of the organization. In this regard, board members have a fiduciary (legal) and moral duty to make sure that primary stakeholders benefit from the organization's activity (see Jensen, 2001). In practical terms, it is understandable that the governance process is necessarily complex as there is a need to manage a wide variety of stakeholders. This need may originate from source or arise when a decision has already been made at board level and it then requires immediate and ongoing consideration.

The literature on the governance of SEs highlights two models that could be followed: stakeholder and stewardship theories (Borzaga and Solari, 2001; Dart, 2004; Low, 2006).

The stakeholder model has prevailed for a long time in academic circles and remains popular due to its roots in social responsibility and application to non-profitmaking organizations (Cornforth, 2003; Letza et al., 2004; Turnbull, 1997). SEs have a shared history with non-profitmaking organizations, prompting a transference of 'values' from one to the other.

The stakeholder interpretation of governance of SEs supports the notional integration of various interests into decisions made within the organization. The premise here is that organizations (particularly corporations) have historically neglected the interests of groups that have no direct, legal power over the organization. Indeed, this forms the basis of criticisms of traditional business models that eschew any social and environmental responsibilities that are not legally prescribed. Therefore, the stakeholder model promotes diverse interests in the organization, provided that the individuals or groups concerned influence or can be influenced by the organization (Freeman and Reed, 1983). Such efforts are intended to enhance the organization's accountability by leveraging the moral rights of marginalized groups.

This model is very popular and has grown in significance in recent times because many organizations recognize the long-term benefit of stakeholder engagement, but the approach can also be problematic (Orts and Strudler, 2002). With regard to recognizing a broad array of interests, the stakeholder model is less radical to non-profitmaking organizations than it is to corporations (Abzug, 1999). The stakeholder model is useful for corporations because it legitimizes a previously hidden or even non-existent dialogue between the organization's internal staff and other neglected though influential groups (Friedman and Miles, 2002). This breaks the mould in management thinking by diverting the focus of the organization's activity *away* from shareholder value, for example. Yet, for non-profitmaking organizations, this model is rather implicit – such organizations *already* recognize diverse stakeholder groups that likely do not benefit from its performance as corporate shareholders do.

For the stakeholder model to be useful to SEs, then, it must help to explain how such relationships can be managed more effectively. At such a descriptive level, stakeholder theory does not go into the organization deeply enough to focus on the rationale behind the mechanisms of governance. Aside from merely classifying relationships and presenting the moral argument for doing so, the stakeholder model does not offer a progressive understanding of how to manage them successfully (Gibson, 2000; Phillips et al., 2003).

The same can be said of stewardship theory. It is useful because it conceptualizes the director and manager as fiduciaries (legal trustees) of organizational assets (Davis et al., 1997; Donaldson and Davis, 1991). Self-serving behaviour on their part is acceptable when their benefit is intrinsically tied to the performance of the organization. This can be said to be true of intermediate labour market organizations and social firms. Both of these kinds of organizations provide pathways to skills development and long-term employment for those excluded from the labour market. In theory, the communities these SEs serve are also (mainly) the same individuals who run the organizations. Therefore, to maximize their benefits, they must pursue the best interests of the organization (Low, 2006; Van Slyke, 2007).

Of course, a realistic appraisal of this would signify that the objectives of one community are recognized but not shared by internal groups. Like stakeholder theory, stewardship theory does not consider other factors that can influence managers and directors to make them more effective. Furthermore, it does not consider situations where such control might not be required – for example, providing effective oversight of individual access to and usage of an organization's finances.

There are alternatives to the approaches that dominate the literature for those interested in the informal and cultural influences on governance of SEs. A prominent approach that provides an option other than the stakeholder and stewardship views is the institutional theory of organizations. This approach emphasizes the importance of relational and cultural influences on governance and places legitimacy at the heart of analysis, which is useful for examining the roles of stakeholders (for example, how they are affected by governance) (Scott, 1987; Suchman, 1995).

The premise here is that how SEs do and should manage stakeholders is partly what makes them unique vis-à-vis other types of organization. This view of their governance derives from their founding philosophy and is expected of them by their key communities. The institutional environment also defines the boundaries for how the SE is governed, according to regulative, normative and cultural/cognitive boundaries (Scott, 2008).

Naturally, the legal (regulative) influences are the formal expectations regarding the behaviour and performance of board members and other staff. These codes aim to regulate individual activities and behaviour to safeguard a set of defined stakeholder interests, while conferring defined responsibilities on the SE and individual roles.

The normative aspect relates to the expected standards of behaviour that prevail within the organization, which may exist beyond the requirements of the regulative component. They comprise the values and norms of the SE. The term 'values' relates to the ideals the organization is striving to achieve. These values should therefore be a prominent feature of the activities undertaken by the organization. The second key feature of the normative environment relates to the expected 'outcomes' from the organization's activities, as well as the accepted practices for achieving them. For example, the Resource Alliance is a progressive organization that seeks to provide support for voluntary sector organizations by supporting volunteers. It has established a strong set of core values to illustrate this and communicates if to its many stakeholders (Resource Alliance, 2008).

- *Excellence* as an organization and as an enabler to other organizations, we strive for excellence in everything we do, practice and demonstrate.

- *Inclusive and diverse* the global alliance is inclusive and diverse in terms of the people and organizations involved and in its ideas.

- *Innovative* promoting and multiplying innovative approaches for increasing and diversifying sources of support.

- *Accountable* the Resource Alliance holds itself accountable to those it works with and promotes the highest standards in resource mobilization and fundraising practice.

The final component in this view is a consideration of the role of cultural/cognitive elements of the institutional environment, which requires the analysis of taken-for-granted aspects of SEs. This aspect asks that we consider the considerable influence that making sense of and the meaning of the external environment have on the internal environment of the SE. In other words, individuals and groups working in the SE behave in ways that are culturally determined and commonly understood. These influences exist even if such activities divert people from the regulative and normative constituents of the internal environment.

This view differs from other prescriptive, formal elements of an SE's institutional framework, instead emphasizing the dynamic and adaptive nature of the 'meaning' of the SE (Scott, 2003). The organization is engaged in an ongoing dialogue, internally and externally, so the collective understanding of values (why the SE exists) and social reality (what it is like to run the SE) change accordingly.

Naturally, for governance activities this is influential because the process is influenced by all three of the so-called pillars of institutions (Scott, 2008) that we have looked at. Regulative pressures on the SE pervade the board – for example, there are the legal responsibilities regarding remuneration of trustees, as well as other relevant legislation (Inglis et al., 1999). The expected standards of behaviour and adherence to common values are also a feature of governance – board members *should* act in the interests of primary stakeholders, as well as championing the cause (as the essence of) the SE. These and other normative aspects, are often strongly communicated and understood – even constitutionally defined. The final aspect, though is perhaps more subtle and emphasizes an individual internalization of external influences, of which the former, of course, is highly subjective. The influence of this on governance is represented by the shared understanding of the reality of managing an SE at board level. Instead, we recognize that boards will operate heuristically, depending on the power and political relations within and external to the board, experience and success in strategic development and operational planning, managing the demands of service users, staff, funders, even local government (Murray et al., 2006; Stone et al., 1999). These factors all add to a highly unique and complex view of what a board is that is quite inaccessible to those unfamiliar with the SE, its history, its board and the challenges the organization faces.

Where this approach to understanding governance differs significantly from stakeholder and stewardship approaches is that is considers the role of deeper influences on governance. Regarding institutional influences on the organization, Zucker (1977) explained that they can be represented as patterns of activity and/or formal constituents of the environment. The former are exhibited in actions undertaken by particular individuals (or groups), in specified roles towards achieving a legitimating outcome or set of outcomes. The latter take the form of objective systems and processes, which exist to ensure the reification and maintenance of institutional norms.

These are both important for governance because they determine *who* undertakes particular internal functions as well as *how*. The *why* is grounded in the search for legitimacy and determined by the ability of internal actors to meet expected legitimating outcomes (Dart, 2004; Goddard and Assad, 2006). Furthermore, these individuals are also guided by cognitive and cultural constraints. These are the internalized understanding of institutional norms that are shaped by external forces discussed above.

This means that the governance of SEs is guided by powerful, enduring and semi-permanent rules, conventions and understandings that bind the organization together. This view of SE governance is very useful because it demands that we examine the formal and informal influences on how the organization is run. Further, it reaffirms legitimacy as the outcome of acceptable performance. Defined stakeholders have the power to assent or relinquish legitimacy if the governance does not meet specified standards. These include standards of financial, social, environmental and ethical performance, which can be accounted for using a triple bottom line approach (Elkington, 1997).

For the governance theories described above, accountability is a unifying concept. Institutional analysis encourages organizations to define processes on three bases; it also focuses on the role of shared meanings and values in organizations. As Golden-Biddle and Rao (1997) outlined, there is a strong sense of identity in non-profitmaking organizations' boards that is grounded in the shared meaning of what the organizations stand for. It is not unreasonable to suggest that this would also apply to SEs, where the shared meaning is geared towards social benefit (Pearce, 2003).

How these factors contribute to trust in an organization with strong values and a social mission awaits further examination in some depth. Institutional views of SEs are useful because they account for the power of shared values within them. Clearly, SEs are organizations built around values (or some definition of social benefit). Therefore, we might predict that SEs can offer something unique regarding how they govern according to these shared values. However, before we determine the value of the governance of SEs to other organizations, we must first outline the key outcomes of governance and why these matter to legitimacy.

Figure 8.1 illustrates a model that shows the relational nature of the groups involved in the governance of SEs. The three main groups, as understood in the academic literature are classified accordingly. The interplay between each part of the model illustrates the interrelatedness and dependency each group has on the other. The major implication of this crossover is on critical decisionmaking, where the interests of one group are (or are not) accommodated in the strategic decisions made by the board. Naturally, these processes are dynamic and different for each SE, leading to an understanding of the complexity of board-level relationships and decisionmaking.

The model neglects the various external influences on the organization from other stakeholder groups that might affect decisionmaking and related activities. The intention of this model is not to be prescriptive, but, rather illustrative of the three key groups in the governance of SEs. A broader discussion of the assortment of stakeholder interests in the governance of SEs is provided in each of the following subsections.

The next section explains how various groups 'fit' within this model and helps us to understand the complexities of governance as experienced by board members, managers and stakeholders. There are also sections that provide an overview of three key governance issues: accountability, transparency and democracy. Accountability provides a barometer of board-level performance, while transparency indicates the openness and accessibility of the board. Democracy relates to the nature of board-level decision-making, voting procedures and inclusive recruitment (see Spear, 2004). Following this,

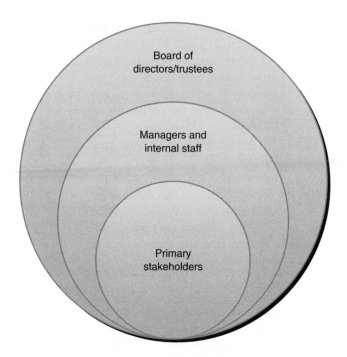

Figure 8.1   An illustrative model of three key groups in the governance of SEs

some of the contemporary issues relating to specific roles in SEs are discussed in relation to each of the three key areas.

GOVERNANCE CHALLENGES

Accountability

The uniting factor between governance contexts is the concept of accountability. In this chapter, it plays a key role in a discussion of whom we owe duties to, and how we can manage the process of accountability in the governance of SEs. Accountability is defined as the 'duty to provide an account (by no means necessarily a financial account) or reckoning of those actions for which one is held responsible' (Gray et al., 1996: 38). There are several different interpretations of accountability and, in this chapter, the major focus is on accountability in governance. This represents the level of 'performance' board members and managers are judged to uphold in their duties to stakeholders. This applies to private, public and non-profitmaking organizations (Ezzamel and Willmott, 1993; Kearns, 1994; Young, 2002). It is essential to governance because it provides mechanisms that encourage good governance. The mechanisms available to achieve accountability in governance are numerous and always developing (Rotheroe and Richards, 2007; Van Kersbergen and Van Waarden, 2004). The value of accountability for SEs is that it symbolize an ethos of proving the effectiveness of its governance, focusing on the performance of individuals as well as management teams and the board.

Exhibit 8.1   A case in point – the Furniture Resource Centre

Based in the North West of England, the Furniture Resource Centre (FRC) has two overarching social objectives – supplying good-quality, low-cost furniture to those most in need and providing employment opportunities to those suffering exclusion from the labour market. Like a number of SEs, the FRC utilizes intermediate labour market opportunities to provide 12 months of paid experience to individuals whom, in many cases, had previously been unemployed for over a decade. The support offered is designed to reinvigorate the trainees back into a culture of work while providing practical experience and qualifications to secure sustainable employment on completion of the training period.

The FRC typifies the values-led approach that is a very familiar SE business model (Westall, 2001), with bravery, passion, professionalism and creativity as the core values that drive the enterprise forward. In order to truly embed the values of the enterprise, regular awards are made for individuals and teams that demonstrate one or more of the core values. To achieve the primary social objectives while maintaining a viable approach to achieving the desired triple bottom line performance, the FRC (2006) has articulated four objectives, which are to be:

- great to do business with;
- a great place to work;
- great for people;
- great for the planet.

Open and honest accountability encourages evolution, thereby creating the possibility of enhancements in terms of sustainable development. Transparent accountability is an integral element of the FRC's values-led approach. The social, environmental and sustainable development reports have embraced the philosophy of more than simply reporting performance, complementing such offerings with realistic yet challenging targets for improvement. The integration of monthly reporting also answers many criticisms of single periodic formal accounting practices, addressing what Gray et al. (1996) describe as the fundamental requirement for such accounting to remain a continual and evolutionary process. It is this integrated and embedded process that enables the FRC to produce annual reports for external stakeholders. The FRC's reports have received frequent recognition from the Association of Chartered Certified Accountants (ACCA), including being shortlisted for the 2006 sustainability reporting award. Having previously received the award for best social report, comments included that the level of accountability for such a small organization was exceptional, setting the benchmark standard for all SEs. Furthermore, the openness and honesty of revealing failings as well as successes, along with objectives for improvement, were cited as significant inclusions (FRC, 2005).

(Continued)

(Continued)

The increasing use of performance measurement techniques by the FRC exemplifies the requirement for continued development in organizational accountability. The transparent nature of this SE amplifies such a necessity, as stagnation could result in a levelling of legitimacy. Introducing performance measurement techniques such as the local multiplier model and the social return on investment (SROI) analysis typifies the two-way 'virtuous' relationship between transparency and accountability.

The FRC is an exemplar of success for SEs. The commitment to prove and improve has enabled the FRC to meet the challenges of managing growth and delivering on its social, economic and environmental objectives. This case exemplifies that embedding the social reporting processes in the day-to-day running of the organization enables a sustainable platform for improving performance.

This continued improvement and commitment to professional excellence have made the FRC one of the growing numbers of best practice 'role models' in the third sector. The degree to which this will be effected across the sector is currently open to debate (Low, 2006; Reid and Griffith, 2006). However, one view is that social entrepreneurs will see the benefits of the FRC's strategy – that ensuring accountability enables them to improve their return on social benefit through a commitment to sustainable governance practices.

Transparency

Transparency is another important facet of governance. Pearce (2003: 191) describes it as when 'an organization, in the interests of being accountable, openly discloses the findings of its social accounts so that stakeholders have a good understanding of how the organization performs and behaves'.

Making activities and decision-making processes transparent encourages trust in them among the organization's stakeholders. Often, ensuring transparency and the efficacy of such activities is achieved by subjecting them to external scrutiny for verification. Transparency is recognized as a central feature of good governance across sectors, including non-profitmaking organizations and SEs (Aguilera, 2005; Gray, 1992; Paton, 2003; Strenger, 2004).

We can understand transparency in terms of the institutional environment. The formal and informal safeguards and pressures that ensure the proper running of an organization represent transparency. Formal, or regulative, safeguards include laws that regulate the organization and define the legal duties of its managers and directors. For example, the new legal form of SE in the UK, the CIC, 'locks' assets to protect them from misuse. Informal safeguards of transparency include normative and cultural/cognitive pressures that, together with regulative pressures, influence the creation and maintenance of the institutional environment (Scott, 2001). Both formal and informal elements are integral to ensuring that governance is transparent and thereby contribute to its legitimacy.

Transparency is valuable because it fosters trust and confidence in key stakeholders about the governance of the organization (Brinkerhoff, 2002). A commitment to transparent governance processes signifies that the board is performing more effectively than if they are not committed to standards of transparency. However, beyond a purely descriptive level, this 'commitment' does not logically equate with 'effectiveness'. Though the importance of transparency in terms of the performance of the board is noted in the academic literature, there are many other factors that will influence perceptions of 'effectiveness' (Nobbie and Brudney, 2003). These include embedded management practices and emerging market forces as well as the performance measures and criteria adopted (Lowenstein, 1996).

The drive for greater transparency across sectors promotes ethical conduct among directors (Fernández-Fernández, 1999). They are bound by a fiduciary duty to ensure that the ethical standards within the organization align with the expectations of its primary beneficiaries (Davis, 1994). Attaining and maintaining ethical standards is central to achieving accountability.

The audit process should enhance transparency and ensure social, environmental and financial disclosure. This process enables the efficacy of governance and business operations to be examined. As Bushman et al. (2004) make clear, there are two types of transparency: financial and governance transparency.

The former refers to the full disclosure of appropriate financial information to investors and other relevant bodies. Financial disclosure is the concern of the board of directors. It has to provide full, detailed financial reckoning for the SE's activities and make this information as accessible to key stakeholder groups as is appropriate.

The latter is a much broader conception of transparency, referring to the accessibility of information relating to a range of key governance activities. This encompasses non-financial processes, such as strategic planning, decisionmaking consultation and the level of stakeholder engagement.

The role of independent directors and trustees must also be considered here. The presence of independent directors on a board is considered to be important in increasing transparency of its decisions and activities (Aguilera, 2005; Roberts et al., 2005; Weir and Laing, 2001). The presence of independent directors requires incumbent board members to be more keenly aware of following legal guidelines for organizational activities and promotes openness. The next section draws attention to the potential role that trustees can have in enhancing board-level transparency.

Democracy

Democracy is a central component of the organizational life of many SEs. The tenets of fairness, equality and inclusive decisionmaking/participation are all easily identifiable with SEs. These principles permeate the entire organization – for example, there might be consultative managerial decisionmaking in an overarching agenda of collective appreciation of the democratic ethos.

Democratic governance refers to how inclusive governance processes are for a specified stakeholder group. Dahl (1991) discusses democracy in a broader political context, in relation to liberty and equality. This exemplifies the interrelatedness of democracy with ideals of fairness and freedom. Political democracy is the process of enabling rational actors to influence the composition of state bodies by means of periodic secret ballots.

Democracy is a central part of governance because it pays heed to notions of equity and trust that should exist in key fiduciary relationships, where powerful internal actors represent the interests of beneficiaries (Courville, 2003). For example, democracy should exist in the fair and honest election of board members within an agenda of board-level inclusion such as in co-operatives (see Cornforth, 2004).

Many issues arise when considering the nature of democracy in organizational governance. In the context of SEs, democracy refers to the achievement of specific objectives, including how directors are recruited, tenure and voting rights. Board members will often serve for fixed terms, requiring re-election to the board as a procedural measure. The election process must be seen to be fair and transparent to ensure democratic accountability, and these activities are generally confirmed during annual general meetings (AGMs). There must also be recognition of any possible exclusion of minority representation on the board. This should prompt the board to seek out these groups and remedy the issue via direct access to the board. Exhibit 8.2 gives an example of how one SE tries very hard to ensure transparency, accountability and democracy.

Exhibit 8.2   A case in point II: Crossroads – caring for carers

Crossroads is an SE organizations operating in the UK to actively support carers and their families. According to its website (Crossroads, 2008), its aim is to improve 'the lives of carers by giving them time to be themselves and have a break from their caring responsibilities. Our aim is to provide a reliable service, tailored to meet the individual needs of each carer and the person they are caring for.'

The board of this SE follows a prescriptive and well-organized process for ensuring board-level transparency. The board meets on a bi-annual basis and there is a good level of representation at these meetings. Service users, managers and interested members of the local community are all invited to attend the meetings. These individuals adopt traditional board member roles, such as trustees, and all regularly attend the meetings.

Each board member forms part of a subcommittee, with terms of reference being set to work on pressing issues, including human resources, finance and fundraising. A nominated, and experienced, board member is charged with reporting financial returns and other relevant information to the board.

As a matter of common practice, the chair rigorously follows procedure and ensures that all matters requiring regular attention are discussed at board meetings in an explicit effort to enhance democracy. Efforts to enhance board-level accountability are an ongoing matter for the SE. Social accounting has been pursued previously, though the practicality of this method is currently under discussion. A willingness to adhere to an established code of governance is also a matter of interest for this SE, and the chair proactively seeks to enhance transparency by inviting independent observers to the board meetings when appropriate.

Democracy is crucial to governance because it demonstrates that the board is representative of stakeholders and members serve on the basis of approval conferred by key stakeholders. Also, democracy is embedded in systems of voting, where all interested parties have allocated rights to influence the management of the organization and its composition. Of course, such allocation must also be representative and be fair, according to investment in or claim on the organizational's interests.

Democracy can be seen to have been established when certain processes are in place. These include the efficacy of voting procedures, the stated length of tenure for directors and the degree of control stakeholders have over the recruitment of directors. In cooperative and mutual organizations, stakeholder access to the board is constitutionally defined. This enhances democratic accountability as there is participatory consultation and it becomes an expected feature of governance (Papadopoulos, 2003).

Critical Issues

Managing diverse stakeholder interests

In addition to typical board member roles and internal stakeholders, there exist a number of groups that can be classified as primary-level stakeholders. Such groups have a close link (financial, social or political) and interest in the performance and continued existence of the SE. The types of stakeholders also depend on the nature of the service provided by the SE, as some enterprise activity might require that particular individuals serve on the board. For example, SEs providing health or social care services might be required to ensure that a number of service users are represented at board level, as well providing access by the local Primary Care Trust (PCT). Their interactions with the board are determined according to specific stakeholder needs that require representation. Other stakeholder groups that can be typically involved with SE boards include funding bodies, local (and in some cases national) government, the local community and trade or umbrella organizations. Similarly, the degree to which these groups are represented can vary depending on the nature of their involvement with the organization.

The acceptance of accountability to an increased number and variety of stakeholders, other than merely shareholders, is a fundamental principle of SEs (Pearce, 2003). Such practices have yet to become formalized as legislation or policy, so remain implicit manifestations of the 'social contract' of the organization (Gray et al., 1996; Moir, 2001). Thus, to achieve accountability, SEs must embed the systems and processes that enable them to be held accountable.

In order to examine the effectiveness of governance, many organizations rely on formal systems of measurement. As the prior sections have asserted, there are many broad challenges for SEs seeking to evidence their accountability. Therefore, in this section we deal with a further issue: how to measure governance performance as part of encouraging good governance practise. Performance measurement typically focuses on 'hard', quantified data, such as a statement of accounts and other financial information. These instruments are required by law and convention, and provide the fulcrum for proving the financial efficacy of the organization. The responsibility for these activities remains with the board and, in so doing, protects the interests of key internal and external individuals and groups.

SEs face a further constraint because the financial and non-financial costs of embedding measurement systems place a strain on already scarce resources. Only larger SEs are likely to have the resources to manage these processes, which are often intensive, annual and continuous in nature. The intensity of the dialogue with stakeholders, which is a central feature of systems of social accountability, provides a wealth of information that requires careful interpretation (Rotheroe and Richards, 2007). Exhibit 8.1 explains how one successful SE has implemented an accountability system.

The role of trustees

The role of trustees in the governance of SEs closely resembles the role of non-executive directors in mainstream governance. Trustees should ensure fair and honest accounting for interests at board level. In some organizations, trustees have a legal responsibility (and liability) to ensure financial probity (Locke et al., 2004).

In the public sector, school and hospital trusts require trustees who have a blend of experience of working with boards. The trustees of an SE need to have these same qualities and are a valuable instrument in ensuring that governance outcomes, such as transparency and accountability, are attained and maintained over time. For example, it is relatively common for service users to be represented on the boards of SEs as trustees.

The effectiveness of trustees depends on a number of factors, including the constitution of the organization, contextualized trustee role and board norms, the individual's own approach, power and political issues between board members and, further to this, the power of board over non-board members. The latter variable is important and raises a relevant contemporary issue: is it 'normal' for trustees of SEs to delegate work to managers, thus becoming more effective in shaping the work of the organization?

In practice, SE practitioners (both board and non-board members) will say that good trustees are hard to find. Typically, problems include poor or inconsistent attendance at meetings, a lack of instrumentality and failure to properly represent the interests of key groups, so they are therefore unable to influence decisionmaking.

Typically, trustees volunteer to serve on boards because they share a belief in the values that drive the organization. That is the true strength of the trustees' role and reinforces why they perform such a vital function: protecting the interests of primary stakeholders and ensuring the efficacy of board processes. Therefore, setting up board subcommittees for functions such as fundraising or service user groups could ensure that trustees are much more effective in their role. This approach makes better use of their particular skills by aligning them more closely with the work done by management and service users. In turn, this approach is also constructive as it prompts board members to engage in strategic consultation and operations when necessary and appropriate. One of the major issues that SE managers have with their boards is that they do not do this or at least on a regular basis.

Salaried or voluntary board members?

The role of the chief executive is, as an executive director, a figurehead for the organization and its interested parties. Typically, individuals in this role are expected to provide the fulcrum for strategic development, to drive forward the organization's objectives. This involves working closely with key staff members and external stakeholders to communicate and implement strategic objectives. They are also responsible for board performance and have a moral and legal responsibility regarding it (Heimovics and Herman, 1990).

Traditionally, the role of chair encompasses being responsibile for managing the board and having the right of veto. The role is associated with individuals who possess a great deal of industry-specific as well as board management experience. Also, the chair has a key role in the management of board-level dynamics, particularly between the chief executive and the rest of the board.

The central issue here is, are salaried board members likely to prove more effective than voluntary board members?

Academic evidence is less than emphatic. Support for voluntary participation indicates that voluntary board members commit to SEs for their intrinsic value, ahead of any financial gain. Salaried board members, however, have a further, financial, incentive to perform well and are then able to commit more resources (for example, time) to the role.

Regarding the roles of chief executive and chair, both face a number of contrasting pressures to reconcile various claims on resources (the strategic management of these demands are covered elsewhere). From the standpoint of governance, we are concerned with the nature of the role of both chief executive and the chair. SEs seeking growth and development require people with the strategic drive and experience to guide them successfully. Also, a certain degree of management and control is required to ensure that the board is run correctly. Therefore, individuals in these roles need a complex range of skills to ensure that both outcomes are met (Mordaunt and Cornforth, 2004; Oster, 1998). Furthermore, the issue of remuneration arises as, in order to attract individuals with the requisite skills, it is common to neglect the voluntary nature of serving on the boards of SEs in relation to this particular role. An emergent view is that directors of SEs with function-specific duties (which the chief executive has) should receive appropriate financial, as well as non-financial, rewards.

There is a similar dilemma when it comes to the recruitment of trustees. Some argue that the philanthropic nature of involvement in non-profitmaking organizations and SEs serves as suitable incentive in itself to perform because people have a particular personal vested interest in the organization's goals (Carroll et al., 2005; Handy and Katz, 1998).

Many SEs do not have sufficient financial resources available to pay their board members, while many would have a moral objection to paying directors, believing that all funds should be reinvested in the organization. There is a persuasive feel to this latter argument, though perhaps the focus of it should instead be on non-executive board members' remuneration: Such directors take a hands-on responsibility for delivering in certain areas, such as marketing, and meeting relevant strategic objectives.

The next section considers a conceptual model for the governance of SEs and provides a discussion of the implications for the various groups involved in this process.

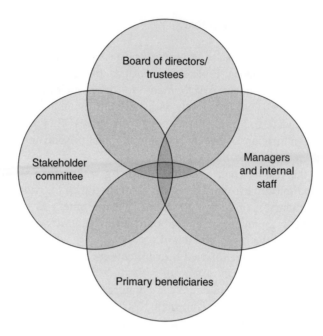

Figure 8.2   A relational model of governance for SEs

A relational model for the governance of SEs

The governance model shown in Figure 8.2 outlines an option for differentiating between key internal and external groups in terms of the governance of SEs. Furthermore, it attempts to conceptualize a stakeholder committee that is more than a notional board subcommittee and aims to integrate stakeholders into a stewardship function on the board.

Four main groups are identified in the model: primary beneficiaries, managers, the board of directors and a stakeholder committee (presently this is represented by a board of trustees). The co-existence of boards of directors and trustees is not common in SEs – usually the latter is commonplace.

Primary beneficiaries/service users

Naturally, the central focus of governance activity is that of creating the conditions for staff to maximize the social benefit to the primary beneficiaries and/or service users. For this reason, primary beneficiaries form the basis of the illustrative model. They have a relevant place in strategic decisions made by the board and are affected by operational matters dealt with by internal staff. Also, the stakeholder committee accommodates their interests. In this way, we can see that the primary beneficiaries group overlaps with the other key governance groups. As recipients of the social benefits generated by the SE, this group has key inputs to make to strategic decisionmaking and consultation on matters including democratic accountability.

Managers and internal staff

Managers (or key staff) form an important part of the SE governance model. They are often instrumental in delivering the social benefits to the primary beneficiaries. This group is also instrumental in achieving the business goals of the SE and has power in terms of its ability to provide legitimacy to the board and the organization. It is logical, therefore, that in the governance of the organization, their interests should be considered as well as those of service users.

As Figure 8.2 illustrates, all the actions taken by the board should positively affect the groups in the model, and managers and staff are often the closest to understanding the needs of the central group. Furthermore, this group should also be involved in governing the organization, which aligns with the democratic ethos described previously. To do this, a member (or members) of staff is nominated to serve on the board.

This opens up the board to participation by internal staff, who, traditionally, have been excluded from the board. This allows them to contribute to the strategic direction of the organization, adding a potentially useful operational perspective. This inclusion might enhance the SEs transparency and accountability, though ensuring that it is within the remit of the stakeholder committee (described below). Hypothetically, this managerial 'layer' also provides useful information to members of both the board of directors and stakeholder committee that can assist them in their decisionmaking process (Brown, 2002).

The outputs could include better product/service delivery, skills development and added value. The more useful this group is at board level, the more the board's credibility to service users and external stakeholder groups is enhanced. This acquisition of legitimacy can become self-perpetuating because the primary beneficiaries receive social benefits as a result of better social performance.

In this model, the board of directors and stakeholder committee shape the appropriate internal conditions that determine their strategic decisionmaking and performance. This is a radical departure from the typical view of the board as a strategic fulcrum. The broadening of the scope of its activities via the integration of manager and service user groups (around a 'core', functional board) allows the SE's board to become strategically relevant and operationally supportive. Its rationale, inputs and outputs are discussed below.

The board of directors

The conception of the board of directors is as an instrumental, functional group of business experts. This differentiates it from the role of a board of trustees – a body that is expected to fulfil two roles: oversight and strategic impetus. This is ineffective because there is no separation of powers. In this model, however the board of directors, serving the key stakeholders, is relieved of the task of holding itself and the entire organization accountable. This role is taken partly by the stakeholder committee. Rather, its members can utilize their time and expertise in driving the SE forward and delivering on strategic goals. This is very important, because it would enable the board to improve its performance and enhance its ability to promote legitimacy-seeking activities. The board also has fewer members than is usual, avoiding the problem of large boards indicated in the literature (Eisenberg et al., 1998; Yermack, 1996).

Directors with the requisite skills and experience are clearly essential here, though, ideally, they would be individuals with a clear understanding of and empathy for the aims of the organization (shared meanings). This opens up opportunities for current managers and other staff with experience of the organization (though they may require some training) to fulfil the roles of functional directors. However, it is more important that directors have the skills to be able to contribute effectively, rather than simply being drawn from the pool of primary stakeholders (as a 'captive market').

The board of directors would accommodate a chief executive, who may be drawn from outside the organization. The chair would serve on the stakeholder committee, to augment the power base of the other of the board of directors.

The stakeholder committee

The stakeholder committee is a body that coexists but is independent of the board of directors. This group is similar to a board of trustees in that it is representative and inclusive of various groups' interests. However, it differs from it because it works with the separate board of directors to ensure the organization's accountability (managing the social audit) and represents stakeholder inputs to decisions made by the board of directors.

Currently, boards of trustees are required to provide a range of inputs on an ad hoc basis. Repositioning this board as an oversight committee could define the exact boundaries of the committee's responsibilities. In addition, it shows where the latter differs from the board of directors.

The constitution of the committee must be representative, so it should comprise staff, primary stakeholders and other parties external to the organization, including funding bodies, local government agencies (as appropriate) and so on. This committee should also have the right to be consulted on key business decisions by the board of directors. It should encourage greater transparency and accountability by bridging any communication gap between the board of directors and staff.

The committee, in addition to consulting with the board of directors on key decisions, adds value by managing the social audit, enhancing inclusion throughout the organization, improving transparency via better links with stakeholders and accountability through better oversight of directors and staff. Its presence fits with the norms of the institutional environment as its purpose aligns with the social and ethical orientation of SEs, yet it also suits the business element of SEs because it reassigns an existing constraint of assuring oversight from the board of directors. In so doing, it frees the board to focus the organization's operational capabilities more effectively.

The committee has the sole task of ensuring that the methods the board adopts to achieve this are transparent, accountable and concordant with institutional norms. The responsibility for strategic development is the remit of both the board of directors and the stakeholder committee. Hence, the committee aids the board of directors in acquiring legitimacy from the SE's primary beneficiaries through open consultation with influencer groups.

There are some caveats to this proposed committee. First, committee members must have an agreed brief and remit in terms of responsibility. This needs to determine where the responsibilities of the group begin and end.

Second, the group must be able to meet on a convenient and relatively frequent basis if it is to influence the governance of the SE.

Members should be able to undergo training to fulfil their roles, if required. This ensures that staff and other members without the requisite skills can still add value to the roles they perform.

Furthermore, the issue of a minimum commitment/tenure for members needs to be determined. For the committee to be effective over time, there must be stability and continuity within the group in order to build trust and legitimize its existence to other stakeholder groups.

Finally, the committee has to be responsive to the dynamic operational environment of the organization. This aspect of the group is one that has to be managed at a 'local' level and this may present difficulties. This is because of the unique contexts applicable to every SE, including the set of skills available to each committee and the mix of different people and their power relationships within the organization. Yet, it is clear that, to remain responsive to change, the committee (and the board of directors) would be adversely affected by dominant key individuals (for example, the chief executive or chair).

EXTERNAL ORGANIZATION

This section of the analysis examines the expected roles and influence of groups external to the core organization – that is, they exist outside of the model presented in Figure 8.2, but remain influential. These have been divided into five key groups: trade/support groups, external verification, funding bodies, government and the local community.

Trade/support groups and consultancies

Trade organizations have influence over particular types of SEs or try to support the sector generally. The nature of this support is typically non-financial, thus differentiating these groups from funding bodies. Their primary interest is in ensuring the success of their members and, to this end, represents their interests.

They provide inputs to SEs in the form of support, training and performance tools development, networking opportunities and championing their cause on a local and national scale. For example, the Social Enterprise Coalition and the Fairtrade Foundation are two organizations with a highly political focus. They both support member organizations through effective political lobbying to ensure that SEs' interests are represented on national and international levels.

The predominant measure of success for support organizations is the creation of more SEs, leading to sustainable growth in the third sector. A specific example of a support group with a focus on engagement with specific SEs is that of Social Firms UK. This organization provides members with a number of accessible 'tools' and 'performance dashboards' to raise awareness of the importance of measuring success. They also place a strong emphasis on support without coercion, recognizing that SEs often require support at specific stages of their development (start-up, growth and closing down). This is not uncommon among other support or umbrella organizations. Co-operatives UK, for example, is highly focused on engaging proactively with members, while the Japanese NGO Centre for International Cooperation (JANIC) provides invaluable information to support its many members, working on a global scale to reduce poverty and medical services.

External verifiers

This group includes those organizations that are involved in the external verification of SEs' financial and social audits (such as the New Economics Foundation). They are important because they form a key part of the process by ensuring the accountability of SEs. Therefore they assist the stakeholder committee in providing an accurate assessment of the accountability of key groups within the SE.

These groups also set the standard for social auditing and accounting, with many different programmes having been developed (including SROI, Local Multiplier 3, Prove It, Looking Back to Move Forward and so on). Utilizing these approaches adds to the credibility of SEs' governance processes by showing that they use (and meet) an 'industry standard'. This can facilitate accountability throughout an SE and influence perceptions of transparency and legitimacy.

These components are central to the governance model as the ability of an SE to prove its accountability also greatly enhances its legitimacy with key groups. Hence, it is crucial that the stakeholder committee has the necessary resources to engage in these activities.

Funding bodies

These organizations play a crucial role in facilitating start-up SEs and offer a fixed-term level of financial support in the short term. They also have a non-financial interest in the organization. However, they have strategic priorities of their own – for example, the pursuance of economic and social regeneration. It is important for these organizations to fund viable projects that have defined objectives and can show evidence delivering on social value. To this end, they exert pressure on SEs to provide proof of meeting defined aims, such as accountability.

The problem for funding bodies is that a proportion of these organizations are content to move from one source of funding to another, ensuring their existence for as long as they can secure funding. This is contrary to one of the tenets of SEs, which is to use funding where appropriate, but with the goal of becoming viable enterprises in their own right. This ideal is held by the, albeit slowly growing, minority of socially minded organizations. Therefore, SEs must be able to develop a coherent strategy to move away from funding, or at least satisfy funders, to enable their future legitimacy and sustainability. The conceptual model promotes this thinking by combining a range of interests at management level: business-focused directors and a stakeholder committee with the authority to contribute to the SE's strategic direction.

Government

The role of government agencies is to promote and support their own agenda and policy for the social economy sector in the UK. Invariably, the decisions taken at this level will affect SEs and could influence individual functions, such as governance.

Government policy intends to shape the sector by encouraging greater levels of involvement. However, it is the role of support groups to communicate this agenda to SEs (the Social Enterprise Coalition is recognized as the most influential in this regard in the UK context).

Like all organizations, SEs will be influenced by macro-level changes in industries. These changes can be often catalysed by government activity. The social economy sector is of particular interest to the UK government for reasons of inclusion, access to employment and social regeneration of communities (DTI, 2002; DTI, 2006). Critics might argue that there is a wider ideological basis, stemming from the dominance of market-based solutions to society's needs rather than state provision through locally based authorities. Either way, SEs contribute to achieving these goals and, therefore, collectively influence the success of these broad policy goals.

Returning to the notion of industry change, government influence is currently pushing the sector towards convergence. The UK government advocates the dissemination of best practice by successful SEs, as well as 'sector champions'. The rationale behind this is that smaller enterprises (or potential social entrepreneurs) can apply some of these learned experiences to their own organizations, and adapt them to replicate success. The degree to which isomorphism occurs, and how, is currently open to debate. However, a steadily growing body of scholarship supports and builds on this prediction (Mason et al., 2007; Nyssens, 2006; Reid and Griffith, 2006). Therefore, we can see how broader, macro-level policy decisions by governments might influence the shaping of the social economy sector, thus confirming the influence the various inputs and influence such agencies have on the typical SE.

COMMENTS ON THE MODEL

The model offers many benefits to SEs. First, it delineates between a functional board and a separate stakeholder charged with ensuring that the business element provides accountability. It also promotes the consultative development of strategy between the board and key stakeholders. This should promote a strategic and operational focus that is relevant to the social and enterprise goals of the organization. Employing experts and specialists rather than overaccommodating trustees better places the board of directors to deliver business performance and maximize social benefit. The intent is to complement the application of stewardship theory to directors in SEs (Low, 2006; Reid and Griffith, 2006). The stakeholder committee provides a new consultative locus for trustees, encompassing an oversight role to create independence from the former board structure. This committee also satisfies democratic tenets that resonate with an ethos of inclusion as stakeholders are seen to operate at a senior level within the organization.

The model recognizes the centrality of the primary beneficiaries in the SE. The central group receives all the value-adding activities conducted by the two management groups. This should provide them with the required social benefit – the primary reason for the SE's existence. In return, the central group confers a degree of legitimacy and helps to assure the continued existence of the organization.

This approach differs from conceptions of managerial hegemony, because the managers' most influential role is to greatly support the primary beneficiaries.

The locus of power for strategic planning and decisionmaking is above the managerial level and, in this sense, the governance arrangements are 'hierarchical' (although the model does not reflect this).

In an effort to avoid overcomplicating the conceptual model, SEs' relationships with external groups were omitted, but have been explained above. The main thrust of their role in the model is the degree to which these groups influence the SE and the duties to these groups that the governance of the SE must accommodate. Attempts were also made to outline the notion of an overlap in interests – that the groups involved in the governance of the SE share interests and rarely operate in isolation. Overall, these groups are important in shaping the SE, from start-up to sustainable enterprise, and they can influence its legitimacy as a result.

THE FUTURE

This chapter has focused on the governance of SEs and issues of accountability. In so doing, it has covered a lot of ground, particularly with regard to the issues faced by social entrepreneurs and board members when involved in the governance process. The central role of accountability and legitimacy in governance places demands on board members to ensure that both are evidenced and acquired. Furthermore, we cannot misrepresent ideas of accountability in SEs by neglecting other key ideas, such as transparency and democracy. SEs are strongly rooted in the social ties to their primary beneficiaries, so we must consider all the aspects that should make their governance ethical.

Contemplation of the likely future direction of the governance of SEs unearths some key questions that we have to consider. The previous section summarized some of the most salient issues facing the governance of SEs and their importance is highly contextual as well as subjective. The two common threads that link SEs together are the drive to provide social benefits and a determination to ensure that the SEs are run effectively. It has been the aim of this chapter to simply map out these issues and suggest that practitioners and researchers can work together to enhance both of these laudable objectives. It is with this in mind that the conceptual model was developed with its stakeholder committee – a mechanism that ensures a pathway on to the SE's board for key stakeholders. At the same time, it encourages the adoption of a more functional board of directors, which has a specific remit to focus on instrumental influence of the areas of the enterprise that need its help the most. In so doing, this smaller board allows improved engagement with management and service users (where applicable) and encourages transparency and accountability. If the primary beneficiaries and key stakeholders are more engaged with the board, helping it to add value, we might expect an effective, relevant and legitimate board as a result. Naturally, this conceptualization requires further robust examination, but serves as a malleable (rather than prescriptive) option for SEs to adapt and adopt as they see fit.

There are other factors that have been omitted from the chapter. Certainly, the role of the CIC legal form will provide some interesting challenges for governance, as specific mechanisms (such as asset lock-ins) apply to them. The particular issues that arise from the board's management of such provisions will be instructive to the CIC's usefulness to SEs. In particular, it will be a worthwhile exercise to understand whether particular types of SE are more suited to adopting a CIC legal form than others. The bases for this phenomenon will shed light on new governance challenges, as well as adding to the aggregated knowledge regarding the governance of SEs generally.

REFERENCES

Abzug, R. and Webb, N.J. (1999) 'Relationships between nonprofit and for-profit organizations: A stakeholder perspective', *Nonprofit and Voluntary Sector Quarterly*, 28 (416).

Aguilera, R.V. (2005) 'Corporate governance and director accountability: an institutional comparative perspective', *British Journal of Management*, 16: S1, S39.

Alexander, J.A. and Weiner, B.J. (1998) 'The adoption of the corporate governance model by nonprofit organisations', *Nonprofit Management & Leadership*, 8: 223–42.

Black, B. S., Kraakman, R. and Tarassova, A.S. (1999) 'Russian privatization and corporate governance: What went wrong?', CEON/CEES.

Borzaga, C. and Solari, L. (2001) 'Management challenges for social enterprises', in C. Borzaga, J. Defourny, S. Adam and J. Callaghan (eds), *The Emergence of Social Enterprise*. London: Routledge.

Brinkerhoff, J.M. (2002) 'Government – nonprofit partnership: a defining framework', *Public Administration and Development*, 22: 19–30.

Brown, W. A. (2002) 'Inclusive governance practices in nonprofit organisations and implications for practice', *Nonprofit Management and Leadership*, 12: 369–85.

Bushman, R.M., Piotroski, J.D. and Smith, A.J. (2004) 'What determines corporate transparency?', *Journal of Accounting Research*, 42 (2): 207–52.

Carroll, T., Hughes, P. and Lukseitch, W. (2005) 'Managers of nonprofit organizations are rewarded for performance', *Nonprofit Management and Leadership*, 16 (1): 19–41.

Cornforth, C. (2003) 'The changing context of governance – emerging issues and paradoxes', in C. Cornforth (ed.), *The Governance of Public and Non-profit Organizations*. London: Routledge.

Cornforth, C. (2004) 'The governance of cooperatives and mutual associations: A paradox perspective', *Annals of Public and Cooperative Economics*, 75: 11–32.

Cornforth, C. and Edwards, C. (1999) 'Board roles in the strategic management of non-profit organizations: theory and practice', *Corporate Governance: An International Review*, 7 (4): 346–62.

Courville, S. (2003) 'Social accountability audits: Challenging or defending democratic governance?', *Law & Policy*, 25: 269–97.

Crossroads (2008) 'About Us' http://www.crossroads.org.uk/index.php?mid=2&pgid=20

Dahl, R.A. (1991) *Democracy and Its Critics*. New Haven, CT: Yale University Press.

Dart, R. (2004) 'The legitimacy of social enterprise', *Nonprofit Management and Leadership*, 14 (4): 411–24.

Davis, J.H., Schoorman, F.D. and Donaldson, L. (1997) 'Towards a stewardship theory of management', *The Academy of Management Review*, 22 (1): 20–47.

Davis, J.J. (1994) 'Good ethics is good for business: ethical attributions and response to environmental advertising', *Journal of Business Ethics*, 13 (11): 873–85.

Donaldson, L. and Davis, J.H. (1991) 'Stewardship theory or agency theory: CEO governance and shareholder returns', *Australian Journal of Management*, 16 (1): 49–65.

DTI (2002) 'Social enterprise: a strategy for success', HMSO, London.

DTI (2006) 'Sustainable construction strategy: report 2006', HMSO, London.

Eisenberg, T., Sundgren, S. and Wells, M.T. (1998) 'Larger board size and decreasing firm value in small firms', *Journal of Financial Economics*, 48 (1): 35–54.

Elkington, J. (1997) *Cannibals with Forks: The triple bottom line of twenty-first century business*. Oxford: Capstone.

Ezzamel, M. and Willmott, H. (1993) 'Corporate governance and financial accountability: recent reforms in the UK public sector', *Accounting, Auditing and Accountability Journal*, 6: 109–32.

FRC (2005) 'Best social report: FRC Group – we do good things'. Liverpool: Furniture Resource Centre.

Fernández-Fernández, J. L. (1999) 'Ethics and the board of directors in Spain: The Olivencia Code of Good Governance', *Journal of Business Ethics*, 22: 233–47.

Freeman, R.E. and Reed, D.L. (1983) 'Stockholders and stakeholders: a new perspective on corporate governance', *California Management Review*, 25 (3): 88–106.

Friedman, A. L. and Miles, S. (2002) 'Developing stakeholder theory', *Journal of Management Studies*, 39: 1–21.

Gibson, K. (2000) 'The moral basis of stakeholder theory', *Journal of Business Ethics*, 26: 245–57.

Goddard, A. and Assad, M. J. (2006) 'Accounting and navigating legitimacy in NGO's', *Accounting, Auditing, and Accountability*, 19 (3).

Golden-Biddle, K. and Rao, H. (1997) 'Breaches in the boardroom: organizational identity and conflicts of commitment in a nonprofit organization', *Organization Science*, 8 (6): 593–611.

Grant, G.H. (2003) 'The evolution of corporate governance and its impact on modern corporate America', *Management Decision*, 41: 923–34.

Gray, R. (1992) 'Accounting and environmentalism: an exploration of the challenge of gently accounting for accountability, transparency and sustainability', *Accounting, Organizations and Society*, 17: 399–425.

Gray, R.H., Owen, D. and Adams, C.A. (1996) *Accounting and accountability: Changes and challenges in corporate social and environmental reporting.* London: Prentice Hall.

Handy, F. and Katz, E. (1998) 'The wage differential between nonprofit institutions and corporations: getting more by paying less?', *Journal of Comparative Economics*, 26 (2): 246–61.

Heimovics, R.D. and Herman, R.D. (1990) 'Responsibility for critical events in nonprofit organizations', *Nonprofit and Voluntary Sector Quarterly*, 19 (1): 59.

Huse, M. (1998) 'Researching the dynamics of board–stakeholder relations', *Long Range Planning*, 31: 218–26.

Huse, M. (2005) 'Accountability and creating accountability: A framework for exploring behavioural perspectives of corporate governance', *British Journal of Management*, 16: S65.

Inglis, S., Alexander, T. and Weaver, L. (1999) 'Roles and responsibilities of community nonprofit boards', *Nonprofit Management and Leadership*, 10: 153–67.

Jensen, M. (2001) 'Value maximization, stakeholder theory and the corporate objective function', *Journal of Applied Corporate Finance*, 14: 8–20.

Johnson, J.L., Daily, C.M. and Ellstrand, A.E. (1996) 'Boards of directors: a review and research agenda', *Journal of Management*, 22 (3): 409–38.

Kearns, K.P. (1994) 'The strategic management of accountability in nonprofit organizations: an analytical framework', *Public Administration Review*, 54 (2): 185–92.

Letza, S., Sun, X. and Kirkbride, J. (2004) 'Shareholding versus stakeholding: a critical review of corporate governance', *Corporate Governance: An International Review*, 12 (3): 242–62.

Locke, M., Begum, N. and Robson, P. (2003) 'Service users and charity governance', in C. Cornforth (ed.), *The Governance of Public and Non-public Organizations: What do Boards do?* London: Routledge.

Low, C. (2006) 'A framework for the governance of social enterprise', *International Journal of Social Economics*, 33 (5/6): 376–85.

Lowenstein, L. (1996) 'Financial transparency and corporate governance: You manage what you measure', *Columbia Law Review*, 96: 1335–62.

March, J.G. and Olsen, J.P. (1989) *Rediscovering Institutions: The organizational basis of politics.* New York: The Free Press.

Mason, C., Kirkbride, J. and Bryde, D. (2007) 'From stakeholders to institutions: the changing face of social enterprise governance theory', *Management Decision*, 45 (2): 284–301.

Mason, C. and Royce, M. (2007) 'Fit for purpose: board development for social enterprise', *Journal of Finance and Management in Public Services*, 6 (3): 57–67.

Moir, L. (2001) 'What do we mean by corporate social responsibility?', *Corporate Governance: A Review of Business and Society*, 1 (2): 16–22.

Mordaunt, J. and Cornforth, C. (2004) 'The role of boards in the failure and turnaround of non-profit organisations', *Public Money and Management*, 24.

Murray, V., Bradshaw, P. and Wolpin, J. (2006) 'Power in and around nonprofit boards: A neglected dimension of governance', *Nonprofit Management and Leadership*, 3: 165–82.

Nobbie, P.D. and Brudney, J.L. (2003) 'Testing the implementation, board performance, and organizational effectiveness of the policy governance model in nonprofit boards of directors', *Nonprofit and Voluntary Sector Quarterly*, 32 (4): 571–95.

Nyssens, M. (2006) *Social Enterprise between Market, Public Policies and Civil Society.* London: Routledge.

OECD (2004) OECD *Principles of Corporate Governance.* Paris: OECD.

Orts, E.W. and Strudler, A. (2002) 'The ethical and environmental limits of stakeholder theory', *Business Ethics Quarterly*, 12 (2): 215–34.

Oster, S.M. (1998) 'Executive compensation in the nonprofit sector', *Nonprofit Management and Leadership*, 8: 207–21.

Papadopoulos, Y. (2003) 'Cooperative forms of governance: Problems of democratic accountability in complex environments', *European Journal of Political Research*, 42: 473–501.

Paton, R. (2003) *Managing and Measuring Social Enterprises*. London: Sage.

Pearce, J. (2003) *Social Enterprise in Anytown*. London: Calouste Gulbenkian Foundation.

Phillips, R., Freeman, R. E. and Wicks, A. C. (2003) 'What stakeholder theory is not', *Business Ethics Quarterly*, 13: 479–502.

Resource Alliance (2008) Vision and Mission http://www.resource-alliance.org/about us/29.asp

Reid, K. and Griffith, J. (2006) 'Social enterprise mythology: critiquing some assumptions', *Social Enterprise Journal*, 2 (1): 1–11.

Roberts, J., Mcnulty, T. and Stiles, P. (2005) 'Beyond agency conceptions of the work of the non-executive director: creating accountability in the boardroom', *British Journal of Management*, 16, S1: section 5.

Rotheroe, N. and Richards, A. (2007) 'Social return on investment and the social enterprise: Transparent accountability for sustainable development', *Social Enterprise Journal*, 3: 31–48.

Scott, W. R. (1987) 'The adolescence of institutional theory', *Administrative Science Quarterly*, 32 (4): 493–511.

Scott, W. R. (2003) 'Institutional carriers: reviewing modes of transporting ideas over time and space and considering their consequences', *Industrial and Corporate Change*, 12: 879–94.

Scott, W. R. (2008) *Institutions and Organizations: Ideas and interests*. Thousand Oaks, CA: Sage.

SEC (2008) What is Social Enterprise? http://www.socialenterprise.org.uk/page.aspx?SP=1345

Short, H., Keasey, K., Hull, A. and Wright, M. (2005) *Corporate Governance, Accountability and Enterprise*. Chichester: John Wiley & Sons.

Spear, R. (2004) 'Governance in democratic member-based organisations', *Annals of Public and Cooperative Economics*, 75: 33–60.

Sternberg, E. (2004) *Corporate Governance: Accountability in the Marketplace*. London: Institute of Economic Affairs.

Stone, M. M., Bigelow, B. and Crittenden, W. (1999) 'Research on strategic management in nonprofit organizations: Synthesis, analysis, and future directions', *Administration & Society*, 31: 378–423.

Strenger, C. (2004) 'The corporate governance scorecard: a tool for the implementation of corporate governance', *Corporate Governance: An International Review*, 12 (1): 11–15.

Suchman, M.C. (1995) 'Managing legitimacy: Strategic and institutional approaches', *The Academy of Management Review*, 20: 571–610.

Turnbull, S. (1997) 'Corporate governance: its scope, concerns and theories', *Corporate Governance: An International Review*, 5 (4): 180–205.

UNIDO (2002) 'Report of the world summit on sustainable development', UNIDO, Johannesburg, South Africa, 26: 92–1.

Van Kersbergen, K. and Van Waarden, F. (2004) '"Governance" as a bridge between disciplines: Cross-disciplinary inspiration regarding shifts in governance and problems of governability, accountability and legitimacy', *European Journal of Political Research*, 43: 143–71.

Van Slyke, D. (2007) 'Agents or stewards: Using theory to understand the government-nonprofit social service contracting relationship', *Journal of Public Administration Research and Theory*, 17: 157.

Vinten, G. (1998) 'Corporate governance: an international state of the art', *Managerial Auditing Journal*, 13: 419–31.

Weir, C. and Laing, D. (2001) 'Governance structures, director independence and corporate performance in the UK', *European Business Review*, 13 (2): 86–95.

Westall, A. (2001) *Value Led, Market Driven – Social enterprise solutions to public policy goals*. London: The Institute of Public Policy Research.

Yermack, D. (1996) 'Higher market valuation of companies with a small board of directors', *Journal of Financial Economics*, 40 (2): 185–211.

Young, D.R. (2002) 'The influence of business on nonprofit organizations and the complexity of nonprofit accountability: looking inside as well as outside', *The American Review of Public Administration*, 32 (1): 3–19.

Zandstra, G. (2002) 'Enron, board governance and moral failings', *Corporate Governance: International Journal of Business in Society*, 2: 16–19.

Zucker, L.G. (1977) 'The role of institutionalization in cultural persistence', *American Sociological Review*, 42 (5): 726–43.

INDEX